Sorry, Dad

EDWARD BLISHEN

Sorry, Dad

HAMISH HAMILTON
LONDON

First published in Great Britain 1978
by Hamish Hamilton Limited
90 Great Russell Street London WC1B 3PT

Copyright © 1978 by Edward Blishen

British Library Cataloguing in Publication Data
Blishen, Edward
    Sorry, dad.
    1. Blishen, Edward – Biography 2. Authors,
    English – 20th century – Biography
    I. Title
    828' .9'1409   PR6052.L57
    ISBN 0–241–89849–8

Printed in Great Britain by
Bristol Typesetting Co. Ltd,
Barton Manor, St Philips, Bristol

To BERNARD and RUTH,
dear cousins

PART ONE

1

I was four at the time. There was, as I recall it, a hole in a hedge, cave-like: big enough, at any rate, to accommodate two of us. Not very big: she was four, too. Her name was Hilda Hawkins. I loved those aitches. Her existence was framed by them—those breaths. Not that I was secure with aitches. But even in dropping them, I was aware of them. She had pinkly white arms and legs, and otherwise a kind of darkness of eye and hair. She told me, in the heart of that hedge, about Hell and Heaven. Aitches again. Heaven, she said, was where girls went. Hell was for boys. It seemed extremely probable. She caused me terror, and I loved her for doing that.

It was just outside our houses, that hedge. We were, most tremendously, neighbours. There were many Hawkins. The boys, Alfie and Jackie and Freddie, were gruff, with broad noses, and knees large enough to draw whole faces on, with indelible pencil. The girls, Ethel and Hilda, had a bigness too, but theirs was red-and-white, and warm. The Hawkins were robust. I was an only child, then, and distinctly frail. Well, perhaps I was not really frail; though I was anaemic, and was taken to hospital for it, and had to consume quantities of liver extract. But I was given a feeling of frailty by the careful way I was brought up. The Hawkins were brought up with a noisy carelessness: I was from the beginning aware that they were, so to speak, created and trained for cheerful bruising, as I was not. It was another difference, like the difference between boy and girl: elevated so satisfactorily, by Hilda, into that huge difference between Hell and Heaven. Part of the excitement of being with Hilda was that of being fragile boy associating with bold, unbreakable girl.

The houses were council houses. They were greyly pebble-dashed, low, with green doors with skeletal porches, and

A*   3

patches of garden, fore and aft. They formed crescents and closes, and brimmed with children. Hawkins, Pratchetts, Hickses, Mallets, Skinners. I loved the way people had names: the implicit descriptiveness of names. And then there were us. I had a feeling we were different. It was again to do with the nervous way I was brought up. I wore kid gloves when on my scooter. Terry Pratchett hated my gloves, and also the woollen suits my mother knitted for me: the jackets secured with strings of wool culminating in bobbles. Terry Pratchett frankly hit me whenever he was in a position to do so.

The neighbours, said my father, were a rough lot. They were nosey, too. There were paths that ran behind the houses, and the Hawkins, the Pratchetts, the Hickses and the rest had no hesitation in using these paths as places from which to stare into our back garden, and our windows. My father longed to escape from this noisy, shamelessly inquisitive pattern of neighbourliness.

The world came to an end, in one direction, at the tin Sunday School to which I was escorted, deliciously terrified, by Hilda. (I shouldn't set too much store, she suggested, by the promises of heavenly favour held out by our instructors: they did not apply to me.) In another quarter, the limits were fixed by the steam laundry, a building half-smothered in ivy that puffed and panted with its hygienic operations. There was a belt that ran out of the building   nd a wheel and then back in again. The whole   ..ed out a thick, dull smell of starch. It seemed to me to   alive.

Two other border posts. The corn chandlers in East Barton Road, where mother bought oats for our porridge. This had a grey, nutritiously powdery smell that turned me, when I entered it, into a chicken. And finally Long Street, named with beautiful truth, the obvious way out to other worlds, if one thought of such a thing: a road that climbed under the railway bridge and away to the very edge of existence, fields and allotments. There was a great dump just beyond the bridge, where we rooted for cast-off motor tyres. We all had tyres which we trundled along the pavements, and hid with uneasy care in our gardens at the day's end. If I had a tyre that Terry Pratchett fancied, he simply took it. My first grievous losses in life were all tyres.

And opposite our house, across the road, was a garage with

4

a steep approach. Whizzing down that slope, I was (though I kept my triumph to myself, and especially withheld news of it from Terry Pratchett) the Scooter Champion of the World from 1923 to 1926.

My father, from then to the end of the story, never did like neighbours. It was a special form, I think, of his natural unwillingness to like people. So many had that loose warmth that was characteristic of the Hawkins. In the case of the Hawkins, it had led to their having so many children. I was early made aware of the notion that to have many children was a form of untidiness, of domestic scruffiness.

I, only child for a while, was a member of a family trimmed and disciplined like the hedges with which my father attempted to give privacy to our garden. I have never known a hedge-cutter to match him. He had a dead straight eye, unfaltering wrists, and endless patience. The Hawkins' privet flopped in all directions and, in summer, was slovenly with spires of white flower. When I entered into metaphysical conference with Hilda under one of her own hedges, that sweet smell became confused with my feeling for her. Part of her was pure privet. But I had little doubt that the disorder of the Hawkins' hedges was one element, a significant element, in that otherness that so displeased my father.

But, come to that, we were ourselves quite untidy in respect of uncles.

They'd come, my father's brothers, on Sundays to sit around our kitchen table and inflame one another. Not Uncle George, who'd become glorious and left the district: but Uncle Harry, Uncle Jack, Uncle Arthur, Uncle Will. They made jokes at each other's expense: and their jokes were deadly.

My father was everyone's butt. It was because he was a civil servant. To work in the civil service was to be, for my uncles, a huge ready-made joke.

'Saw Dick coming from the station in his little bowler hat,' Uncle Will would say.

'Carrying his little umbrella.' This detail from Uncle Jack.

'Christ!' Uncle Harry rarely went beyond ejaculations.

I was not much aware of the detail of such exchanges. What I sensed was that my father was often on the defensive.

He had made himself quite spectacularly vulnerable by becoming an office worker. It was not in the tradition of a family given tortuously to unkindness among themselves, and bitterly quarrelsome.

I loved my uncles for their occupations. Uncle Will had a greengrocer's shop, in a parade close to the station. He would come to our house carrying cabbages, beans, carrots. The shop was not doing well : he was in partnership with a rogue. 'Damned rogue'. 'Rogue' was a word I enjoyed, partly because Uncle Will himself seemed to enjoy it. 'Do you know what the damned rogue did this week . . .?' I would not understand the story that followed, but I loved the loud laughter that accompanied it : my four uncles laughing, enjoying the unkindness of the situation. Uncle Harry, who was curiously dwarfed (as a result, I later understood, of a childish illness), would laugh himself to the point of death by choking. My uncles, and my father, standing round Uncle Harry and beating him back to life! Uncle Harry drove a van for a department store in London. He wore a cloth cap. even when he was in the house. 'Hullo, Teddy,' he would say, thickly, when he arrived, and shake me by the hand. He had a kind of jokey courtesy, and smelled of tobacco and London. I loved him.

Uncle Arthur was a plasterer, and his fingernails had the character of stone. He was famous (I *thought* he was famous) for being married to my Auntie Joan, who had such alarming good looks that she was always spoken of uneasily. At least, as a child I had the impression that her being so pretty was rather like the Hawkins being so lax in respect of hedges : it was a mark of some delinquency against which self-respecting life had perpetually to struggle. Uncle Arthur was handsome (but so were all my uncles) and added his note to that general noise of theirs; but he was clearly diminished by marriage.

Uncle Jack was himself a rogue, in the strict sense in which the word was applied to Uncle Will's partner in the greengrocery. He wore steel-rimmed spectacles, behind which his eyes gleamed with hard angry mischief. I knew he was a rogue, because no one, not even himself, made a secret of it. His occupation had no name; he was always fishily engaged in transactions. Quantities of this and that were being purchased for amazingly small sums, and sold at once for amazingly large ones. His pleasure was to learn that someone was in need

6

of anything whatever: he knew how it could be obtained to the disadvantage of all concerned but himself. An idea I early acquired was that no one knew where Uncle Jack would end up. It was what they always said of him in his absence: or, if they were in brawling mood, in his presence.

Childhood, it strikes me, is a little like being drunk. There is the same difficulty of knowing who people are, the same indistinct grasp of the geography of things. My family, and the world they lived in, pieced themselves together by guess and rumour and inadvertence, during those early years in East Barton. The heart of it all was my grandmother's house not far off, near that pulsing laundry.

My Cornish grandmother, Martha.

She had come to London as a girl, handsome and passionate and bad-tempered: had been a maid, somewhere: was seduced: had a love-child (a term I caught on the edge of conversations, and cherished): married my grandfather, whose family had long lived in the West London slums. He, by day, drove a van for a department store in Oxford Street: before that day began, worked another, as a porter, in Billingsgate fish market. A jolly, ill-tempered man, they said—amiable among his friends, stern and irate at home. A wife so discontented, sons so headstrong! My father remembered that at noon every Saturday one of the boys would stand in an agreed spot in the Edgware Road, waiting for their father's van to come along. He'd lean down, that grandfather I never knew, and hand the boy a sovereign, wrapped in tissue paper. The boy would run home with it: until it was delivered to my grandmother, there was no food for the next meal. It was the *running* my father remembered—the true urgency of it.

My grandfather would drive on and stable his horse and van—then he'd go to the pub. He was welcome there, among his cronies, for his singing, and for certain feats he performed. Family lore suggested that among those feats was the lifting of pianos. I could never quite imagine that—my grandfather, as part of the weekend fun, lifting a piano, for a wager! Did he lie on the floor and support the piano on his chest? Or hold it aloft with raised arms? Perhaps it was a legend only; though there must have been some basis for it . . .

At home, the shopping done, the Saturday dinner would be

7

prepared, and my grandfather waited for. As often as not, he put in no appearance. So a boy was sent to fetch him from the pub. 'Dad—Mum says dinner's ready.' 'All right, boy. Shan't be long now. Wait outside.' That's how my father remembered the exchange . . . Hours of anxious waiting. The boys were caught between their mother's mounting fury, their father's mounting guilt and need to justify himself. *Her* revenge, when he came home at last, was to name her children for whippings. 'How you expect me to keep your sons in order while you drink yourself silly . . .' And *his* revenge was to give the beatings she asked for. They had grown up, my father and his brothers, among these angers that looked for easy targets.

A trim man, my grandfather, with a sad, rather furious face: tin photos show him at a stile somewhere, three or four fellows in rakish bowlers, with three or four girls as feathery as chickens: or one in a row of moustaches, firemen at the department store where he worked.

Then, at forty, on his early way to work, he fell dead in the street. Was it because he'd lifted too many pianos? Was it an accumulation of rages, so that his heart burst with anger and disappointment? My father was taken to the mortuary, to identify the body. He was only thirteen. 'Queer thing I've never forgotten. They lifted his head up, and water came out of his nose. His nose was running. I just thought how funny it was that he was dead and his nose was running.'

2

The East Barton of my childhood had been created by the railway. That's to say, there'd been a village of the name for centuries, but it was a drowsy scrap of a place until the neighbouring town, Barton-on-the-hill, turned the railway down, halfway through the nineteenth century. Barton-on-the-hill, lofty in all senses, lapped by green fields, seems to have

thought of the railway as a vulgarity. So a site for the suburban terminus was found at the foot of the hill, giving rise
rapidly to New Barton, which had soon begun to absorb the
village. By the 1920s, it had become a patchwork of old hamlet
and impatient new suburb . . .

So we lived in a sourly damaged countryside: and specu-
lation had its eye on all the fields around us.

An afternoon I remember: when it was rumoured that a
bull was loose in doomed fields facing us. A curious horror
preserves the memory of that afternoon. I had no idea what
a bull was. There was this rumour, tensely floated: and all of
us children were rounded up and confined to our gardens.
What happened next was that a pair of carts drew up, with
nets thrown over them, and from these carts came men, stocky
men carrying pitchforks. We stood in our front gardens, our
mothers with us, and watched these men walking slowly into
the field and across it. Some time elapsed before anything
else happened: somehow the absence of the quarry, those men
moving carefully, peering up the field towards the brow of a
low hill, was more definitive of what a bull was than its appearance: which it made at last, shaggy and frightened and
frightening, coming over the hill and towards us, followed by
other men who'd approached it from another direction. The
two groups of men came nervously together, with the bull in
between, and there was much galloping about, and snorting,
and shouting and cries of alarm from the women, before the
creature was cornered and driven, foaming and furious, into
one of the carts . . .

How full of mystery, a child's world! Had I been told that
bulls had their uses, I think it would have made little difference. Life was subject to bulls, who were simply every kind
of fear on four legs, and they were obviously difficult to control. For this sort of reason, life was also full of warnings. I
was warned against entering Ferguson Road, which ran up
beside the corner shop, over the way, where I bought far-
thingsworth of sweets, handed over in cornets rapidly twisted
out of old newspaper. I suspected that Ferguson Road was
crammed with bulls, any empty spaces being filled with burglars. I was not sure what burglars were: but that did not
prevent me from imagining them very precisely. They were
men with foxes' heads. They entered houses at night, that I

knew; and if they had a purpose in doing so, it could add nothing to the simple horror of their power of entry. Even today I do not think comfortably of Ferguson Road, though I now guess I was warned off it because the children who lived there were 'rough.' I could not, anyway, have imagined roughness worse than Terry Pratchett's.

Was it my mother who had that strong feeling about the roughness of the children in Ferguson Road?

Throughout my adolescence I had the greatest scorn for my mother's horror of whatever she could call 'common' or 'rough': earlier, I often groaned under the consequences of it. 'You could eat', she would say of a neighbour who had her approval, 'off her floor.' It was a phrase my father greeted with some of his worst sarcasms: 'I'm damned if I want to eat off her floor—or off her—' 'Dick!' Mother, quick to interrupt when one of my father's coarsenesses threatened . . . We were always clean, our clothes were always decently darned: the house was always spotless. In time, I came to understand what lay behind her dread of all dirt and disorder.

It was partly a matter of temperament. By nature she was dainty. My father, in a tone of surprise that never quite vanished—I think he never came to terms with the unlikelihood of their union—used to say that what drew him to her in the first place was her 'wholesomeness.' 'I can't put it any better,' he'd say. 'Always sweet. You could eat her.' Father, as wicked a thirteen-year-old as you could imagine when they first met, being thrown off course, for life as it turned out, by mother's edibility!

But temperament was reinforced, rather terribly, by experience.

My other grandmother, too, had a love-child. A common enough consequence of being in service, at the end of Victoria's reign. In her case, it led straight to an unhappy marriage—with a cousin, willing to take her, as the phrase was. Here was another grandfather I never knew. My mother's account was of a man of moods: sometimes adorable, more often hateful. She remembered his making a doll's house for his daughters: and once, seeing how pale an organ-grinder was in the street below, making up a sandwich and taking it down to him—and turning the handle of the organ while it

10

was eaten. But there was a darker side—or just, perhaps, a desperate side. He was a builder's labourer—often out of work, sometimes for whole winters. He drank heavily—and mother never forgot an occasion when he came home mad with drink and . . . 'the table was set lovely and suddenly there it all was, on the floor.' And my grandmother was always inventing respectable reasons for the marks of the beatings he gave her.

Two families in one, it seemed. There was my grandmother, a gentle woman—gentle and warm and in love with the idea of quietness and friendliness, like my mother: and there was my mother herself, with her pride in being neat and clean already complete in her. A matter of temperament that was, for both of them, also a matter of their capacity to survive. Paying fierce attention to being tidy was an answer to drunken angry anarchy. One winter my grandfather was simply unable to support his family—so he and my grandmother and the baby went into the workhouse, and my mother and her two older sisters were sent to a residential school. 'I had my lovely long hair bobbed,' my mother remembered, 'but we had school uniform: ooh, that was nice: and each of us had our little basin for mealtime and our little pinny.' The intense pleasure with which, all her life, she talked about clothes and their neatness and the materials of which they were made! And their cost—she never, all her life, forgot the cost of anything. When it was time to return home, my grandfather having work again, mother's sisters were jubilant—but mother, miserable.

On one side of the family, mother and daughter—setting great store by cleanliness and freshness and prettiness: and on the other side, my grandfather and his eldest children, Daisy and Violet (my mother was the only one to be unflorally named)—they being what my mother always called 'loud and common.' It came to a head one day when she was fifteen and the drunkenness, the beatings, the sneers made this child who was my mother, three years already out of school, resolve that 'life could be better than this.' And she packed a bag and left. 'I said: "Annie, they'll only *leave you* astray."' Scrappy schooling left her with a lifelong tendency to miss, by a sometimes dazzling inch or so, the target of any idiom. And if what was already happening to Daisy and Violet was anything to go by, she could have been left, or led, far astray. 'Daisy', mother would hint, 'had a *bad name*!'. . . . She found work as a maid, living in, in a boarding house much used by students—an experience that gave her another lifelong trait : a habit of claiming easy acquaintance with Indians 'and Italians and all that,' which was combined with a considerable actual nervousness about anyone who didn't speak English . . .

She didn't lose touch with her mother, but never went home if there wasn't a pot of flowers in the window—an agreed sign that her father was out . . .

And that was how they met, my mother and father. He was thirteen, she was sixteen : and he a van-boy for yet another department store, a dashing, desperate lad in an overcoat so long he was inclined to trip over it : and he delivered to the boarding house a special daily loaf for one of the lodgers who was diabetic. Such an odd fatality, their meeting! This simple, brave, gentle girl, who always remembered in detail what she wore when he came (ready at once to pinch her bottom) to deliver that important loaf. 'I had a very pretty lilac dress, and a cap with streamers down the back—and used to wear alpaca and . . . fancy aprons in the afternoon.' One day she didn't answer the door, and he came back with some excuse about not remembering if he'd made his delivery. 'Well, you did,' said the mistress of the house, 'and if you're looking for the pretty little girl who works for me, she's gone for a walk in the Harrow Road . . .' And he went in search of her, and was successful, and . . .

It had begun. Nearly seventy years of what was too complex to be merely described as misalliance . . .

Being warned off entering Ferguson Road—being given kid gloves to wear when I rode my scooter—having my interest in Hilda Hawkins delicately frowned upon :—much of my awkward childhood stemmed from mother's experience in goodness knows how many West London lodgings twenty and thirty years before I was born . . . 'I swore my children shouldn't go through what I went through.'

It was my father who, at the time, I thought of as Hilda's enemy. Or, given what I felt about Hilda, as her victim.

On our small journeys round the green in front of the houses, she obliged me to walk in puddles, without the benefit of wellingtons—which, I think, I did not possess. This was bound to lead to trouble at home: but exposing oneself to danger by accepting a dare propounded by a girl was clearly an inescapable feature of life. Life was defined by such things. I saw Hilda, and without surprise, as my father's foe. If Hilda could persuade me to do whatever would cause my father distress, that was perfectly natural. Girls were agents in a chemical explosion in which the hostile components were a father and a son.

It came to a head in the matter of the pansies.

Left alone, I don't think I'd have conceived the idea of sneaking a carving knife out of a drawer in the kitchen and, with it, cutting a great bouquet of pansies from the front garden—my father's favourite flower. It was, and remains, my favourite, too. A bed of pansies was a bed of grinning harlequins: on the short green bodies of their stems, those hilarious faces . . . With the same instrument, I hacked my way through a privet hedge to present the bouquet to Hilda, coolly expectant on the other side. It wasn't an activity I'd have embarked upon without that atmosphere of the *dare* she generated: or without that sense that the dare must be taken up to the interesting injury of my father.

My mother, appalled as never before, sent me to bed. There I stared at books—from a box under the bed, the only books in the house—until angry steps on the stairs reminded me why I was there. The attack on my bottom produced tears and soreness, together with the familiar, always rather baffling sense of having stumbled into unpopularity. Sometimes you were liked, the luck of things kept you in people's good books: and sometimes you weren't—you most terribly and completely were not. In Hilda, who'd heard it all through the wall our houses had in common, it produced a gleeful sympathy.

Having a bottom at all seemed a very great weakness. To me, at such times, my father was those powerful hands, square-nailed, with rings on the fingers: hands that laid hold of gardens, newspapers, hammers and cobbler's tools (he mended all our shoes), and subjugated them. My father was a square of power, smelling of cigarettes: terrible when angry, marvellous when friendly. At best, there was riding on his foot, *The Galloping Major*—up in the air you went, at the end, thrillingly unsafe, but perfectly secure in that square-handed grip.

At worst, that merciless misuse of one's bottom.

Most of my uncles had this square quality : I mean, as if the basic shape involved in their making, of spirit as well as of body, was a stern, able, angry square.

They came together on those Sundays at home, but also in Sutton Villas, their mother's home. To me, Sutton Villas was a name as big as, later, such names as Asia and America were to seem : it was the name given to all the mysterious past of the world—which consisted of the old photographs, the tasselled overmantels, the little polished needles of marble everywhere that had been the work of my great-uncles, all stonemasons. There were so many of these needles that every mantelpiece was a little cemetery. It was my grandmother's voice, Cornish, a sharp burr of a voice . . . and her spiteful apple of a face, and the white silk of her hair. It was apples especially : there was a little orchard, and a lavatory, apple-smelling, that thrust itself into the orchard, and never had I seen a lavatory seat of such amplitude; the business part of it was framed in such levels of pale scrubbed wood as you could have made a desk of—and I often did, laying out the scraps of newspaper that were kept ready on a hook, and which spelled out the first pages of the *News of the World* I was ever, haltingly, to interpret.

But Sutton Villas was especially granny's bedroom, where she spent so much of her time, a room crowded with photographs and with articles of furniture, so many tallboys and wardrobes, such a plethora of little tables with cloths laid on them, and the great bed with a brass knob surmounting each black metal post : and, chief of all, and source of the smell of hospital that was always in the room, the table at my grandmother's bedside, jammed with medicine bottles and pill boxes and boxes of ointment, the spoil of her everlasting hypochondria. 'Granny isn't well'—it was Granny herself who was always saying this, smiling sadly at me from the pillow, her sadness that was always for herself. 'No, poor Granny isn't well,' she would repeat, and her plump white untrembling hand would go out for a bottle, or a box, and I would watch, while she sadly gave me the corner of her eye, her pouring out of a medicine, or the funereal ceremony with which she administered to herself a pill.

It was from Sutton Villas that my parents were married in the summer of 1919. My mother remembered that as she stood at the altar of St Margaret's Church, East Barton, listening to the clatter of my father's military boots as he approached her up the aisle, she had an overwhelming desire to release him from what she suddenly saw as a most unsuitable commitment. 'For two pins I'd have said, "Dick, you needn't bother, you know."' Instinct must have supplied her with a last-minute desperate awareness of the rather large element of error in this arrangement. Half of her own nature had always joined with the frank horror of her friends and relatives to protest against her obstinate interest in the former van-boy—now uniformed, employed as a clerk in the War Office since his wounding in France two years earlier. But the other half of her, to the confusion of all emotional arithmetic, was the bigger half. She did not speak that day in 1919. I think you could have showered her with pins, and she would not have spoken.

'The bride,' said the report in the *Barton Record*, 'was attired in pale grey crêpe-de-chine, with veil and wreath of orange blossom, and carried a bouquet of white and pink carnations . . . The bride and bridegroom left later for their honeymoon in Cornwall; the bride travelled in a fawn tailor-made costume with hat to match.'

With that sentence the report, carefully composed by my father at Sutton Villas, should have ended. But it was given to Uncle Arthur to take to the *Record* offices : and on the way he added a final sentence. 'The gifts,' he wrote, 'were numerous and costly.'

It was the occasion for a brawl. They were given nothing, said my father, worth more than half a crown. His mother, Cornish Martha, gave them less than nothing : she emptied her own salt cellars before the wedding feast to ensure that the happy couple provided their own salt. Such gifts as there were had been sparse and cheap.

But in making unkind jokes at each other's expense, my father's family had no equal.

3

The most secure objects in my early life were Tate and Lyle treacle tins. I had a cupboard full of them, of all sizes. I have never quite lost the feeling that almost anything can be built out of treacle tins. When I first heard of the Tower of Babel I saw it in those terms—as a tottering attempt, green and gold, to outdo what, often enough, I had aimed to do: to reach the ceiling of our living room.

Treacle tins, and tin toys. On some Sunday School occasion, quite beyond my understanding (I had such need of Hilda's hot hand), I was lined up with other small creatures and informed that I should run, with them, towards the other end of the room. Slow, suspicious, appalled, I gave the cry of 'Now!' my full consideration before deciding, largely because all the other children were nearing the opposite wall, that the event was under way. Wandering indecisively in their wake, I was seized by a Sunday School teacher and presented with a tin motorcyclist on a tin motorcycle. It remains the most astounding unsolicited gift I have ever received. The adult world managed somehow to persuade me that it was mine. I remember being poignantly aware of the way the motorcyclist's face was joined, down the centre, by tin tabs. I was, I think, rather frightened by the principle implied: that people could be made of tin, and held together by interlocking tongues of the same metal. I guess like all small children I did not for a long time manage to think of toys as mere toys. They were rather appalling alternative forms of life.

For a long time I preferred treacle tins, which claimed only to be tins: and books, those in the box under the bed, out of which tunnels could be made.

It was among the lodgers' feet that I remembered making my tunnels. It was a fairly brief business, our having lodgers,

I guess, and I do not know how my father, to whom neighbours were natural enemies, managed to accommodate outsiders under his actual roof without bitter warfare. Perhaps he did not manage it. I remember a club foot, as the main and (for that sad reason) most memorable lodger, and several pairs of pointed ladies' shoes—I do not tidy up the phrase, because, if it was the shoes I knew most about, down on the floor with my tunnels, I did find the ladies (who were nurses) quite pointed, too. Two thin women supported by the slightest bases you could imagine, those brilliantly shining shoes. Everybody smelt of the shoes they wore. The club foot was over-nice to me. How does a small child know there's some disparity between what an adult says and what he feels? But perhaps the poor man was trying to do something about the fact that, down there on the floor, I must largely have seen him in terms of that huge boot.

People were towers to look up at.

Some of the best people were my mother's friends—women she had been in service with. There was May, frail and, I think, the most unmarried person I have ever known: who had great ear trouble, for news of which I was always eager. Bulletins on the state of May's ears were at the heart of current affairs, for me, for a long time. They made my father impatient: 'Oh, damn that woman's ears!' And as if created to balance May there was Sarah, who was unable to read or write, and who was fat and stumbled over words—I loved listening to Sarah trying to get words into line, as, for her, they were always unwilling to be got. I suppose I loved Sarah's discomfort with words, which ought to have made me uneasy, because I loved Sarah, her total clumsiness, and the wonderful oatcakes of her own making she always brought with her: a huge, worried woman, a grown-up child, I think, who was in her middle years in the early 1920s, and had never been educated. She was happy, for all her worriedness, being in that sort of service that had become an odd kind of companionship: with old Mr Parker, a widower, a man mostly given to silence, though he delighted me by always addressing me, when he spoke at all, as if I were of his own age: he was the first adult, for example, who asked me for my views on the recent weather. It was all part, all this, of a confusing social pattern. There was mother's cousin Gladys, for example, who had married her employer, and lived in a house that, when I was old enough to be aware of it, *felt* to me like a product of the powers of one of my favourite characters in a comic: the magician who, with his striped wand, could enlarge anything he touched . . . It took hours, as it seemed to me, to walk from the front gate to the front door: for a long time, I thought of that distance as the very mark of domestic magnificence . . .

Somewhere, in the pattern, there were lodgers: and May and Sarah and (involving quite a different idea of Sarah) Sarah and Mr Parker: and my uncles, including Uncle Arthur, who kept pigs. Can I have had any feeling about the social value set on pigkeeping? Yet I think, as I spent Sunday mornings in his piggery, intoxicated by the marvellous stench of pig-food, that thick green ooze that smelt, as it were, of its appearance—I think I had caught from the atmosphere a sense of one's being up in the world, round at Mr Parker's, and rather down in it, alongside Uncle Arthur and his pigs (whose grunts, come to that, *sounded* much as their food smelled).

And there were the Bees: Mr Bee had been the gardener at my mother's last place. He seemed to live almost non-stop among his vegetables and flowers: I always had a sense of discomfort when I saw him actually inside his little house, just up the road from ours. I loved and hated the Bees' house. Loved it because it had the hugest mantelpieces, all hung with velvet mantelcloths—and those fringed with balls of velvet: and on the mantelpieces, and on every surface in the room, little houses made of thin wooden sticks—I have no idea where these came from; but I suppose it was back—I mean that I loved it because it was back—to the magician with his striped wand, mantelpieces too large for the rooms, a little actual house filled with tiny model houses. I hated the Bees' house because it smelt of caraway seed, and because there was always seed cake for tea, which I loathed: but you had to eat it, because Mrs Bee was censorious about children's feeding, and my mother was too much in awe of her to come to my aid. But I loved listening to my mother complaining, in other company, of Mrs Bee's intolerance in the matter of seed cake: and speaking of how much her heart ached when Mrs Bee frustrated my plan of taking the most fetching gateau, or the grandest slice, from the plate.

Mother sang me to sleep. My favourite song was called *Peggy O'Neill*. All I remember of it is that it celebrated, repetitiously, this lady's sweetness. 'Sweet Peggy O'Neill.' The thought of her makes me somnolent to this day. In some ways, I think I confused her with my mother. I had various mothers—one was always turning the handle of the wringer, and had bare, muscular arms. She was not the heroine of the song. *That* was my mother in her best, her faded but beautiful best, the lilac dress she'd been photographed in ten years before: with loops of coffee-coloured lace on the broad collar.

One of my mothers brought to an end, rapidly, our possession of a dog called Bob. I was disappointed when this dog arrived, long promised, because it wasn't edible: they'd talked of it being thoroughbred and I believed this was a variation of gingerbread. My mother was harassed by Bob—largely, I think, because it went about on four legs. Uncanny, almost as bad as spiders. Mother was then in favour of living things being on two legs, strictly. Later in life she became more relaxed about dogs . . . Bob went also because of his incurably slapdash attitude to excretion. In any case, he certainly wasn't a thoroughbred. He was an unkempt anthology of many sorts of dog. I wept when he was suddenly not there. Poor daft Bob—he'd come to the wrong house. A canine Hawkins.

But I think now of the quiet bothered passion with which she must have struggled to keep the house, my father, me, clean and orderly and decent. Her own father had used the obsession with cleanliness, hers and my grandmother's, to torment. The lino had to be pulled up and the floorboards scrubbed. A meaningless labour: it must have been imposed out of simple cruelty. It was my mother who had to do it: her sisters were set free by their coarse indifference to housework, of which he approved.

I try to imagine that beginning of hers, in those many different lodgings in West London. She liked school, but was rarely there. She had to be at home, looking after the baby, while my grandmother went out, nine till five for half a crown. At times my own schooling, especially when it showed signs of going on rather beyond the age of twelve (the age at which she'd stopped going to school herself), filled her with wistful reminiscence. She liked particularly, she often said, map-drawing. There'd been an afternoon when she stayed on, after the last bell, to draw a map: couldn't remember exactly what it was a map of, 'but it had O-C . . . in the top corner.' 'Ocean, Mum?' 'That's it—ocean.' It was the teacher who brought her to her senses. 'Won't your mother be worrying?' It was worse than that: she had to buy a loaf of bread, on the way home, and the shop was shut. 'My father thrashed me.'

When she fled from home, her comfort (leaving aside the stormy comfort that came from her encounter with my father) lay in the support of her mother's relations. These were mild people, much given to chapel-going. Mother herself was a Methodist; and was, it seems, much wooed by respectable young men of this persuasion. She was, and never stopped being, in the wild slipstream of my father's career: *he* was handsome and strong and dangerous and dreadful and irresistible: but that did not prevent her from considering very seriously the other offers she had. ('Oh yes, I had other offers.') But by then her father was in disgrace, her mother was in a mental hospital. She was afraid that these decent, apparently quite eager, young men would find out about her background. It was one a Sunday School teacher might flinch from. It would take much more than that to make my father flinch . . .

Oh, in any case, she used to say, they were dull, those others. They were nice dull men, some of them devoted to their mothers beyond all endurance. How much more exciting my father was . . .

Not that there seemed much real hope that she'd net that strong-flavoured youngster. It had been marvellous at first. They couldn't afford to go to theatres, but they walked the streets happily. He had, she remembered, a habit of leaning against lamp-posts. That's when he was at his best, with a lamp-post at his back. She'd wondered about it so much that she asked why he did it. He laughed at the idea of anyone thinking it remarkable. It was to be part of the pattern of their long life together: her amazement at what he did, and his astonishment . . . sometimes, alas, his sullen anger . . . at her amazement . . .

Other parts of the lifelong pattern were there from the beginning. He, aged thirteen, took her with him when he bought his first bowler hat. When he tried one on, in the shop, she found it impossible not to giggle. He was very angry. Didn't it suit him, then? But it did suit him, she thought.

Everything suited him. He wore things with such an air. It was only . . . And she struggled to say that his lovely solemnity, with that stiff black hat on his head, made laughter inevitable, though it also made admiration and adoration inevitable. He sulked. For nearly seventy years he was to sulk when she expressed her love in the fashion he did not understand, through laughter. Later I was to be involved in the disfavour she earned this way . . .

But it didn't last. It wasn't just that he lacked the graces of a lover. Once she saved up, saved up desperately, accumulated an entire half crown, bought him for his birthday a set of cufflinks and studs. Went off with the gift to the little half-house where my widowed grandmother was living with her quarrelsome sons. And he didn't even thank her. Took the gift—said nothing. 'Well,' said my father once, when the story was told, 'I suppose we weren't used to it. We never had presents—never gave them. I didn't know what you were supposed to say.' His disturbing laugh. 'Expect I sold it next day.'

It wasn't hurts like this that caused a break in the affair. She was used to enduring hurt: though such incidents must have given fresh force to the lamentations of her aunts and cousins, all of them opposed to the relationship. What broke things up was simply my father's attachment to other girls. They were, mother said, in that phrase that never varied, 'loud and common.' They wore great feathers in their hats, and were no better, were vastly worse, than they should be. They were versions of her own scornful sisters. They absorbed my father, bore him off, out of Annie's reach.

Well, of course. He had this cheeky handsomeness, which could become sulky and cruel. He was of medium height, not impressive that way, but chunky: an attractive body . . . I was proud of him in a bathing costume, used to find occasions to show photographs of him to schoolfriends. He was always dapper, his fingernails always trim and clean. In a photo taken when he was fourteen, he has the air of someone four or five years older: his hair smoothed across a high forehead, as it always was: full-lipped, the eyes wary. He wears a double-breasted suit that seems a little too large for him, and what looks like a celluloid collar. In another photo are all the brothers, and all their suits are out of scale. It was Will and

21

Arthur, my father once told me, who were the 'knocker men' —a phrase, I guess, for those who had the gifts of doorstep salesmen. They could charm anything out of anyone. They charmed, out of heaven knows who, suits for themselves and their brothers. They stand, in this photo, all of them, in a powerful half-circle round their handsome mother. A wilful strength and charm is the mark of most, as they thrust hands in pockets, lean on the backs of chairs, staring out with their wary, ambitious eyes. Among the smiles, only that of Uncle Harry, his nature simplified by his early illness, is quite easy . . .

A double-breastedness of brothers.

So my mother and he drifted apart. She gave her half-hearted attention to other steady young Methodists. He had several girls, and several jobs. It was always necessary to support their mother and the younger boys, not yet at work. Even at school the need to keep the family going had made learning seem remarkably irrelevant. 'Played hookey, all of us. Over the wall.' He remembered thin meals: sixpennyworth of bits, that was crumbs of beef, twopennyworth of potherbs, a penny packet of desiccated soup. He also remembered how they slept: five in a bed—three one way, two the other. The youngest slept with my grandmother . . . He left school at thirteen, excused on the grounds of his mother's need. Was a harum-scarum sort of chap. Remembered one job, as assistant to a photographer. Lost that, as he recalled, for mixing wrongly, carelessly, the chemicals for a flash. Then he became a van-boy. First task every morning, polishing the brasswork on the front of the shop, in Oxford Street.

And for fun, and to get into the ultimate trim, a soldier's uniform, he joined the Territorials. Horses. Gunners. It was in the family blood—his own father had been a regular soldier, and he had military uncles. There was the ex-hussar, who ran a gymnasium in a country town: when they were small it was there they had such holidays as they enjoyed: scaled-down glasses of beer with meals, and drill in the garden. Up and down with books on their heads, learning to be upright: and then, to round it off, to make them smarter yet, uncle pouring icily cold water over them, from buckets.

It was a keystone of a word, to my father: smart. Where philosophers worried over the 'true' and the 'good', he worried over the 'smart.'

Then came the move out to the green edge of London, to Sutton Villas. That was just before the war broke out. In early August, 1914, he was to go to an annual camp, as a Territorial : instead, he was called to the colours . . .

My first overcoat was made from my father's military greatcoat. It was often talked about: how it was cut down by a jobbing tailor, and how dashing it was, this miniature form of the khaki my father had worn throughout the Great War.

The war itself, which formed the substance of much of the imaginative life of my childhood—so many forms of the *Bumper Book of the Great War*, so many films, so many toy soldiers—the war itself was cut down for me, as a small set of anecdotes my father told, and certain objects that were kept in cupboards throughout the house. Here, for example, was the monocular he had managed not to hand in : it had a bright leather sheath, and I used it during my adolescence to examine nearby bedroom windows. Here, also, was his swagger stick, with its soft leather grip. The anecdotes were few and fixed. There was one about a trench, in a bend of which was embedded an officer's leg, still in its shining boot. He could not forget that boot—so appallingly swish. There was the time he was sent along a much-shelled sunken road to deliver a message to a forward position. Arrived, he tethered his horse to a post : but when he came back for it, the horse had freed itself and was gone. He had to run back along the sunken road, under shelling—and remembered sobbing as he ran. And finally, the memory of being hit, which had brought his active service to an end, a year before the armistice. He'd been carrying a cup of tea across an orchard, and a shell had landed nearby. He was taken back to England in a hospital ship that had been the King of Belgium's yacht, and remembered how a soldier in the bunk above him kept crying out from the pain of the arm he'd lost. 'Oh my poor bloody arm !' the man had cried, again and again.

He would say : 'There were horrible things. I didn't care much for anybody then, but some of the things I saw were very horrible.' Out of it, and out of that hand-to-mouth existence in West London after his father's death, he came with a bleak view of life : with some kind of innate chemistry, I guess, also at work. 'No such thing as a conscience in this

23

world,' he'd say. He regarded the very idea of friendship with scorn. 'All anyone's interested in is Number One.' There was, always likely to appear, that quality of cheeky charm, but it was set in a nature deeply suspicious, inclined to be coarsely and quite angrily derisive of any generous or aspiring quality in anyone . . .

4

The very best furnishing of my childhood was our living-room table. My father had bought it at an auction—an occasion that was part of family lore, since Uncle Will and Uncle Jack had attended the auction, to bid against my father and so make his purchases more expensive: it was, again, that cruel sense of fun.

It was a big, solid pine table: its best feature being that it had a shelf running all the way round, underneath. I sat under it and turned that shelf into a private universe. You could run toys along it, a totally secret system of roadways. You could simply *put* things on it. I think it was the perfect privacy of the world under the table that made it so marvellous. Hang cloths over the side and you were free even of the rare grown-up bending down to see what you were doing. It was often crowded down there: magicians, charming imaginary young women aged three or four, pliant replicas of Hilda Hawkins, Tiger Tim and his friends—we were all under the table.

It was from under the table that I watched my brother's teddy bear burning in the fire. It had fallen from his high chair over the brass rim of the fireguard. Helplessly I watched it burn. It was a horror of impotence, combined with my first and definitive experience of the inexorable destructibility of things. Helplessly, all my life, from time to time, I have watched it burn. I watched it burn when I saw London ablaze, in 1940.

24

It is one of only two memories I have of my brother, born the day before my third birthday, in 1923. The other I can date exactly. It was his first birthday. I am standing with a neighbour at a front window, watching my mother, the baby in her arms, hurrying across the green, and over the road, past the corner shop, and into forbidden Ferguson Road, which would take her to the station. Puzzlingly that night I went to Sutton Villas, and slept there with my grandmother. I remember her watching over my dressing on the morning of the following day, my fourth birthday : the enormity of dressing under an eye not my mother's.

What happened that night was that my brother died. He had been treated for constipation : what he really had was inflammation of the bowels. The treatment destroyed him. I feel a helpless distress, still, together with a sense that things *have* changed—things *have* changed, in the fifty years since— at the thought of my mother carrying her dying child, in her arms, up Ferguson Road to the station, and then by train to London, and then by bus to the hospital. I try to imagine how her simplicity dealt with the terror of it, and how they both felt about the arrival of the birthday card they'd sent him . . .

I still have the birthday card. It was one of the 'little things' that my father, in his last years, believed the heartless survivors would throw away. 'All these little things,' he'd say, bringing out some neat file of documents and photos. 'Straight in the dustbin when the old man's gone.' 'No,' I'd say. 'Don't talk to me. You won't be able to wait to get rid of them.'

One reason, but only one, why I've kept all his 'little things'.

Betty was born six months later. 'Come,' said my father, scooping me off the couch in the living room, 'and see your new sister.' I remember, as a sequel to this astonishing invitation, being carried up the steep stairs, into mother's bedroom, and seeing this fat stranger, herself so unexcited by the event, this is what struck me, that she was fast asleep.

The most precious things could be destroyed, easily : but new creations were amazingly possible.

When it came to school, my mother, I think, felt quite complacent about my prospects. After all, as she often told me, she'd tempted my embryo, according to a theory strongly adhered to in her family, with music and fish: the first was believed to aid the baby to beauty, the second to brains. I was born, as it happened, in a rather pessimistic manner, with forceps, and was not only badly bruised, but turned out to have what my mother always referred to as 'a sugarloaf head.' Years later she'd shudder when talking of it. 'I thought I must have been listening to the wrong music.'

But there'd been no evidence yet that her efforts with the fish had also misfired . . .

I should, of course, not have been there at all, with any sort of endowment, if mother hadn't written to my Cornish grandmother, after the outbreak of war. Mother's official recollection was that she'd been moved by the thought of the widow having, at such a time, six sons, most of military age. I guess she'd really been looking for any opportunity to renew an old acquaintance: and her simple guile worked. I can't, looking at wartime photos of my father, mischief itself in French studios, his cap at an angle he never permitted me when I wore another sort of cap as a schoolboy, his putteed legs confidently astride—I can't imagine that his taste for showy girls had faded. Whatever the French is for 'loud and common' . . . In that hell where he 'didn't care much for anyone' but 'saw some very horrible things,' did the thought of my honest mother, so eager of nature, so straight (her straightness was to be against her later, when he recovered his taste for crookedness), offer the only intelligible possibility of a way ahead, towards some unfrightened kind of life? They exchanged letters (I imagine mother writing hers as she did all her writing, with sternly compressed lips, nodding now and then as though to reassure herself amid the hazards of composition). And, against all the odds, they made their way towards marriage.

Their first problem, at that point, was to decide if he should leave the War Office, where he'd been sent as a clerk after he'd recovered from his wounds, and return to the service of the Oxford Street department store: or if he should sit as an ex-serviceman, for an exam that would give him, if successful, an established post in the Civil Service. His decision meant that when my mother was cramming herself with fish to make a scholar of me, my father was engaged in scholarship of his

26

own. He passed his entrance exam at the second attempt . . .

And here I was, going to school. Mabel Street was the biggest, most unlovable building I'd yet seen. It was of the oldest style of Board School : constructed to accommodate giants in need of restraint. I could not have imagined ceilings so far above my head : corridors so long and echoing : such a maze of rooms and doors and ways in and ways out. The air of the place seemed to hold the shouts and groans of generations of children. There was a bruising noisiness.

The playground was worse. The playground was unspeakable. In it, so far as I could make out, children were done to death. Well, there was no being sure that they weren't. Early on there was an event I cannot believe anyone explained to us. Suddenly we were in the hall, all of us, in the staggering immensity of the hall, and singing 'Abide with me.' Was the world about to end? Yes, it was : for at that moment a maroon went off, outside : and the entire hall fell silent. There was a great stirring coughing silence, and then we sat down and someone talked.

I didn't know what to do about standing up again. In fact, there was nothing to do, but stand up, and let everyone see the pool I'd left on the floor, on Armistice Day, 1925.

But there was Miss Stout. Miss Stout was stout, and she somehow reduced to kindly size the great crate of a classroom we occupied. Under her rotund care I learned to read to myself. I can recall the exact moment when it happened, and the odd, almost physical feeling I had of the words being inside me instead of outside. They were like so much fluff, falling lightly into my mind from the page : or perhaps not into my mind, for it was a feeling much like eating, except that what one was eating had practically no body, only this fluff-like quality, sinking down inside. It definitely went down—your mind was in your stomach, perhaps that was it. Something, I remember, about a farmyard.

Round the walls were boards painted with blackboard paint, and on these we were allowed to draw, with chalk. I can't remember ever drawing anything but a sheaf of corn . . . a series of concentric curves to the left, and another to the right, and a cummerbund of chalk lines across the middle, to represent the string. It was a great thing to draw what, even given this limited model, was clearly one's own sheaf of corn.

B   27

I wore boots for school, and for years afterwards. Preparation for school was a momentous matter of lacing these up. Done while reading Rupèrt Bear in my father's *Daily Express*. Laceholes to a certain height, then metal tags: then round, and through the leather tag at the back, and round again, and a bow in the front. By which time Rupert was either out of trouble, or so much in it that you didn't know how to wait for tomorrow.

A man sitting in the kitchen, crying. It was my father.

He'd been to his doctor. 'Ah,' said the doctor. 'I can't do anything for you neurasthenics.' He told my father to concentrate on gardening. This was not helpful, since what he needed was help simply in enduring the journey to work. He suddenly could not bear to travel. The underground was worst: quite impossible. In the underground he was back with the terror of the trenches, the dread of being buried alive. But to go anywhere must for him have been to move through country shrieking with phantom bombardments.

He cured himself. One day he would take a penny bus ride, and walk back. When he had mastered this distance, he took twopenny bus rides, and walked back. He kept at this until he could ride the whole way to Whitehall.

His certificate of discharge from the Army says he was dispensed with, on 11 May 1920, as being surplus to military requirements, having suffered impairment since entry into the Service (Para 392 (XVIa). K.R. 1912). He had served with the colours for five years, two hundred and eighty one days. Marks and scars, says most curiously this Army Form B. 108D, had he none.

We were going to move. We were going to have a house of our own . . . that's to say, one mysteriously more of a possession than our council house.

It would bring to an end our Sunday ritual, when we went down the road, past the Sunday School, and up the lane to the cemetery, to tend my brother's grave.

What a strange experience to have become part of the pleasanter memories of a childhood! But I liked it in the cemetery. I liked walking with my father, down the lane, and the occasional meeting with someone my father knew: lovely, hanging about at the edge of a meeting of adults. How extra-ordinarily versatile and competent, their conversation! How marvellous they were at making jokes! I wished their talk would go on for ever . . .

In the cemetery, the sickly sweetness of flowers. And the curious, untroubled interest one took in individual graves. I had feelings about particular graves quite like the feelings one might have about particular people. Our own quarter of the place felt very much our own. We had acquaintances among all these grave-tenders: grew accustomed to queuing up with them to draw water from the slanting tap. If I felt any dis-quiet, it was caused by the bowls of waxen flowers on some graves: for these seemed truly deathly, ashen, stiff and airless, and appallingly white, and their burial in glass seemed much worse than the idea of bodies being buried below those grassy humps.

While my father used his shears and trowel, I made my way with our dead flowers to the copse at the edge of which the cemetery, for the moment, halted. Here there was a dump into which dead flowers were thrown. The sweetness here was sharp, and here death was very apparent, the death of flowers.

But there'd be Sunday dinner to think of, to begin to smell . . . And we were going to move, whatever that meant. I hoped it wouldn't be like our experience of having, and then not having, a dog.

PART TWO

1

So we moved up to Barton-on-the-hill : to Number 10 in a row of semi-detached houses at the bottom of one of its slopes. The rest of the road was lined with large villas, all different in design, with names, not numbers. We were the road's humble appendage. It was to be the same, in time, with all the roads—some of them not modestly roads at all, but avenues—that ran down the hill. The big, comfortable houses, built early in the century, had not reached to the bottom : that would have involved too tedious a trudge to the railway station, at the top. Barton-on-the-hill had welcomed the railway, belatedly. It bore hundreds of bowler hats daily to the city.

I had an awestruck sense of the difference between us at the bottom, and those at the top whom it would have been impertinence to call our neighbours. It was part of the strongly-felt social geography of Barton. One end of the town was working-class : the names of the roads there were blunt and direct. Mallett, Perkins, Soper, even Jakes. The Avenues were ambitiously sonorous : Shakespeare, Worcester, Granville, Wickham. It was a complication, living at the velvety end of town.

Number 10 wasn't a mere house—it was, to me as a child, a creature, almost alive. I even thought of it as having a face. Since it was semi-detached, it was one face yoked to another. Next door was old Mr Folkestone, a retired sailor, with his famously disgruntled wife, and their half of the total house seemed to frown, in her manner, but also to hint at snatched laughter, in his. Ours had my father's tidily handsome but shut-off look. There was a blindness of lace at the windows. All twenty houses were the same, yet minutely dissimilar : certain elements, especially red tiles set in simple geometrical patterns on the roughcast, varied from house to house. The red tiles on ours made diamond shapes. On Mr Folkestone's they made circles. I had, as a child, some vague notion that these dissimilarities had a sly reference to the characters of their owners.

To my father the house was certainly a creature, to be tended, groomed, intimately watched over. He kept it as neat as he could, and I took from him a simple sense of difference as between our neighbours: there were those who treated their houses as he did, with tireless care, and those who were indifferent—or incapable of caring. I admired my father's sheer competence as an owner of property. Nothing that belonged to him, from the smallest tool to the fabric of Number 10, was ever allowed to fall into the mildest disrepair.

There were long narrow competitive gardens, and these too became part of my view of their owners. Mr Folkestone's was transformed into a curiously uncertain little pixieland, with ponds and paths that took cramped detours for the sake of a curve, abbreviated mysteries of destination. Walking in Mr Folkestone's garden made you very dizzy. Mr Bailey's, on the other side, was practical, full in season with wigwams of runner beans. The Baileys had a curious immunity from my father's usual scorn of neighbours. They were childless, both thin and shy, she always thickly made up, her bony arms in short sleeves. They had won a small car in some lottery: it was the only car among the twenty of us. 'Bailey,' my father would say, 'is always turned out like a new pin.' He very much admired Mr Bailey's hats: stiff pearl-grey trilbies. The target they offered—the sad absurdity of her make-up, their having a car (my father regarded the possession of a car as a despicable attempt to impress others)—was refused because of Mr Bailey's tidiness. 'Never a hair out of place.'

Mr Folkestone was saucy. He was a saucy ex-tar. His arms were works of art, anchors and mermaids. He made chuckling jokes that I did not entirely understand; but part of my love of them was rooted in my father's disapproval of them. 'Old Folkestone is a fool,' he would say. 'He can make as many jokes as he likes, but his bloody apple tree, that's what he calls it, though I've never seen a bloody apple growing on it, it hangs over my fence and he'll damned well have to prune it, or I'll do it for him.' 'Your dad,' Mr Folkestone would wink, 'is upset because my trees grow faster than his.' I would stare

34

fascinated at the mermaids swelling on his biceps, and would grin disloyally. That's what mainly Mr Folkestone contributed to my life—the curious thrill of being disloyal. 'Your dad's not about?' he'd whisper, coarse and throaty, a whisper that had surely once been audible over square miles of ocean. 'Then I'll nip his rose bush. It's half an inch over my side of the fence.' His secateurs flourished: my treacherous grin. He'd snap the shocking metal in mid-air, cutting nothing: then wink. Mrs Folkestone would appear. 'What are you doing there, Fred?' Mr Folkestone would make the secateurs snap several times in quick vicious succession. 'Cut your tongue out, old girl,' he'd whisper, mysteriously.

My father had a whole range of responses to other people's gardens. There were habits of mockery in respect of someone's roses. He was always on the lookout for horticultural pretension. 'Who does he think he's impressing—?' He vastly enjoyed his own scorn or indignation: and was always keeping easy greetings at bay. 'I don't go into the garden to gossip.' Neighbours were people who, given half a chance, would chat a morning away. They would also, if you didn't watch closely, tie their obstreperous bushes to *your* fence. It was part of the lore of my childhood—that this fence was my father's, to be kept free of intrusive vegetation: the other, Mr Folkestone's, to be constantly inspected for any sign of deterioration. 'Time Folkestone slapped some creosote on that fence of his. I shall have a word with him.'

'Oh Dick!' My mother knew very well what my father meant by 'a word'.

'Of course I shall have a word with the man. I don't want his fence to start falling into my garden, do I?'

So the quick word over the fence: not to be mistaken for conversation. 'What's going on there, then?'

Mr Folkestone, quite placatory when it came to an actual exchange with my father. 'I'm thinking of planting another apple tree.'

'I don't want its roots growing under the fence.'

'Oh, I don't think they'll do that.'

'They will, you know. I'd prefer it if you planted it a bit further away.'

I loved being in on one of these prickly conferences. I admired my father's dangerous crispness—and sensed the uncomfortable chumminess with which Mr Folkestone would try to turn a sharp encounter into a sequence of jokes. 'Your missus will be able to make apple jelly out of the apples that fall on your side.'

Bad move. My father's eyebrows lifting.

'I don't want any apples to fall on my side. And we have apple trees of our own, if we wanted to make apple jelly. As a matter of fact, we don't care for apple jelly.' My father in his element, with such a full hand of negatives to proffer.

'I'll watch where I plant it.'

'I should, if I were you.' My father's crisp, final nod. Upstairs a curtain would fidget: my mother, grieving over yet another infringement of the vast smiling neighbourliness it was so dangerously natural for her to feel.

My new school was Barley Road . . . less awful than Mabel Street, being single-storey. Building Mabel Street, they must have had fortresses, prisons in mind: the place was full of Gothic references. Barley Road was a rambling educational cottage: though like the other it was, for me, too inclined to stress the business of entering and leaving. There were so many doors, and such a ritual of penetration and escape to master. Watching films with Ruritanian settings, the point of which so often turned on the complex facilities available for smuggling oneself into castles and struggling out of them, I felt at home: it was just like school.

Inside, Barley Road at first was Miss Chadwinkle. She was very tiny, she seemed indeed to be one of us, dressed always in black, but wrapped rather than dressed. Her clothes made a small, kindly parcel of her. As a teacher she was totally empirical. That's to say, we were encouraged, in the matter of counting, in the bold use of matchsticks and fingers. She had cut-outs of all the letters in the alphabet, and these we moved about bodily, fitting them together to make our guesses at words. Miss Chadwinkle, whose name gave us such delight that we left it as it was, almost—in a hurry, she was The Winkle—was wholly opposed to abstraction. There was the feeling that, given the chance, she'd have made all knowledge tangible and portable. History itself could be turned into a sort of matchsticks . . . well, dates hung about the room, sometimes with no legend to account for them. So if you turned from what had become the pure manual labour of counting or spelling, your eye might be met by an urgent sheet of cardboard that simply shouted: 1066.

I was beginning to have that idea of yourself, as a dangerously exposed public person, that you're given by the need to write your name on the outside of an exercise book. At Barley Road an exercise book was used with great economy. So, at one end it would announce itself as an English book: turned upside down, and working from the other end, it would be an Arithmetic book. For Arithmetic you earned great blue-pencil knots, 'R's for Right: or, of course, blunt crosses for Wrong. In all subjects you had your Excellent, or your V.G. for Very Good, or G for Good or F for Fair, or S for Satisfactory. (How tepid that S was! Worse than F.G. for Fairly Good, and in some ways less preferable even than Poor, which was always spelled out.) Then there were your marks out of ten. You were always being stamped, in this complicated fashion, assessed and placed. I was soon aware of having the Barley Road seal of approval. I was one of nature's spellers. Had spelling not existed, this was the impression, I should have invented it. Put me in front of a picture and ask me to describe it—it was a favourite way of getting composition going—and I'd respond with a meticulous report, like a small policeman: beginning, 'In the picture I can see . . .' ('One little girl has a white overall on. The other little girl has a blue overall on'). We were barely out of Miss Chadwinkle's before we'd taken the soul-changing step from pencil to ink. On the middle finger of my right hand is still visible the distortion around the nail that resulted from becoming a young master of the inkpot at the age of six and a half. The metal of the nib-holder impressed itself, with the intensity of my grip on the pen. It made a hollow that was always black with school ink. I was altogether, in some deep sense, black with ink. I became an adept at Transcription which, in 1927, as a surviving exercise book proves, was an exercise given to the most tender: who were required to print this word at the top of the page. (I hadn't yet learned to join up my writing. 'He joins up' was another fine thing to have said about one, when the time came.) 'Transcription', I guess, was copying from the blackboard. Teachers are strange people! How curious to make no effort to translate this technical term for the understanding of its tiny users. We might as well have headed the page with some such word as 'Tergiversation' . . . Except that I suspect the human ink-blot I had become might have enjoyed that.

Briefly, incredulously, under Miss Thrift for Arithmetic, I ran out of favour. Not for my work, but for that other great compartment of oneself, its existence revealed by the busy paperwork produced by the school: one's Conduct. In this area I was perfect until I met Miss Thrift. She was an impatient woman, and choleric—not unlike my father: and perhaps it was this similarity that made me do, in her class, what I was already in trouble for doing at home. 'One thing I can't stand,' my father would say, 'is bloody giggling.' My mother and I, alas, were bloody gigglers. I think it would not have helped if we'd laughed frankly and aloud, instead of giggling, at those junctures which my father viewed as unsuitable ones. He would still have been angry. But it was for giggling that he pointed his square and excommunicating finger at us. 'Get out!' (It was I who had to leave the room— but there was no doubt that I was being exiled for the crimes of both.) Something about Miss Thrift's own ready angers made me giggle: and the knowledge that it was dangerous to giggle made it worse. She must have felt I was fooling her to the top of my bent. Anyway, she beat me, and I'd go back to my seat and giggle, and she'd beat me again, all in a sort of nervous daze. Indeed, it was the nervous thrashing the nervous. I find it horribly easy to remember how the hands grew puffed and red, great painful cushions.

How strange, again, teachers are! Caning on the hands was common throughout the school—and odd, very odd, when you think that our hands were the prime tools with which we were expected to work . . .

The playground at Barley Road was firmly divided. For a brief period, while we were in Miss Chadwinkle's care, some sort of innocence was presumed that made it acceptable for us to play together, boys and girls. But as soon as we were into ink and exhibiting other signs of ominous maturity, like joining up our letters, we were divided, and the division was expressed in solid terms, as walls. It was as if the girls suddenly took veils . . . of blue engineering brick.

It was great, and it was horrible, to be promoted to the

boys' playground. Great because we all accepted the view that promiscuous contact with girls would cause a sensational decline in our manliness. Horrible because I didn't, when it came to the point, much care for being manly. Or rather, I wanted to be able to make a selection among those acts and habits that were identified as masculine.

All right, games with your 'faggies'. That was playing with cigarette cards, in any of three or four different fashions. Your enemy cocked his cards against a wall, and you flicked at them, taking those you knocked down. Or you flicked with the aim of covering cards already lying there. It was, in effect, a series of ways of bringing about an increase or decrease in the number of 'faggies' you possessed. It was the nearest, I think, I've been to knowing how it is to be a millionaire, or totally down-and-out. There were times in the 1920s when I had such quantities of cigarette cards as I swoon about, even as a memory. I was one of your bloated cigarette card-owners. I've known, too, what it is to be down to half a dozen caricatures of lesser members of the Australian cricket team, 1928.

Playing with 'faggies' was gentle enough, even for a child like myself, virtually born with kid gloves on. So were such games as 'airplanes'. In 'airplanes' you simply were . . . airplanes. Cap back to front, arms outstretched. A friend to swing your propellor—actually, your tie. 'Contact', he called, and you stuttered and vibrated before allowing the engine to come fully alive: half a turn, a bit of taxi-ing, and you were airborne, in a cluster of tense-faced aircraft arbitrarily given to ramming each other or shooting each other down. ('Go on—you're in flames!' 'I'm not!' 'You are!' 'Fred saw me! I put in twenty bursts! Didn't I put in twenty bursts, Fred?') Some of the consequences of playing airplanes could be nasty, but could be avoided, as they were by myself and other milder boys, by keeping to the air-lanes alongside the wall of the girls' playground.

But I didn't like not being able to go to the lavatory, sit-down, without being turned into an exhibition. There were no locks on the doors. You'd sit there, praying, but they'd come crashing in, the big boys, running the whole length of the lavatories, throwing doors open with immense cries of 'Poppy show! Poppy show!' They'd have smaller followers, who'd shout, 'Take a look at *that*!' They struck me as having knowledge and experience of quite an appalling kind, lying behind these exclamations of theirs. It was the sort of mysterious acquaintance with things that dictated another of their habits—of running through the playground, demanding: 'How many balls you got?' I knew the accepted answer was two, and would provide it rapidly—the convention was that failure to answer such questions was punishable with punches —but I didn't know why it was the answer. I did not know about balls. I didn't, for a long time, know about valves, either.

That was wireless valves. 'How many valves you got?' they'd ask. Even if you had no wireless set—especially if you had no wireless set—it was a dangerous question to answer.

Much of our life from about 1929 onwards revolved around the wireless. Until then, we'd had, as a family, only the most fitful encounters with this invention.

My own first was about 1923, when wireless was still quite raw and improbable. The Dockrees next door had one. This was enough to earn them the reputation of being stuck-up, if not high and mighty. ('I hope they don't think I'm impressed', my father would have said—never able to believe that people had other motives for possessing anything.) However, when they invited him in one evening, to listen to this pretentious acquisition of theirs, he did not demur. He took me with him. It was a crystal set, and we donned earphones. Very tiny music tickled our ears. Minute voices murmured. I took it that these marvels were occurring at the edge of, if not deep in, some bleak ocean. The wailing of gulls could be heard, and the surge and collapse of distinct waves. At times a whole orchestra was swept away, amid screams, to be tossed up again, its music desperately watery, a moment later. I did not take to it. It was altogether too calamitous.

All the same, it was a misery of my early schooldays that we did not possess a wireless. It left me particularly vulnerable in that matter of how many valves we might have. With time I came to realise that the acceptable answer to the question was anything from three to five. You could say seven, but this might be a punchable answer, because it involved making a pretty lofty claim. Safer to say 'Three'—or 'Five' if your interlocutor was of the milder kind. For a long time, for me,

40

this was part of the same phantom arithmetic as the answer about one's complement of balls. We could not afford a wireless.

So I've never forgotten the almost intolerable excitement of being able to say, one day, to members of my intimate circle, who knew the truth about us—that until then we'd had no valves at all: 'My dad's bringing a wireless home tonight!' Oh, that shameless exhilaration! And running home—to find we had this box of tricks and its companion horn. The horn was a slender question mark, black, and the programmes, not much more robust than they had been in my earlier experience, took place in the depth of the horn. Uncles and aunts were scratchily jolly, down there. More music was drowned: comedians made shipwrecked jokes. And the saga of the accumulators began.

The wireless depended on accumulators, and I was their slave. That is to say, I was responsible for taking them to be charged, and for fetching them home again: the domestically sensitive essence of this task being that there should always be an accumulator ready for fetching when the one in use petered out.

Someone living down the road did the charging, in his garden shed. I'd stand among all those bubbling accumulators, anxiously. Was ours ready? Make a mistake, and we might miss Saturday night's vaudeville. Harmony in the home came to depend quite gravely on those glass boxes of acid, and on high tension batteries. Sometimes it depended on even greater mysteries. For no known reason, the horn would fall silent. Then my father, with no gift for such things, would fume over the dead marvel, making angry disconnections and reconnections: resorting, often enough, to ignorant bangings and shakings. In the garden, our aerial, fifteen feet high, appealed to the air for a croak from some comedian like Stainless Stephen, for the crackling cry from the announcer that heralded an hour of indispensable comedy.

Most of the time, I think, whatever answers I gave in the playground to those terrible bigger boys with their merciless curiosities, we had two valves only—just about, I guess, the very smallest number possible.

But then we were distinctly poor. One of my worst memories is of a moment at the end of a holiday. We'd had a week in Hastings, staying in a boarding house—marvellous, that, because my father was so interestingly severe about our landladies, on such holidays. He was inclined to be generally severe on landladies, as he was on bus conductors ('Can I have your number, please?') and cinema usherettes ('Will you give me your name?'). The seaside landlady had no number, and he already knew her name, but he always had the air of someone preparing a long and scrupulously documented complaint. 'Wonder what made her give us the room overlooking the gasworks?' I liked being in on these dissatisfactions. They gave a sort of political edge to the felicities of being by the sea. 'What did you think of the breakfast, Annie?' Seaside breakfasts were always marvels, to me: such surprising insights into other ways of cooking bacon, such amazements as to cereals. But it was agreeable, as we set off into the huge but anxious libido of the day (would we go on the pier? oh, *would* we go on the pier?), to listen to father's equally surprising objections. 'Suppose you could call it fried bread—gave it a sniff of the cooking fat, perhaps. Sorry for that little husband of hers.' Sorry for her husband? 'Doesn't get a word in, poor bugger. Excuse my French.'

On the occasion I remember, he suddenly found he had lost ten shillings. It was awful to see my strong, capable father crumble. There was terrible despair. The day vanished as we hunted through pockets, through cases, turned our bedrooms upside down: went through the town to every place we'd called at the day before. We went back to shops and made hopeless inquiries. It turned the holiday ashen. Ten shillings was all the margin between serenity and horror.

Well, as I know now, he had never moved above his first rank in the civil service, as a clerical officer. Anger grew in him: he suspected that it was because he'd left school at thirteen. Hadn't the right voice, the right background. Among the *dramatis personae* of my childhood were those seniors of my father's who, in his view, kept him down. Ching, Aston, Maclagen. When he cut my hair with particular ferocity, and before it needed cutting, it must often have been as an outlet for furies with their roots in Whitehall. We rarely went to the barber's—my father saved the money by cutting our hair for us, my sister's and mine: and this task he performed with his usual efficiency, and in my case with that habit he brought to so many things of stripping to the bone. My whole head bristled when he'd done with it. At times the hedgehog nature of the stubble rising up the back of my head made me whimper. My father had no patience with whimpering. I'd daydream under his brisk scissors. He'd move my head to give himself easier access to the part of my hair he'd reached, and in my absentness I'd turn it back at once to where it had been; whereupon he'd spread a big square hand over the top of my head and turn me with a jerk into the position he wanted, hissing impatiently. I'd weep then, with the shock and roughness of it, and he'd grow angrier yet. 'For God's sake keep your head still! Think what you're doing!' 'Dick!' My mother's habitual protest at his lack of patience. At the worst, there'd be crying, floods of it, which might well catch on, so that my sister would cry, in sympathy or rivalry : and sometimes my mother would add tears of her own : and he would at once enter on some disagreeable task chosen for its untimeliness and the general inconvenience and distress that it caused. 'I'm going to have a jolly good clear-out today!' That meant once that the model theatre I'd built out of cardboard, with characters cut out of magazines and mounted (Sinbad and the Forty Thieves, with certain ancient Romans intervening, because they'd been available in the *Strand*), went onto the bonfire in the garden. What had Ching, Aston and Maclagen done that week?

So much of what I was as a child was defined by my father's hands. They knotted my tie for me every morning. I was fourteen before I learned to knot a tie for myself. His angry capacity to do practical things well made it impossible for him to leave such things to others—even when they concerned matters so personal as knotting your tie. He bathed me with painful rigour, as if he were dealing with some disorder in the garden. Once a week, standing nervously out of the water, I'd gaze at the distorted image of us both offered by the copper casing of the geyser, watching as he spun me round, scrubbed and polished, as if I'd been copper myself. 'Ow!' 'What's the matter now? For God's sake stand up straight!' When I set off for Barley Road, it was a stinging, throttled child who ran out through the front gate and loosened himself, screeched himself into untidy readiness for the school day. Not that I could do anything about the thick shirts that were always

43

bought too large, to allow for growing, with tails that had to be folded as best they could between my miserable legs. I had burning excesses of shirt, always, stuffed into my shorts with their perpetual, careful creases. I was one of Dad's artefacts, impossibly groomed, a groaning target for boys—and that meant nearly all boys—less unwillingly dapper than myself.

So well-meant, much of the time! I was a living retort to the notion that, given his background, my father must be indifferent to appearances. In any case, the men in his family had always been careful with clothing. It was their riposte to the world of the slums—but also curious evidence of their notion of manliness, which depended on the curl of the brim of a bowler hat, the set of a suit. Behind that, I guess, lay the family's experience of soldiering. They wrote pipeclay and polish into their private lives. When, years later, I became my own man, my father was tirelessly scornful of my dress. 'Oh my God!' he would cry, of some shirt I wore as a thirty- or forty-year-old. 'What do you call that?' He was uneasy about being seen in my company if I was wearing corduroy, or suede shoes . . . Anyway, whatever happened, I was not to be allowed to be a cause of gossip among the neighbours. 'I'm not having a child of mine looking like a tramp.' There seemed, alas, to be no compromise between looking like a tramp and looking like a drawing in the draper's catalogue . . .

But for all his angers, his tendency to treat us as slovenly privates in his army, I admired and loved him. Of course. He was the best of nurses. Show any sign of illness, and he'd be gentle, attentive, tirelessly concerned. He had lost a child, and nearly lost my sister with double pneumonia, and his impatience vanished at the first cough, any childish sickness. And on the other side of his refusal to see life as anything but a callous conflict of egos, Number Ones, lay his boyish charm. He made Christmas a great occasion, always. The gaucherie of his youth as to the giving of presents gave way absolutely, then. We didn't hang up stockings, my sister and I: we hung up pillowcases. He had one little child-pleasing gift which was a feature of all those Christmases—he'd convert walnut shells into mice, with string tails and inked eyes. There might be residual annoyances about the precise timing of the feast— his obdurate sense of life as a timed military exercise was never in abeyance. When he was at the table, bow-tied, giving the carving-knife its final edge, you were ill-advised to do anything but scurry to your place. But then, I never wanted to miss the spectacle of my father carving. He was famous for it, and never was a turkey more beautifully dissected. I'd tear myself out of the world of the *Holiday Annual, 1929*, Billy Bunter fatly triumphant (it was a grief of mine that I could never persuade my father to read those stories, to share my weekly *Magnet*), in order to watch him at work, achieving slices paper-thin.

Christmases! The annual entry into our lives of the exotic date, rare tangerine, wastefully fragile biscuit, Christmas pudding almost as black as his bowler hat! Chestnuts baked on the edge of the grate, splitting to reveal the hot yellowing flesh . . .!

And on Boxing Day we might very well go in quest of leaf-mould, in our local woods. You weren't allowed to take this rich deposit away, it was against the byelaws, but we'd creep out for this Christmas crime, he and I, early in the morning—with a suitcase. I think it seemed to my father that a suitcase might strike any forester who was about as an unlikely receptacle for leaf-mould. So there we'd be, man and boy, sneaking out of the woods on this festive morning— with such, I've since thought, highly suspicious innocence, wrestling with an appallingly heavy suitcase—in which, and this was the real cunning of it, the incriminatory tool we'd used, a trowel, was safely hidden.

As I think of those Boxing Day mornings, a nine-year-old grin, even now, spreads over my face.

2

At Barley Road one of my studies was love: I was in it, in three different ways, with three different teachers. They were Miss Baker, Miss Wilson and (so it happened) *Mrs* Wilson. This triangular love was given an extra richness by the faint difference of title between Miss and Mrs Wilson. I puzzled over that. Some point was obviously being made, but I couldn't guess what it was. If they'd been addressed in exactly the same way, the ladies would have been perfectly distinguishable. Mrs Wilson was heavy, dark and whiskery. I liked her moustache, which in certain lights had a bold existence. Miss Wilson was slim, fair and, somehow, sad. What came from her was a lovable sort of melancholy. I think in truth she may have been rather a dull woman. But her lack of liveliness felt to me like sadness.

Miss Baker I loved, I believe, precisely because it did not seem to be what she was made for. She was a tall spike of a woman : severe, brisk. But she gave me, very often, ten out of ten; marked my work Excellent; expressed, in her crisp manner, her sense of my promise. I felt I was in stern favour with her : it was like being rather coldly caressed.

In Miss Baker's class, we were each encouraged to make a poem our own. So Jack Spriggs was *A Boy's Song*, by James Hogg. Fred Burgess was *The Sound of the Wind*, by Christina Rossetti. And so on. At some point, Miss Baker would say : 'Jack, come out and recite your poem.' And Jack would go to the front and stand very stiff and tense, and rattle off his title and the poet's name. Jack was pure devil : he used in the playground to ask me rude riddles, extensions of that one about the number of one's balls, to which I knew and anxiously gave the answers without at all understanding them. Now he'd throw himself into his poem, which he recited on the principle that a poem should become faster and faster, the further you got into it. He was going at a pretty lick by the last verse but one :

> Why the boys should drive away
> Little sweet maidens from their play,
> Or love to banter and fight so well,
> That's the thing I never could tell . . .

None of us blinked an eyelid at that, though a little irony might have been justified—especially from the little sweet maidens of the class, who, as far as Jack Spriggs was concerned, were little sour maidens : having good reason to doubt the sincerity of that innocence he expressed by way of James Hogg. The last verse he'd fling off with rattling haste, and have done with the whole thing. 'A little more *expression* next time,' Miss Baker would observe, with amazing self-possession, and Jack would scuttle back to his desk, looking relieved, proud and furtive, all at once; and out would come Fred Burgess. In the course of months Fred, a quiet boy, had virtually *become* Christina Rossetti. Miss Baker never had cause to complain of a shortage of expression in his case—he gave everything in his little poem (his and Christina Rossetti's) more value almost than it could bear.

> The wind has *such* a *rainy* sound,
> *Moaning* through the town,
> The *sea* has such a *windy* sound—
> *Will* the ships go down?

This query was always pitched very high, so that you felt uneasy because you couldn't give an answer : there was the imperative quality in it that was found in other questions which we knew had to be answered, such as : 'How many ounces in a pound?'

> The *apples* in the *orchard*
> Tumble from their *tree.*—
> Oh will the ships *go down, go down,*
> In the *windy sea?*

'Good for feeling', Miss Baker would observe, perhaps translating that opinion into figures (8 out of 10); and Fred Burgess-Rossetti would hurry back to his seat, while we still disturbedly struggled with our sense that the question really ought to be given an answer. Well, would the ships go down, or wouldn't they . . .?

And some time during those afternoons it would be my turn to step out : I being William Brighty Rands. I don't think I ever really believed this name stood for anything so commonplace as an actual human being. It was obviously an invention of the order of the poem itself—my chosen poem, and so, to me, the most archetypal of all poems : more so even than *The Forsaken Merman*, with which *Mrs* Wilson used to rake our bowels on dusky winter afternoons . . . my own poem : *The Pedlar's Caravan.*

47

> I wish I lived in a caravan,
> With a horse to drive, like a pedlar-man!
> Where he comes from nobody knows,
> Or where he goes to, but on he goes!

I can hear my childish voice in it still, expressing immense astonishment.

> The world is round, and he can ride,
> Rumble and splash, to the other side.

I concluded it was an amphibious thing, a caravan; I saw him driving it through the very sea.

> With the pedlar-man I should like to roam,
> And write a book when I come home . . .

(Ah! myself, seconded from Barley Road for the purpose of writing a book about my voyage round the world!)

> All the people would read my book,
> Just like the travels of Captain Cook!

It was my poem, totally. Ever since I could remember I'd had that curious desire to write books. It was *my* poem for reasons of love, as mysterious as the three varieties of passion that drew me to Miss Baker, Miss Wilson and Mrs Wilson. I loved the romantic elation of certain phrases: 'He clashes the basins like a bell,' for example. 'He can ride, Rumble and splash, to the other side . . .' Superb! 'He has a wife, with a baby brown . . .' I loved that, especially. I liked the idea of a brown baby, but even more I liked the delay of the adjective: I liked the adjective appearing on the unaccustomed side of the noun. *That* was poetry!

The love got into me so much one afternoon, and in its turn so penetrated Miss Baker's severe casing, that she sent me to recite my poem to our headmistress, in her room. She, Miss Mason, was a sad, hunched little figure. We didn't know then that she was suffering from a hopeless slow illness—I guess that was what made her seem sad: a little woman, gently stern, holding herself together against pain and the grief of being fatally ill. I remember her smile when I'd spoken *The Pedlar's Caravan*: her nod: 'You like that poem?' 'Oh yes, Miss Mason.' 'Do you know any other poems by William

48

Brighty Rands?' I could not take in the implications of this question: that my poet, far from flaring once into splendid existence to compose *my* poem, and then expiring, might have been around for some time in a common busy way, composing others. I smiled and received another sad smile in exchange, and went on my way, feeling almost unbearably famous (for having been despatched to give this command performance), and quite powerfully confused (for having been introduced to this notion of William Brighty Rands as a sort of poetical navvy).

Prose was another matter. Prose I devoured—without, at first, causing my father alarm. Later, when reading became with me what he saw as a disease, he was bitter about my passion for books. 'Go out and get a breath of fresh air. Where do you think all this . . . sticking your nose in a book is going to get you?' But I remember gratefully—I think he mercifully forgot—that the first memorable reading I ever did was thanks to him.

He belonged to the Westminster Public Library. The name of that institution, matter-of-fact enough, gives me a thrill of pleasure to this day. It was stamped on the books he brought home. His own reading was surprisingly sentimental: he was very fond of Warwick Deeping. On the whole, though, he thought of novel-writing as the art of padding. It was a term he often used. 'All padding.' 'After all,' he would say, 'you can tell a story in five minutes. That's all one of these books is—a story anyone could tell in five minutes. Less.' He'd laugh, as though pleased to have this opportunity of putting you wise to the rascalities of writers. 'Well, reading a book . . . you can get the gist in a quarter of an hour. When I come to pages where they look at the flowers, I skip over them.' 'After all,' he once added in later life, when I was a writer myself, 'they're only—'

'Padding?' I volunteered, drawing on decades of familiarity with this speech of his.

'Trimmings,' he said, triumphantly.

The first book he brought home for me from his library was *Alice in Wonderland*. It had olive-green covers and the curious, heady smell of a library book. It was a smell as of a concentration of such covers, of millions of pages living with

49

each other, squeezed together, on miles of shelving. I try to define that smell because it had such an effect on me. I was made dizzy by it as by the fumes of some powerful drug. For years, thereafter, I was readily overborne by the sheer smell of literature . . .

I read *Alice* on summer evenings, in bed. Ah, the clean sheets, the white light, the sounds of such of the world as was yet unbedded! Especially the clink of my father's spade, as it struck a stone out in the garden. I've never, anywhere, been in a happier posture for reading. And there I was, in two worlds side by side: the secure world of the murmuring garden, of mother moving below in the kitchen, and that world, all magnifications and minimisings, shrinkages and telescopings, invented by Lewis Carroll. I know people who say that *Alice* is really no book for a child. They, as children, were aware only of some audience Carroll was addressing over their shoulders. Alas. I can't think of a better book to have started with: because it *is* about transformations, all those rapid changes of scale. Reading it makes one ready for a basic feature of life—its simple marvellous ambiguities of measurement . . .

Reading *Alice*, I was committed, among other things, to a lifetime as a library-user.

My first library was in Barton-on-the-hill and opened its doors for two hours only in the evening. Or rather, it kept its doors closed until someone inside was ready to leave the small room the library occupied, when he would change places with whoever was at the head of the queue on the pavement. In my memory, it is always winter, always very cold; I suppose because in winter it was a particularly exhilarating experience to step into that room. There was a roaring fire, and it brought out the smell of the books wonderfully. Literature was a fume, a smell you could step into and disappear in. Transformations, vanishings. Every book offered both. Where would you choose to vanish today? How transformed? Into the desert, as a Foreign Legionnaire? Into the year 17—, when you might one dark night have been seen riding hell-for-leather in the direction of York? I welcomed all offers of transmigration for my small self, but had a special liking for becoming a pupil of some faintly tragic boarding school, circa 1880.

In the middle of the room, the volunteer librarians, mostly

50

large ladies with immense hats. At one end, the junior section. At the other, the adult section. Most of the time I was happy enough to be a literary junior. But it was possible to explore the other end, make a choice and—selecting a moment when some particularly large hat was particularly lost in the business of using the date-stamp—escape with a book you oughtn't to have . . . It was among my earliest crimes, and led now and then to baffled reading.

A book a day, much of the time. Up to the library, reading the last pages, bumping into lamp-posts. Fairy tales. Any story about brothers leaving home to seek their fortune was a story about my uncles . . .

And at school, Mrs Brown read *Black Beauty*. She did that at the end of the day. Again, in my memory it's winter; the gas is on, the serious equipment of the day is stowed away; we have permission, ah marvellous permission, to fold our arms on the tops of our desks. Mrs Brown, with her round, comfortable voice, *is* Black Beauty. I definitely and affectionately equate this motherly teacher with the horse—which I don't, perhaps, altogether think of as a horse. Sensitive, mane-tossing Black Beauty—she's rather like Pam Rice, whose own wild black hair makes her beautiful : but the boys' playground says she's 'dirty'. 'Gyppo!' . . . More transformations . . .

I guess now that Mrs Brown believed the graver business of teaching language had been completed earlier in the day : a matter of commas and fullstops, nouns and verbs and those adjectives always defined with such circularity . . . being describing words because they describe . . . because they describe . . . But in that gaslit classroom, here, for me, was the real teaching of English : as the words came together to form sentences, the sentences composed a harmony for which one might invent the word paragraph, and inverted commas thought themselves into existence as Mrs Brown read of her . . . no, of Black Beauty's conversations with Ginger . . .

My father was not a religious man; but there was a time when he decreed that my sister and I should say our prayers after bathing. I can't remember that it was ever on other occasions : there was plainly some connection in his mind between ablutions and piety. We bathed in a tin tub. This was already a strain, because my father was also rather

51

precise about the need for me to stand, at any moment that might be thought to imply display, with my back to my sister. I don't know what sort of moral rot he thought might result from my standing otherwise. I remember the shock this mysterious prudery caused me; for though I could not imagine how anyone could be disgraceful when seen from the front, I did hold quite severe views about the other aspect. To make a show of the bottom was as wicked as anyone could get. I sought an explanation, but in vain . . . So there was already giggling, as part of the business of bathing, when prayer was added to this moral topsy-turvydom. Embarrassment was complete: and led only too easily to scenes quite unlike those my father must have had in mind. Giggles: shouts of reproofs: at last, slaps. On the bottom, in the stumbling middle of the Lord's Prayer. Once again, I regretted the very existence of bottoms.

Piety was a mystery altogether. At school we seemed to pray at the oddest junctures. There was an insistence on the full convention: hands clapped together, heads bent, eyes closed. It was a posture that led at once to the nervous comedy of the sly glance, the exchange of murmurs. Miss Thrift came round to see that our hands were truly sealed, our eyes genuinely closed. Defaulting hands she would jam together, fiercely. The preamble to prayer—that irritable tour of hers, her cry of 'We're not ready! We're *still* not ready!'—made us ache with unholy impatience. I believed, however, in the general idea surrounding these activities. God *was* above, watching. He *was* making notes.

Suddenly our headmistress, Miss Mason, was away: was said to be ill: was said, one dreadful morning, to be dead. It was too much to take in. The chief effect on me was that, for long afterwards, I would suddenly remember that she, too, was above us, on watch. It was always in the middle of a moment of mischief that I reminded myself of that sternly gentle *voyeuse*, struggling to digest the knowledge (unfairly gained, I could not help thinking) that I was *not* the entirely excellent lad she had taken me to be, when limited to earthly vision. I felt the unbearable shame of being wholly known. She must have made a heavenly note, for example, of the fact that I stole comics.

I had discovered that you could pick up a comic from the

52

newsagent's counter, and seem undecided about having it, and pick up another, slipping the first under it: and then display, and pay for, only the comic on top. It was amazingly easy. I did it again and again. One day I told Freddy Fletcher about it; then offered to give a demonstration. Leaving the shop, giggling in anticipation of Freddy's astonishment, I ran into Mrs Wilson, going in. Did she not look at me sharply? Could she not, being Mrs Wilson, divine at once the cause of my excitement?

I poured out my horror to Freddy: and we ran along the High Street, through the church passage, and didn't stop till we were in what we took to be the relative sanctuary of our own road. But in a universe full of teachers alive and teachers dead, how safe was any place for the wrongdoer? Somehow it struck us that the only thing to do was to bury the evidence. This we did under a hedge bordering one of the bigger houses. For weeks afterwards, I trembled in Mrs Wilson's presence, hurried past the scene of that appalling burial, waited for the arrival of the police . . .

How difficult to be good! How easy to be wicked! One never stopped quivering, morally. Such sternness everywhere! I would wake in the night, remembering the loveletters stuffed into my desk, at school.

Such a small playground—I've been back to look at it—and we were only children of nine or ten; but that playground seemed then a grey Sahara, and the boys in it were bigger than camels. All except me, that is; I was as small as you like, a kind of metaphysical smallness related to the fact that I'd earned the hatred of Brian Green. All I clearly remember of Brian now, apart from that illusion of hugeness, is his teeth, very large and white. He hated me, and so his gang hated me, because I was his rival for the love of Jean Rawlins. She, I suppose, was a scrap of a child, in fact; but to me she was whole ripe womanhood—golden hair, rounded arms, large bright eyes. There was a general feeling in the class that she was queen of all the girls—her attentions must be reserved for the king of the class, and that was Brian Green, obviously, he and his great white teeth and his loyal gang. But Jean had confused the picture by also leaning towards me—the swineherd: or perhaps the piping shepherd lad, for what she liked

53

me for was my good marks in English. She expressed, at times, quite unrestrained enthusiasm for my compositions, as read out by Miss Baker. So, though I was thin and polite and a palpable weed, she had chosen me as her consort. At the same time, she had chosen Brian Green. Herself, she was happy to leave it at that: she was a two-fellow girl. But having to share her formed a cloud over some months of my life at Barley Road. I had no gang, to balance Brian's—I had nothing like a gang. Oh, I had friends, but our bond was the swapping of comics, the sharing of fantasies, long talks in safe parts of the school corridor. We were always adding to our plans for an adventurous tour of the world which should be embarked upon as soon as the trifling obstacle of our infancy was surmounted. We formed nothing like a military unit.

So life became very chequered. In the classroom it was all brightness. We must have done something other there than pass notes, but much of what I remember is the passing of notes. Those loveletters, stuffed into my desk!

It was something we all did—a curious amorous traffic. The notes always, as I remember them, took the same form: *Do you love me?* they asked, and they followed this with the formula, *Ans.* This is an abbreviation usually associated with arithmetic —A-N-S = Answer—but we gave it a new literary setting. The loved one was to make her reply in the space that followed: and usually it was *Yes* or *No*. Can we really have spent so much time asking the same question and receiving, usually, a teasing negative: the old, familiar, expected teasing negative, which made the heart thump, the blood race? When it came, you tried again: and on, and on, until—just before the day's last bell went—the note would come back with, on it, that blessed affirmative: and all was well, then, until the following morning, when it would start all over again.

That was the classroom, and glory; but there was also the playground to be faced—the great Sahara across which Brian Green and his army would come streaming . . . I would lie on the asphalt beneath them, sobbing, and that was my playtime—suffocation, plain suffocation, till the bell went again and I was released. There was nothing for it but to turn to the teachers, and to assume for their benefit the frailness that might be expected to go with continual top marks in composition—a general plea of headache, and overall malaise, that

54

sometimes earned me a playtime indoors, a happy reprieve cleaning the inkpots or clearing the blackboard of its last spot of chalk. It was at this time that I found I could very easily turn white, simply by concentrating on the idea of being that colour. It was the only way to avoid being, every playtime, at the bottom of the great spiteful pyramid of Brian Green's gang.

Nights were the best of all—the great white summer nights when I lay in bed and over and over again destroyed all the might of Brian Green and his gang. I had complete command of the situation then. There he was, Brian Green, invading the town—he and his gang horsed and armoured, traitors every one. The shock it caused when the town discovered that Brian Green was really a Saracen, a wicked baron, a German!—the revelation varied from time to time, but the substance remained the same. Traitor! To whom could the town turn for protection against those revolted schoolboys? To whom but to that gentle writer of praiseworthy compositions, that hero whose tendency to earache and dizzy fits had hitherto masked the nature of his heroism? There was I, at the head of my army, and my lieutenant weed, frail little Freddy Fletcher, at my side—at my side, but much lowlier, of course—and we rode through the town and met the enemy in the recreation ground. We drove them through the bandstand and the flowerbeds, through the churchyard and into the High Street, into Sainsbury's and out through the yard at the back, down through the printing works and so (marvellous coincidence) to the school playground, where the final critical battle took place. School was going on as usual, of course, but soon the windows were lined with astonished and admiring faces—especially the faces of girls—especially the face of Jean Rawlins. And when the battle was over and Brian Green and his friends were neatly tied up, in a great sobbing bundle of villainy, and stacked by the wall under the chalked cricket stumps and the portrait of Mr Gridley hanging from a gallows—when that was done, then I rode my horse into the school hall (all rules being waived for the occasion) and reined him in there under the bell rope. In front of the girls drawn up in lines fluttering with relief and admiration, the Headmaster started a lengthy speech of thanks. But I modestly waved this aside, and descended from my horse, and clanked to where Jean Rawlins

55

was standing: and . . . she invited me to tea. It was what all the carnage had been designed to produce—that invitation to tea. This was the final tableau—me in my armour, clanking still a little, and my plume very much in evidence—and Jean saying would I please, please come home with her to tea . . .

This was something the real Jean never did; but she did suddenly announce that she meant to choose between us. We must come with her after school, she said, to the recreation ground, and there she would choose . . .

We waited for her together, silent: Brian Green's gang dismissed, his hostility in abeyance, this plainly being an occasion for mufti and diplomacy and other arts than those of war. I remember it was raining a little and we both began with a sense of discomfort and irritation—there was common feeling between us, right from the start—and that feeling grew when Jean tripped up to us, for her face was full of a trivial liveliness, and her conversation was mundane, chirpy, unfitted to our noble mood. We came to the recreation ground and made without hesitation for the solemnest part of it, a great tree overhanging a pond, and we stood among the roots of the tree, he and I, our hearts full, waiting for our mistress to make the great speech out of the fairy tale, in which she weighed us out aloud and announced which one of us was chosen. But the wretched girl made no speech at all—she prattled at us, about school, about teachers, about (very soon, this) having to get home because her mother didn't like her being late. She prattled and giggled, and Brian and I stood there, grim and pale and waiting. It became clear in the end that she had nothing to say, and at last she tripped off, waving and bye-byeing, and Brian and I were left alone, empty . . . Oh, he could have thrown me at once into the pond—he could have driven me up the tree until, timid-footed as I was, I fell from some midway branch—he could have done anything, for I was quite at his mercy. But instead he asked me if I was going his way, and though I wasn't I said I was, and I went with him and we talked gruffly about football—which I didn't understand—and about books—which he didn't read—and what we were really talking about, though it was years before I realised this, was the impossible frivolity of creatures like Jean Rawlins, and the way we might have to press on without them, into the stern worlds of football-playing, and commanding gangs, and writing

56

compositions, and having the headaches and earaches that seemed somehow to come from writing compositions . . .

The fact is that those scraps of paper piled up in my desk. The crime of having them at all was compounded by the use of our exercise books as a source of paper. Anyone with an ounce of sense would have smuggled those notes out of the classroom in his pocket. I failed regularly to do this. I thought of doing it—fully understood the grave importance of doing it—only at useless moments : the middle of the night being one.

I was always on the edge of total ruin. How could the day of reckoning not arrive? My father's angers, directed at my everyday faults, seemed to me only rehearsals for the terrible occasion when all would be discovered. God, Miss Mason, Mrs Wilson, the newsagent, the school caretaker—did he never wonder why my desklid stood at such an angle?—would report together to the police, who would report to my father . . .

It would happen, I was certain, some night when, giggling nakedly and damp from the bath over my sister's wilfully in-accurate echo of my rendering of the Lord's Prayer, I was in that condition that the foolish existence of the bottom made most ripe for disgrace and . . . unspeakable battery and assault.

3

The Barton I knew when I was a Barley Road boy, in the second half of the 1920s, exists as a ghost under the brimming Barton of today. Then, we went to London: now, it would seem an affectation to say one did that. There was a rim of fields, and old ponds, and Victorian roads petering out in villas, snoring in summer under eiderdowns of leaf. There were allot-ments, and untidy meadows in whose hedges, all thorns and old birds' nests, we crouched over nerve-racking fires of our own making: more than once I, and the rather refined gangs I

57

belonged to, fled from blazes out of hand, and for days went in fear of farmers. It was in the heart of one such hedge (come to think of it, I spent much of my childhood in hedges) that I and Freddy Fletcher were lashed to a hawthorn by the Smiths, and threatened with death by incineration. They rattled matchboxes, and when we escaped, probably with their connivance, for it would have been awkward to have had to carry out the threat, we felt charred, and thought our lives were not worth a day's purchase while the Smiths remained at liberty. They lived only round the corner, in houses very little smaller than our own : but there was a strong sense that they were a cut below us, and that it was this social difference that made bullies of them, and victims of us. Aghast at their parting promise to chip pieces out of our ears at our next encounter, we ran to the house where they lived, and hammered at the door. Their grown-up sister opened it, Polly Smith, whose name was chalked on every local fence, with hints of her abounding readiness to be kissed, as we took it; and we poured out our wrathful story. We felt certain of her aid, that she would grow indignant at the brutality of it, but instead she said, 'I can't do anything. You must fight your own battles,' and slammed the door. It was horrible enlightenment as to the limits of the protection we could rely upon.

By our parents the social peril was felt to be far more awful than any physical one. 'I don't want you mixing with boys like that,' my father would say, as if mixture was the danger. There were fine distinctions between acceptable and unacceptable companions. Freddy and I took it all in, and grew as uneasily exclusive as our elders could have wished. I remember realising that I must not speak at home about having to share a desk with Birdie, who was a gypsy. I loved Birdie's proximity : he smelled of fields and somehow of grain gone hot and sour, with an overlay of smoke. Birdie copied my work, with my permission, but did so with such an unconvinced pen that no one ever guessed. In return he taught me to make knots. If the scholarship that was the mysterious goal of a handful of us had been concerned with string, Birdie would have topped the list. He also provided golfballs, which we enjoyed picking to pieces under our desks : yards of crisscrossing elastic, the trick was to unreel as much of it as possible without a break; and in the centre, a white goo that secretly made me feel sick. I was worried about thinking of that goo when eating. 'You never know,' it was another of my father's statements, 'where things have been.' Out walking, I'd pick up a fragment of old newspaper or a tantalising sheet of a comic, and my father would snap: 'Put that down! You never know where it's been!' I could induce nausea in myself at any time by thinking of those yellowing pages, or of a fountain pen I'd once found on an allotment, but had to throw away, because my father's voice growled in my inward ear: *'You don't know where it's been!'*

You didn't know where people had been, either. This truth was hammered home by the visits of the district nurse, with the disinfected sticks with which she hunted through our hair for lice. It was another kind of sorting out: an underlining, as the lice-free smugly thought, of the need for our parents' constant wariness on our behalf. We heard about germs and microbes in Hygiene, and I prickled; there were lice, I was suddenly certain, cohabiting with fleas and germs in my every crevice. Miss Thrift took us for Hygiene, and was doom itself in respect of our hope of retaining our teeth. Finger nails were simple execution squads; they narrowed our already laughable hope of survival. In Miss Thrift's hands the subject might frankly have been renamed Decay and Degeneration and Death.

That this was not merely material to make lessons with was demonstrated by the first actual deaths among our twenty semi-detacheds. Mrs Collis died of dropsy, and the great patch outside the Collis gate was the water that had run out of the coffin. Mr Sexton said one morning to his wife, 'Oh my dear, I think I'm going to die,' and did so. I made my way complicatedly to school for weeks, avoiding the Sexton house. A brisk, neat man: my father's bowler and his rose to each other, in passing. I had an absurd feeling of anguish which amounted to horror at the thought that his briskness and neatness had not saved him. Death became the twenty-first of us, living in an appalling invisible semi-detached of his own.

The prejudice against gypsies, and nervousness about lice, reached a peak when the time came for the town's annual fair. Every road trit-trotted with horses, on their way to be sold by fat men with switches and watch-chains you could have secured an ocean liner with. My father, who had at ordinary times a ritual of door-locking last thing at night—at the same time inspecting the weather and shouting a verdict back into the house ('Might be a decent day tomorrow, for once'—one saw the clerk of the weather, Mr Folkestone-like, tipping an ironical hat)—would double-check his locks. Then the showmen would come, huge caravans with entire round-abouts folded up in them: winged beasts, gaudily mythical, flaring red nostrils in cursing traffic jams in the High Street. The fields that ran down the hill, green vacancies the rest of the year, grew marvellously unrecognisable: mazes of hooting pleasure, flaringly brilliant at night. A hundred strands of brutally happy music met together above the scene, in a shining cloud of dust and smoke. Sleep was impossible, splendidly so. How important it made us feel, being residents of this Mecca, as the trams and buses came in crowded from all directions, and the fairgoing crowds spilled into the road, on to the hill, on to the Great North Road itself; and the trams inched their bagpiping way up, taking hours to go from bottom to top. Then we saw our daily acquaintances anew, garishly lighted, flushed with the fair fever, all flinging their pennies around, suddenly rich and reckless, and the more heroic among them clutching coconuts fairly won, vases or furry toys. Then my father became a hero, devastating with darts, without rival at the coconut shy. Bold men and women spat on their hands and spun great skeins of toffee, hanging them on hooks. It was sexually exciting, too—Good Lord, there was Milly Strang, the most quietly beautiful girl in the class, suddenly all roundedness of knee, on a roundabout, her skirt, all her clothes about to fly over her head and . . .

Enormous dizziness. But all improper, when it came to it: a gala for germs, surely. You'd have heard the lice cheering if it hadn't been for that music. Back home, with our coconuts, we washed thoroughly and felt uneasy about our hair.

Elsewhere and at another time there was the hay harvest. Freddy and I made sensuous tents out of the hay, sat inside the heat of it, and Freddy asked me, with enjoyable slyness, which part of my body I liked best. I gave teasing replies, coming late to the answer he wanted. It was, at that point in our development, the bottom. Freddy heartily approved. He made it clear that one's bottom had his vote, too. It was all extremely chaste and verbal. When Freddy sought to enlarge our seminar, by alluding to certain female bottoms—he even referred to Jean Rawlins, who, as far as I was concerned, was constructed without this feature—I became unco-operative. I never thereafter quite trusted Freddy.

Why did I find it necessary to bribe myself into friendship? Curious recollection: stealing books from among our small hoard, those that had introduced me to literature in the penitential beds of my infancy, and giving them to boys I wished to grapple to me with hoops of . . . most inappropriate paper . . . How could I think I would win Ronnie Brooks with a novel by the author of *East Lynne*? Enormous young anxiety for allies. For lovers, I suppose. Sexual rehearsal. But when it came to it—paradigm of what might actually happen—I didn't have to buy my best friendship of that time. Reggie Oliver was to be secured without gifts.

The Olivers lived at Number 16. Reggie's father worked for a publisher of light fiction, and brought home books in galley proof. Reggie passed them on to me. Even now the thought of those absurd books, and of reading them in that form, a couple of feet of a page at a time, is an excitement. We also collected titles in the Readers' Library. These cost sixpence. They were bound in thin board, the colour of ox-blood, and had pages that from the beginning were mildly sallow. They smelled dusty. The pages fell out at once, and it was necessary to hold the more seriously affected volumes together with elastic bands. Our favourite newsagents in the High Street always had a row of them in the window. I remember long weeks of impatient waiting to amass the sixpence for Tolstoy's *The Cossacks*. Well, we'd seen the film. And the great thing about the Readers' Library was that, where there had been a film—and there usually seemed to have been a film—a selection of stills from it, in brown photogravure, formed an inset of illustrations.

Books and films. They were what cemented my friendship with Reggie Oliver—they were also what held me in thrall, and eccentrically shaped my view of things.

But except that the cinema went deep into my imagination, I'm not at all sure now how I thought of the weekly drama on the screen. I don't know that I can find words for the tangle there was of everyday life and the pervasive life of

61

cinema . . . Reggie and I read such film magazines as we could get hold of : we cut out pictures of film stars, and pinned them round our bedrooms. In 1929 I was fairly desperately in love with Vilma Banky; she was followed by Anita Louise and Madge Evans. Those names, so young, look now so old . . . No film was hopeless of our appreciation. The small boys we were took in, with matter-of-fact hospitality, the wettest romance, the absurdest cardboard drama of high life. We were often moved deeply. There was a film based on the sinking of the *Titanic*. Certain liberties were taken with the facts. There was for example a love affair, which met its own icebergs, between the captain, quite the most handsome that any shipping line had elevated to that position at the age of, I suppose, twenty-five, and one of his passengers. There had been a misunderstanding between them, leading to one of those scenes when he leaves the room, haughtily and for ever (I suppose it must have been a cabin), and she throws herself against the closed door, weeping bitterly. I could never bear such misunderstandings, in film or novel. I always wanted to step into the fiction and put the matter right . . . Came the collision with the iceberg : the captain stood grimly on the bridge. She made her way to his side and began a timid attempt at reconciliation. Whereupon he snapped : 'Never speak to the man at the helm!' Reggie and I often reconstructed that moment. It clutched at our hearts. Lying in bed, weaving fantasies in which certain small schoolmates of mine attempted to revive my affection for them in various conditions of crisis, I would snap out that superb response : '*Never* speak to the man at the helm!'

We went to the cinema on Saturday afternoons. I liked going with Reggie : he was the solidest person I had ever known. Physically compact, he was bluffly compact of mind, too; in his presence I felt like a small boat in the shelter of a cliff. One needed a sturdy friend, in the foyer of the Barton Cinema on a Saturday afternoon in the late 1920s. All the kids were there, never managing to form the queue the commissionaire had in mind. For us, and it was a grief, this official never appeared in full evening rig. No Ruritanian uniform, no white gloves under the epaulettes. He wore his peaked cap, but otherwise was in mufti—ready for the rough work of keeping us within some sort of bounds until the box-office opened (we arrived anything up to an hour early), and then siphoning us through in a fashion that made life possible for the cashier. Once inside we hurled ourselves into the body of the cinema, and there was a nerve-racking clatter of seats being claimed and then abandoned as friends or enemies were spotted in other parts of the house. The manager, stripped for action like the commissionaire, hurried from one unallowable tableau (it could be a battle as dramatic as anything to be seen later on the screen) to another. One curious delight arose from the existence of the cinema's programmes, and their being always left in batches at the back of the hall. They were sumptuous : and the centre pages, which offered a resumé of screenings for the next month, were of thick white blotting-paper. I don't know why the cinema didn't hide those programmes away on Saturday afternoons. But they didn't : and that delight of ours lay in running, during the showing, to the back, and stuffing our jerseys with programmes. Half the juvenile population of Barton and their families blotted their writing with stolen blotting paper for a decade thereafter, I guess . . .

And our lives were peopled with film stars. Across every horizon came Tom Mix, on his white horse. Charlie Chaplin, whirling round like a baggy-trousered top, dodged with the exquisite timing of, as it appeared, pure accident, the murderous fists of the bully with the huge black square beard. We laughed with our bodies as well as in the usual way, and translated our amusement into blows aimed at our neighbours; the cinema shrieked with our joy, and the manager and the commissionaire ran up and down the gangways, as if the response of laughter was the last thing they wanted. You could be thrown out for excess of appreciation. I was ordered out once for standing up and shouting instructions at Rin-Tin-Tin, who, given this encouragement from me, had every hope of rescuing the heroine from a fate that, in the convention of the time, was not worse than death, but *was* death. We believed devoutly that girls might be tied to railway lines for being diffident about being kissed. On that disgraceful occasion—being essentially law-abiding, I did feel the disgrace of it—I didn't leave the cinema. We had a perfect reply to ejection. You simply found a place in some row further back . . .

Such great sadnesses, too. To be in love was to opt for sadness, as often as not. Janet Gaynor was always wet with tears. We could hardly bear knowing so much more of the plot than the characters ever seemed to know. Our advice was generously offered. When Mary Pickford buried her face in her hands, in some garret, our sympathetic silence was a kind of noise. You could be thrown out for responding too obtrusively to tragedy. When the end of the programme came, and the ultimate sorrows were endured by the characters to the music of our seats, clanging upright as we readied ourselves for the stampede into the real world—by that time, Reggie and I were usually quite limp. It would take a time, out in the High Street, in the surprising late afternoon light, among the undramatic shoppers, for us to readjust to being no more than boys.

When Reggie knocked for me at home—'Can Ted come out?'—it was as often as not to inform me of some item of news from Hollywood. Marie Dressler was in this or that. We could hope to see John Gilbert in that or this. *She* had a new husband. Let's go down to East Barton and look at the stills outside the Regal. Let's go walking and discuss the various virtues of the extremely various Bennett sisters . . .

4

If my father's relatives were hard and dangerous and dramatic, my mother's were the reverse: all gentle, soft, like herself. Though soft is not quite the word. They had, in their mild way, the tough quality of people who'd weathered lives of poverty, sickness, disappointment. They were toughly soft.

All were, as a matter of address, aunts and uncles—though some were really, I believe, of the order of great-second-cousins. I could never quite add up my mother's family: given what had happened to it, to go on visits was like inspecting

64

the rump of a regiment after some ghastly battle. Mere corporals tended to be addressed as colonels.

But Uncle Bill and Aunt Polly were real . . . she was my great-aunt. They lived at the bottom of a tall tenement in St John's Wood.

We'd stand (it was always a Sunday) outside Uncle Bill's front door, with my mother adjusting our dress, Betty's and mine, on her usual massive scale. In my case, cap and tie straightened, buttons undone and done up again, braces re-hitched. Plenty of time for that, because Uncle Bill took ages to reach the door. There'd be the slow sound of him dragging himself from their one room across the kitchen: the long fumble of his fingers on the doorknob. Then there he'd be, blinking out at us, a little tobacco-coloured hoop of a man, his pointed beard the colour of the shag he smoked. His legs made a nearly perfect circle: the story was that they'd been damaged when a lift at the dairy where he worked got loose and shot down the shaft. His sight was poor, but he wore his spectacles only to read the *News of the World*; he rarely left this tiny flat, and seemed most of the time to feel no need of anything but the vaguest vision. This meant that he took some time to identify us at the doorway. 'Ernie?' he would venture, and 'Jack? Is it Harry?' He was deaf, too. 'Ah—Dick and Annie!' The blue eyes, whitening with blindness, would quite fail to take us in. 'Don't stand at the door,' he'd say, as though the delay was ours. As we went in, I'd feel that we didn't ourselves quite know who we were.

In there, when he'd shufflingly taken us through, we'd find Aunt Polly. For twenty years—again, it was the story—she'd lain in bed. My sister and I were thrilled by the idea of this. I'd boast about it to boys at school: that I had an aunt who had been in bed for twenty years. When we came into the faded, clean little room, there she'd be, her body hardly making a heap at all under the bedclothes—the tiniest face, a trembling smile, a white cotton bonnet, and under the coverlet, lavender-smelling, the faintest worn-out traces of body. There was really nothing much of her but eyes—large, bright eyes that wel-comed you with an awareness wholly unlike Uncle Bill's washed-out indifference to the identity of visitors. Always I was struck by this distinction—between my uncle, living in a world colourless, vague, all its features worn away—and my

65

aunt, bright and watchful and aware as she lay there in what remained of her body.

'Dickie!' she'd exclaim, and she'd run through all our names, each name being a summons for a kiss. Then she'd look at us, watch us as we moved about the room, as if we'd returned after fifty years from the ends of the earth; her eyes shining with welcome, and nothing else of her alive, her bony hands crossed and still on the coverlet. And we'd turn—sensing, I guess, that all she needed was to listen to us and watch us— to Uncle Bill; who always at this point would back up against the fireplace and begin to fill his pipe. This took him a long time, because his hands were stiff and amazingly knobbed— only in the vaguest sense were they hands any more, and I'd watch them with fascination, plucking, stiff and pincer-like, at the shag in his pouch, and spilling it as he brought it up to the pipe trembling between his lips. 'Nice weather, Dickie,' he'd say, or 'Nasty day': and the talking would begin. I never knew how he acquired his information about the weather.

It was always the same talk. The joy of all those visits was to hear, again and again, the same things said. Uncle Bill's deafness meant that my father had to raise his voice and repeat remarks, and this made it necessary to replace any mildly difficult word with a synonym. 'And how are you, Dickie?' 'Well, mustn't grumble.' 'What's that?' 'I say—one can't complain.' 'Eh?' And Aunt Polly would join in: 'Dickie says he's all right.' 'Oh, he's all right, is he?' 'Yes, we're all right,' my mother would say, anxiously confirmatory, as always. 'What's Annie say?' 'She says they're all right.' 'Ah.' The pipe would be filled now, and a match would be trembling, weakly, along the side of a matchbox. Then, 'We mustn't grumble,' Uncle Bill would say, more likely than not, having a habit of coming, at the end of one of these bouts of talk, to the very phrase that had caused trouble at the beginning.

It would take half an hour or so—this exchange of elementary information, with Uncle Bill saying at intervals, 'I find it hard to get about now. I find it hard.' He'd never say it with much feeling; it had been true for so long, for both of them. He said it, I guess, to keep the thing going. But after a time his eye would travel to the *News of the World* lying on the little table by the fire. The hint was taken: we got ready to leave. Aunt Polly would try to hold us, her bright eyes longing

66

for it to go on. But we'd be shuffled to the door after final soft kisses, and the bright eyes following us out of the wistful white prison of the bed. 'Come again, Dickie,' Uncle Bill would be saying as the door closed.

We'd stay with my parents long enough to hear their verdict ('The old boy's getting very feeble') and then race up the stairs, from landing to landing, enjoying the separate smells of each, the smells of different Sunday dinners. In the top flat lived Uncle Jack and Aunt Madge. Aunt Madge was a daughter of Uncle Bill and Aunt Polly. It was another world up there, younger and brisker, and the noise was welcome after the exhausted slowness of life downstairs. The noise of Radio Luxemburg ('Noticed it, Dick? That's my new All Mains D.C. receiver . . . a Royal Sovereign') and of Uncle Jack's perpetual laughter. He was a great anecdotalist, Uncle Jack, and all his stories had the virtue of being true. They were rueful tales of his life as manager of a newsagent's. The owner of the shop was always having bright ideas, which always turned out to be rash ideas. So he'd install a cigarette machine full of a brand totally unpopular in the neighbourhood. 'I told him—blimey—they'd smash 'em up! "Never," he said. Oh, what a nut he is!' Long seizure of laughter. Smell of cooking from the kitchen. We dreaded, affectionately, Aunt Madge's meals. She was fixated on toad-in-the-hole, for which my mother had set an exacting standard. Mother's batter was always crisp, brown, feather-light: her sausages perfectly cooked. Aunt Madge's batter had the quality of worn-out bolsters, and her sausages kept much of the pallor they'd had before cooking. 'Well—went in next morning. And blow me! Bloody machine in pieces! Front smashed in! Then they must have bounced it up and down! Blimey! Another fifty pounds down the drain.' Enormous laughter, all round. Uncle Jack having to retire to the lavatory, his amusement often seeming to have a dramatically laxative effect.

I'd be exchanging shynesses with my cousins. Hilda and Mary: one thin, one not. Hilda was a stick insect of a girl. Mary, as I noted in a diary I was keeping—using for this entry a perilously penetrable code I'd picked up from the *Wizard*—had a distinct bottom. Mary having this sort of plumpness made me cruelly conscious of Hilda's emaciation. The grown-ups after dinner, laid low by Aunt Madge's bloated batter, would divert attention from their exclamatory stomachs by making jokes about me and Mary. 'Who's your sweetheart, then, Mary?' Reddening, I would glance wistfully towards the *News of the World*, which I was not allowed to read. Mary would shoot me glances that laid quite remarkable burdens upon that code I'd taken from the *Wizard*. 'Does she love me?' I didn't really doubt it.

'Don't know how they manage', my father would say on the bus, as we made our way home. 'Pays Jack a pittance, you know.' I had dreams of rescuing them all from poverty. I'd written these famous novels, Sir Edward Blishen, all mains D.C. receivers in every room, Radio Luxemburg on tap, and I'd set Uncle Jack up in a shop of his own. No ill-judged cigarette machines. 'You run it just as you like, Uncle Jack. No—it's a pleasure. Like to come down to the dress shop, Mary? Choose what you like. Excuse me—I'm just going to read the *News of the World*.'

How many years before had all these gentle, battered people —in all senses, battered people—been advising my mother not to marry my father? Uncle Bill had been very much against it. He was a soldier, my father, they had that against him—and in objecting to his being a soldier they must, given the background of the times, and given even that my father was a sparetime soldier before the war broke out, have thought of soldierliness as a mark of undesirable character. They meant that he had a soldier's taste for the 'loud and common' women my mother said he was always being drawn to. How could a soft-spoken girl like her, who'd embarked on her own brave campaign against commonness, be a match for such a man— and from such a family! Sitting there, laughing and burping, on those marvellous Sundays in St John's Wood, we were among my father's ancient critics. But we didn't know it. You'd not have known it. I never knew what, precisely, my father thought about his in-laws, in all their wryly amused endurance of tenement life, of livelihoods gallantly scratched. But he always seemed at his best on those occasions. There was—perhaps this was it—so little quarrelsomeness in them. Impossible to imagine Uncle Jack, say, writing abrasive letters on toilet paper.

As Uncle Will did.

It was always a problem, knowing at any moment which of my father's brothers was friendly, and which was not. Uncle Will became hostile, as far as I could make out, over the matter of my grandmother's maintenance. This was an issue that dragged on for years, and at least once was to rise to a dramatic climax, claiming the attention of the entire neighbourhood. The Board of Guardians came into it, somewhere. Efforts were made, within the family and by officials outside it, to secure a steady allowance of money for my grandmother, from each of her sons. My father was, in this context, among the responsible ones. But to require the brothers to come together in a compact involving money was to ask for trouble. There *was* trouble—tortuous trouble, in the family tradition. Brothers kept sore and wary eyes on brothers. The latest arrangement, sketchily agreed upon at some summit meeting at Sutton Villas, was always falling to pieces, on the grounds of some brother's ingenious new notion of the inequity of it. I knew the names of all the officials of the Board of Guardians, having so often to carry appalled messages to one or other of them. My grandmother's visits to our house were often occasions for tears, remonstrances, complicated arithmetical disputes. I'd be fascinated, overhearing these, by her collar.

She always wore, as part of her outdoor dress, a fur collar that was, in fact, the pelt of a fox. The claws hung fiercely in their places, and the head and tail met at the front. Head so flat and narrow, with glass beads for eyes! And rows of tiny sharp teeth! As a child, I was fascinated by that collar, and felt menaced by it; and looking back I see this was only partly because the thought of a fox being emptied of flesh and bones and slung around someone's neck was horrifying. Partly it was because the fox's head duplicated hers! My grandmother's head, too, was small and narrowed as if for speed and capture; her teeth were small and sharp! Her eyes had a glassy hardness—though they were pale grey where the fox's were brown.

Uncle Will believed, anyway, that he was at the other end of a fiendish piece of injustice: and that at the business end of it was my father. Thus, for some months, these letters—on toilet paper. Only now does it strike me that the gesture fell short of the scorn Uncle Will must have fancied was conveyed

69

by it. In Uncle Will's own lavatory, as I well knew, you were offered only scraps of newspaper, impaled upon a nail. For him to use toilet paper proper for his correspondence was rather like his using high quality notepaper.

5

Whatever it meant, I was backed for a scholarship. This obscure expectation was a halo round me, as I made my way through Barley Road. It did mean, clearly enough, that I had to do extra work at home. Winning a scholarship rested partly on being confident that the phrase 'as black as—' was completed with the word 'soot'. Anything that was black was as black as soot. Anyone who was rich was as rich as Croesus (whoever he was). I've reflected since that it was a good thing, if I was to win the scholarship, that I wasn't influenced by some of my grandmother's turns of phrase, including one about rich people. They were so well-to-do, she'd say, that their backsides might have been studded with diamonds. God knows what the snobs at the grammar school—it was among us the accepted, almost affable word for them—would have made of that, if I'd used it in the scholarship paper . . .

To become a snob myself I'd also have to write compositions to order about almost anything: though rather often it seemed to be about the advantages and disadvantages of a Channel Tunnel. My father was an agitated supervisor of this homework of mine. All my daytime attributes—of being Excellent and Very Good and 10 out of 10—fell away in the evening, under his angry eye.

I think it was a pity that my father became a clerk, when he would have made such a fine gardener. He had green fingers—ink didn't suit him. But I am unspeakably relieved that he never became a teacher. Given the occasion—or, in his case, taking the occasion—to instruct anyone about anything, he was instantly flooded with vast annoyance. He had a whole stock of problems with which, in five minutes at most, he could reduce me to tears. Three or four of these, and he would have my mother in tears, too. Education would turn into a universal blubbing.

'Listen again,' he'd roar. 'For God's sake wipe your eyes, sit up, stop fiddling with that pen, and *listen*! The street's a hundred yards long, there are lamp-posts at intervals of ten yards—how many lamp-posts are there?'

Presented with the question by Miss Baker I'd have solved it serenely in no time. Presented with it by my father, his square hand becoming a fist to punch the table with, his eyes blazing, I began even to doubt the meaning of the word lamp-post. 'For heaven's sake draw the bloody street, then! Make a bloody plan!' But through the huge tears in my eyes I couldn't see to draw the bloody street. 'Oh, let him be, Dick!' mother would weep. 'But an idiot could see the answer! It's so bloody simple!'

If anything, it was worse when he took in hand my writing of compositions. His lack of confidence in me was here so great that in no time he'd be dictating to me. 'The English Channel is reputed to be 21 miles wide.' 'Is what, Dad?' 'Is *reputed*. R-e-p-u-t-e-d. Well, write it down, then.' 'But Dad, I can't write that. She'll know I never thought of that!' There wasn't a child in the class on whose lips this incredible word would sound natural. 'What's wrong with the word, then?' 'Oh, let him be, Dick!' 'She'd know it wasn't me.' 'I don't know what the boy's talking about!' 'Oh Dick, he's had enough for one evening.' My father's enormous, hot sigh. 'How that lad thinks he's going to win the scholarship, I don't know.' But Barley Road had no doubts. I was confidently haloed . . .

I think now what a solemn school it was, compared with any primary school fifty years later. Those Transcriptions! The heavy density of the Arithmetic we did—so much division of unlikely numbers or quantities by divisors so unworldly! There was, I see, looking through an old exercise book, some attempt to give numeracy, to use a phrase that won't quite do, a human face. The sum, 350 x 6, would have the heading: bricks. Not blank numbers, but bricks and pigs and cakes and buildings. Someone had 5,735 cakes, and was imperatively bound to divide them into four heaps. Someone else, going to the table for what he'd fancy was a normal high tea, would be faced with 1,433 cakes. Rem (= remainder): 3 cakes. Well, a manageable scenario, if you brought your whole imagination to bear. But what about the quarter of a pig that some phantom farmer found trotting about his farmyard, in my work of 18.4.28?

And what a little muff I was! It was partly, I guess, because I was so anxiously groomed by my parents for a future of unspeakable respectability. Behind their ambitions for me lay their intent that I should never be such a child as they had been doomed to be. As to the adult I should grow into, my father saw me already as a civil servant: but I should be a civil servant fully armed against Ching, Aston and Maclagen. Did he have fantasies in which, risen spectacularly above them, I would subject them, perhaps, to positive demotion?

I was prodigiously protected against the ordinary hazards of being a boy. For a long time I was not allowed to go into the town, except in the company of one or both of my parents. I was tended as awfully as one of my father's best roses. I was relentlessly weeded.

And such a muff, as a result! One memory: of being told that I was to take part in the district school sports, down in East Barton. How could I have had such a total lack of understanding of the character of commonplace athletics? The word 'sports' might have been any dreadful word, for all the meaning it had for me. Up the road, then, and to the tram terminus to take the journey down the hill. And sitting in the tram, waiting for it to start, I was overwhelmed by the sheer horror of it. Terror rose, a great chain reaction of gulpings and gaspings, in my throat. I left the tram and ran, driven by these convulsions of breath, all the way home. Did my mother for once lack sympathy? I remember next running, the long way, still with terror acting as a pump for my breath, to East Barton . . . It was a relay race. Why did I not understand the nature of a relay race? My team-mate ran at me with his stick, and I stared at him as he attempted to thrust it into my hand. I remember, and wish I did not remember, staring with idiotic incomprehension, among the howls of all the school-children in the world, at the boy who was trying to make me take over the baton . . .

All the same . . . I'm glad I was at Barley Road, from 1926

72

to 1930. Glad especially for the anarchic edges of the experience. Muff though I was, I was still, in those distant days, Charlie Chaplin, Buster Keaton, Billy Bunter, Harry Wharton, the Scarlet Pimpernel, and the boy among others who had his free existence in the very skirts, the very hems of the skirts, of the adult life of the town. No, the *hair* of the adult life of the town. I think now that we were often a sort of *lice* in the hair of the grown-ups . . .

I see children nowadays being ferried to school by car, and wonder what it's like to miss the walkings to and fro, those marvellous patches of time when you were not at home and not at school, but came into possession of a curious kind of freedom. It felt like not being observed by anybody. Time and town were ours.

Up the road, and into the big street; vanish into an alley (we had a strong sense of vanishing); clatter through that, made noisy by appetite, and into the shop that we always took to be our shop. The formal owner of it was a big man who was never without an apron or a smile. It didn't feel quite like other smiles . . . was meant to help you to spend your money. Not that I had any slack for spending on impulse: it was usually the basic farthing—though now and then the relatively wanton-seeming ha'penny, and rarely, guiltily, certain rich moments when, alas, I'd slid my fingers into my mother's purse . . . There, after long noisy hesitations, while Mr Hobbs smiled patiently, we bought gobstoppers that changed colour as you sucked ('Hobbs, Hobbs, sells suckers for your gobs!'), or thick hunks of liquorice, or triangular bags of sherbet, with a paddle of toffee to suck and dip with; or cylinders of chocolate shreds called tobacco; or hundreds and thousands; or little rubbery loaves of some white substance that tasted like milk gone sickly; or cachous; or cough drops; or enormously long strips of very narrow toffee, which almost tasted of toffee, but did not melt readily in the mouth; or humbugs; or hateful, dry locust beans, that nevertheless got eaten because, at much less than a pinch, we could eat anything. And so loaded, to go and knock on doors and run away. I pass sometimes today a house at whose door I used to knock regularly, on my way to and from school, fifty years ago: I have an absurd impulse to apologise—to the door at least, which looks to be the same. It's on a corner—you knocked, and nipped down the road on

73

the other side. The owner in the end complained to the school : all boys whose journey took them through that quarter of the town were gathered for a sensational homily : the rest of the school was rather disgusting in its innocence . . .

And when you got to school, the sticking of transfers on the back of the hand, the arm, the knee. The skill of licking the back of one, and the attempt at patient waiting for it to take; too often, the misery of lifting it too soon, and the colour not staying flat and firm on your flesh, but rising with the paper, in strings—however fast you banged the transfer back into place, there'd have been distortion. The satisfaction of having a transfer take, unspoiled, could make a whole school-day worthwhile.

How gory and scabbed our visible skin was, and covered with transfers, and sketched and scribbled over! Clattering through the town, knocking at doors and running away, shouting after the roadsweeper, inhabiting a Wild West, sands and Arctic wastes invisible to our elders, who were barely visible to us—still we'd note evidence of the existence of another world : for example, what we didn't know were election posters. These gave me the conviction, which I've never quite lost, that the adult world is divided into three parts, and their names are Ramsay Macdonald, Stanley Baldwin and David Lloyd-George . . .

We had no real understanding of the scholarship. If you won it, the future would sparkle with vague splendours. If you failed, you would become a lesser creature, somehow. You would become, I uneasily knew, Reggie Oliver : because he was not even sitting for the scholarship. My friend's light burned low, for that reason. It was a sort of dowdiness, not winning the scholarship. About being picked to take it there was, altogether, something rather shamefully distinguished.

We sat the exam on a day whose very weather I can still remember. That trembling spring sunshine—when the shadows tremble : uncertain brightness. We'd been given so much that was brand-new : penholder, nib, blotting paper, ruler. We ran through the town, five of us, with lumps in our throats. A totally unfamiliar town; nobody about . . . only grown-ups. Came to the cruel gate of the cruel grammar school. The gate bore crowns, and a date difficult to believe :

74

1584. The old hall was red and turreted, it was the sort of building we'd seen in the background of pictures of beheadings, and hangings, drawings and quarterings. It wept ivy.

Received by the Head. He wore mortarboard and gown. That seemed part of the cruelty. Had he chosen to wear a white sheet with slits for eyes we could not have been more terrified. We sat at worn desks, under windows and roofbeams that mounted to points. It was all sharpness. There was a dictation, which the master delivered in a voice sonorously lordly. It included the word 'cannonade': it seemed to be the word that caused one of us to burst into tears. A sudden wild passionate howling, which spoke for us all. The master was so scathing about this weakness that the rest of us decided not to resort to overt weeping . . .

A few weeks later at Barley Road our own plainclothes Head came into the classroom and announced that Willy Cox and I had passed. We did not even need to take the oral exam, whatever that was: we were unconditionally in. At once we were surrounded by admiring dislike. The boy sitting next to me said, in the calm manner of one using a purely technical term: 'Snob!' I heard Jean Rawlins whisper: 'Look how red his face is!' At the time I was rather more struck by my success in being red of face—and so interesting to Jean Rawlins—than I was by that other puzzling triumph.

PART THREE

1

Going to the grammar school was a dizzying business of severance from all things familiar. I was intoxicated—and terrified. It was marvellous, for example, but also oddly horrifying, to be wearing school uniform.

I'd had a badge on my cap at Barley Road. But it was chosen arbitrarily from a range of loose heraldic inventions obtainable at the haberdashers. You could have a lion, a stag, a crown and anchor—it was more like setting up an inn sign than a school badge. For a long time I sported a sort of aggressive pig, holding in its mouth what looked like a banana. But now—my badge was splendidly, appallingly genuine. A silver crown, red roses, and foreign words underneath. Purple ribbons crossed it, hot-cross-bun fashion, to show that I was in Ravenscroft House. On my back I carried my strong-smelling new first satchel. My socks were rimmed with stripes in the school colours—gold and red. I had become, it seemed to me, a creature of fiction.

From my reading of Talbot Baines Reed, Harold Avery—all those Victorian school stories—I knew what to expect. It was a fiction oddly melancholy, sadly moral. Bedecked as I was, in a setting so ancient, I could look forward to boys . . . drowning, or dying of consumption; and, always, struggling with their souls. School at this level was a tragic business. All the high jinks moved inexorably towards the deathbed, or the river. There was no river in Barton, but there were several serviceable ponds . . . My first sight of the school captain clinched it all, for me. He was taller than any boy would have dreamed of being at Barley Road : he had a golden smudge of moustache; he wore a tiny black gown; he limped. He was also very handsome, and obviously doomed. He had three Christian names, being Longbone J.F.C. You could tell from

79

that that he was a paying pupil. Any paying pupil who had only two Christian names was clearly exercising forbearance. Longbone was an obvious candidate for the honours board in the old hall—the one that commemorated old boys who'd died in battle. If you got through without recourse to the river—or the pond—or the death-bed that followed from your not drowning instantly in the river (or the pond)—then you were booked for a bullet in some spot in . . . on the whole, it seemed to be India or Africa.

In the paying pupils I saw all the handsome and fascinating snobs and heroes and bounders of the school stories. The sense of distinction was very powerful. They wore flannels that did not, like the cheaper trousers worn by scholarship boys, turn yellow and baggy. Every day they wore the silk tie in the school colours that we wore only on very special occasions. An alternative was allowed : a narrow black tie that rapidly became a dispirited string, capable of producing only the most minimal knot. They had different voices; and some hammered home the difference by wearing plus fours. Difficult now, I think, to make it clear how assertive of social superiority this form of trousering could seem in 1930. I had simply never imagined that a schoolboy could so garb himself. It was more arrogant than top hats.

A cruel place, I thought—without surprise. Architecturally it was cruel, for the old hall itself was a sort of academic dungeon, full of shadows and carved and scribbled over as by generations of prisoners; and you moved on from the hall to the playground, a desert of pebbles, on all sides of which gloomed the Victorian additions—doors designed to resist a siege, tall peaked roofs, the sharp tips of windows rising above meshes of wire . . .

I hated and feared and worshipped it : for it seemed right that it should be so awful. That's what one had won the scholarship for—to pass into a world whose superiority was measured by the dread it roused in you.

Timetables. That first morning we had dictated to us by Haddock, our form master (it was days before I discovered that Haddock was not his actual name), our weekly timetable. It seemed to include a constant commitment to what I took to be 'Mass.' I wrote it down as such in the relevant squares in the printed form we were given, which had to be stuck to

80

the underside of our desklids. Mass. I understood vaguely that the word had cruel religious connotations. There was little sense of anti-climax when it turned out to be Maths, and I found it meant that Arithmetic had been only the thin end of the wedge of a subject quite shockingly complicated. Maths was no less exotic than Mass.

It was a world where almost everything you did, at first, turned out to be a mistake. Approach a master, and you discovered he was a prefect. Walk round a corner in the pebbly yard, and you were out of bounds. Look up 'thou' and 'art' in your new Latin dictionary (Latin! my heart fainted from the start at the very idea of Latin—how majestically remote from anything we knew as life!): write down 'tu ars' and it was wrong; it was wrong enough to bring the world down on your head. A master called Hammer took us for French (how could he be called Hammer? Willy Mead addressed him as such, and there was the world, again, falling on him), and alleged almost at once that we smelled. He walked about the room, sniffing. 'Does someone need to make himself comfortable?' That was French. We clearly hadn't even the right smell.

My own first serious mistake arose from the loss of my cap. It was not where I had hung it—it was on no other peg—and appalled by the thought of having to tell my mother she must buy a new one, I rushed into the presence of Mr Knott, classics. Driven by my sense of major disaster, I poured out my story as if I expected this large, frowning man to halt the world, to set going an investigation that would turn the whole school pale. 'I hung it,' I kept repeating, 'in the lobby.' 'Lobby' was the Barley Road word for the place where you hung your clothes. Mr Knott sighed and said:

'Where did you hang it?'

'In the lobby. Sir.'

'Here,' said Mr Knott, 'we call it the changer.' He began to move away.

'What shall I do?' I asked.

'Look here, laddie,' said Mr Knott. 'I'm not here to look after your clothes for you.'

'Oh, but—'

'We don't have nursemaids here, laddie. We care for ourselves, you see.'

81

'But my cap—' I groaned.

'What's your name, laddie?'

Mr Knott received the information about my name with great indifference, and was gone—leaving me feeling very frightened. I did not understand the workings of this place at all. I did not understand its studied lack of concern for what seemed to me very large agonies. Incident after incident, in my first weeks, seemed designed to bring home to me my total unimportance. There was the day when I had a cold, and my mother told me to say that I'd not be able to play rugger. Foremost (E.J.), the games captain, looked me up and down with impatient amusement.

'You have a what?'

'A cold.'

'And your—Who told you you weren't to play games?'

'My mother told me.'

'Your mother.' Foremost (E.J.) laughed, apparently at the idea of anyone having a mother. 'We don't,' he said, 'stop playing games every time we have a little cold.'

'But my mother said—'

Foremost (E.J.)'s lip curled. He was almost as tall as Longbone, more a man than a boy, and he too had a strong trace of moustache. He laughed with a cruelty that I could not help admiring, though I was stung by it.

'I'll make a special point,' said Foremost (E.J.), 'of seeing that you're on the field this afternoon. Now, off you go—and—ah . . .'

I was wondering how to tell my mother that her command could be set aside by an insolently handsome eighteen-year-old called Foremost (E.J.).

'And what's your name?' asked the games captain.

It was how so many of these incidents ended: with the collection of my name. I felt it was being disapprovingly pigeon-holed by half the cruel giants who now ran my life.

Queen's had been, until lately, a sleepy school—where, on the whole, the sons of local tradesmen and professional men acquired a little polish, learned some forgettable Latin and History. Now, in new hands, it had sterner ambitions. There was a story I heard later of the way these aims were formulated: 'Gentlemen, what this school needs is three years of calculated snobbery.' It meant whipping us new lads from the town into shape—it also meant a campaign against an old style of senior boy, jolly, coarse, disgraceful, unambitious. There were still boys among us who'd been cast in this mould: mostly, now, for that severer regime was a year or two old, in the fifth forms.

We always went nervously into Room D for French, for that was the Upper Fifth's room—and often, dreadfully, the Upper Fifth were still there when we came in.

'Charmain, Charmain!' they'd be singing. 'Do it once and do it again.' They used as an aerial gymnasium the network of beams that supported the ceiling, and what one saw was an intricate rudeness of plus-foured legs and bottoms: all those tweedy roundnesses and lengths suggesting such a coarse, reckless power. It was not strictly imaginable how one could be a boy and yet, in so jungle-like, so muscular and impudent a fashion, not at all a boy. For me, it was pure Victorian school story. They represented the world of bounds being broken, pubs being visited and barmaids embraced. The Bounders of the Fifth. Cads. To be barged aside by one of them was to be touched by an unthinkable future.

'Charmain, Charmain, Do it in the High Street, do it in the lane.'

They had a strong smell, which I vaguely believed was the smell of what they did with Charmain, whatever that was. Now they were down from the beams with a thunder of boots, and were a hoarse heaving scrum, from which one of them fell, awry, with a shout of: 'You buggers! You rotten buggers!' His plus fours had been unlatched, had become shapeless bloomers. The others thrust at his flyfront, and the whole mass of them, all that raging tweed, tumbled through the door, out into the passage, down the stairs . . .

How could I tell them at home about the Fifth? Or rather —since that was not really the problem—how make any connection between life at home and such bawdy scenes?

There was a social aspect to games, too. We played Rugger —and I was snobbishly pleased by that, as an idea. Rugger was so plainly upper crust. In practice, I quickly came to hate it. I did not—never did—understand the rules; I had no gift for

83

doing anything whatever with a ball of any shape. I was dismayed by the air with which it was played—that keen manliness and excitable aggressiveness. 'You can't say you've played Rugger,' said Argyll, junior games master, 'until you have broken a collar bone.' It was meant as a joke, perhaps: I thought I had never heard a more horrible joke. Oh, what an awkward nature I had! No readiness to have a collar bone broken! Absolutely no desire that my team should conquer the other one! I didn't care what the result was: I only wanted the uncomfortable experience to be over. I had no heart at all for the dreadful things that masters in charge of games were given to shouting. 'Oh, you idiot! You *dim* idiot! Why did you pass forward?' I was not stimulated to greater effort by these ringing insults; instead, I shrank with misery. Damned Rugger! Damned mud! Why did they so happily whip us into such meaningless competition in a setting so dispiriting? Shirt and shorts that didn't keep the wind out—and so much mud!

'Sit on it! For goodness' sake *sit* on the ball!' Argyll shouted during our first game; and I obediently, but gingerly, lowered myself on to the thing, as if I'd been a hen and this some curious muddy egg. He laughed, and flicked me with the strap on which he carried his whistle. I was a forward. The scrum collapsed. Claustrophobe, I began to scream and bite my way out of this intolerable burial: I was dying under a heap of boys. 'What the devil's wrong with you, laddie?' Argyll cried. Oh, indeed. What the devil was wrong with me? It was like my being scared of climbing trees; or being, when they played soccer in the field facing our houses, at best, and with disgusting eagerness, the fellow who placed himself lackey-like behind the goal (jackets thrown down) and retrieved the ball for the goalie.

Soccer. The scholarship boys from East Barton, aggressively proletarian, played perpetual soccer in the playground with a tennis ball. It was frowned upon, as a social lapse. They did not care. It was their natural game, and they persisted with it. But they were good at Rugger, too; and they put up with Rugger. I had mixed feelings about them. Of course they were letting us down. In theory, incorrigibly, I sided with Rugger, when the social implications were at stake. Boys who demonstrated their allegiance to soccer were enemies of the queer glory of being at Queen's. But I also, sneakingly, admired them. They were not easily to be won over. In an odd way, their demonstration of this awkwardness of theirs seemed to be a demonstration on my behalf. I talked soccer with them at times, inaccurately, and felt an obscure relief. Such a muddle I was of loyalties and disloyalties, mysteriously strong, bewilderingly irreconcilable.

Peter Bunce and I—he was then my best friend, an alphabetical friend, for we sat next to each other in class—preferred reading. Together, Peter and I could accept our muffishness, without dissimulation. He was worse than I was at games: Rugger made him open-mouthed, startled and worried, absorbed in a private activity—that of being, so far as he could manage it, out of all contact with the ball. Peter playing Rugger was a boy in retreat from the action. Our delight was to have been somehow left out of all games, on a Wednesday afternoon or Saturday morning. We would walk through the town, glorying in being sensibly dressed, in being able to saunter, unathletically. We were both, at one time, reading Francis Iles' thriller, *Malice Aforethought*, which was being serialised in the *Daily Express*. One of the characters, we discovered, was going to have a baby, but there had been no mention of physical contact between her and the apparent father. From this we deduced that a mere feeling of desire was enough to cause pregnancy. Peter's mother was pregnant at the time: it gave a curiously awful edge to our deliberations. Idling slackly round the town, muffs, refugees from Rugger, we concluded that it was best to avoid even looking at girls. One warm glance and we should have confirmed what we both secretly felt was true about those not drawn to the playing of games—that they were particularly likely to end up in moral disgrace.

Part of the bewilderment of things was that I now had a new library to borrow from. The Queen's library was a rich one, a marvellous haphazardry of books gathered over a period of sixty years or more. Happiest moments of those early days at the school—galloping up the spiral staircase in one of the towers of the old hall, and ending breathlessly in the tilting library. The old floor ran hastily, quite sharply, from one wall down to its opposite. It was like borrowing books from a sinking ship. So warped was the room that the squareness of the books themselves came as a surprise.

Among my first borrowings were bound copies of the school magazine. They went back to the seventies of the last century; and they caused me what I can only describe as a splendid gloom. Here were schoolmasterly jests, as cruel as those of drill sergeants, receding through the decades. Chappelow A. F. C. would be a better scrum half were his fingers not made of butter. Jones B. J. had sung 'Who is Sylvia?' in the school concert in the tones of a police constable making inquiries on the scene of a petty crime. Occasionally someone dared a poem: but how impressively unenjoyable was the verse:

> When methinks swart fate embraceth me
> And death's dark fingers circumscribe my throat . . .

That was Wilson F. B. C. (1889-96), who figured in a rather later volume: 'News from Wilson F. B. C. (1889-96), now manager of the Trinket Trading Company in Hong Kong.' How hateful it seemed—curiously hateful that Wilson should be managing the Trinket Trading Company with those dark fingers still, one supposed, circumscribing (circumscribing?) his throat—and how correctly hateful. When I found myself in the magazine for the first time, misspelled (*Avete*: Anderson X. Y. Z., Best P. M., Boshen E.), I felt myself halfway to Hong Kong.

It was the verse that fascinated me. So much of it—though I hadn't the words for it at the time—was so precociously sombre. There was always a sort of Wilson F. B. C. around. In 1901 he was wishing himself a worm:

> Would I were a worm,
> Burrowing in the soil . . .

Or once again, in 1921, he had got himself into Canterbury Cathedral:

> The light's chill fingers trace the massive arch . . .

He was joined now and then by someone occasionally called Harris B. J., who was usually stirred to astonishment by one of the seasons:

> Winter! with its fingers of frost wrapped round the rough

86

boles of the slumbering trees, from which, one by one, the leaves of dead summer have fallen . . .

My first technical belief in respect of poetry, a belief later discarded with hasty horror, was that it revolved round the use of the word 'fingers'.

But as I read these magazines and wondered nervously how I could take my place in that repetitive dowdy pageant, it was the sense of masters coming and going that impressed me. Again, *gloomily* impressed me. Old Mr Pottle once more retiring ('He will be missed by the Philatelic Society') and young Mr Pottle once more joining us ('fresh from Cambridge and triumphs with the javelin'). These men, in some form or another, were still with us.

There was Winstanley, known for reasons long forgotten as Eros, who gave us cubes and cube-roots: 'Take,' he would shout, '333, 974'. Huge numerical burdens that blackened the day. Rubber Wrightson—Rubber?—was kindly, stone-deaf, maddened by his infliction, armed with an actual eartrumpet; an expert on the lesser sixteenth century clergy of his home town, who threatened but rarely beat us with a length of gnarled stick. It was known as the knob. 'Knob him, sir!' was the cry. 'Eh?' poor Wrightson would demand, turning his helpless trumpet in all directions. Boys would run up to address him directly through this unfortunate instrument. 'KNOB HIM, SIR!' 'Get back. Sit down. Be decent,' Rubber would snarl. What other occupation could have reduced this dull, gentle man to snarling? Ma Rutherford, the last woman on the staff to survive from the desperate arrangements of the Great War, gave us passages from the Bible to learn. The trick was to misunderstand her and commit to memory, for the public performance she required, a passage of erotic quality. For some reason it was believed that any passage containing the word 'begat' was disgraceful. Johnny Ash took us for a period called 'Architecture', an attempt to introduce a civilising element into the curriculum: he was full of a private rage against speculative building. Fido Philips, in our class, was the son of a local builder. Cruelly, Johnny would make him stand in front of us while he expounded the virtues of the Parthenon. The idea seemed to be that Fido's father should have been filling Barton-on-the-hill with classical temples

87

rather than semi-detached villas. I once failed to define 'horizontal' correctly and was made to lie on the floor for the whole period. This left me with the useful idea that horizontal meant lying on the floor.

With what rages these men filled our days! But none was worse than Sergeant Clinker, a veteran of the Boer War who, in full military fig, gave us drill once a week in the playground. The Sergeant remitted no parade ground rigour in his treatment of his wretched, shambling charges. Marching, trotting, forming twos and fours—or a square which we were to understand was under attack from howling tribesmen—we generated, in an hour with Sergeant Clinker, such muttering distemper that revolt was never far away: we were always on the point of becoming the howling tribesmen ourselves, and he increased this possibility with his repertoire of soldierly insults. His chief victims were boys who wore plus fours. These he seemed to regard as flamboyant declarations of softness, cowardice, even pacificism. He called them 'bloomers'. A plus four leg, with all that pounding, would lose its anchorage, and begin to slip downwards. 'Never mind your bloomers! Left right, left right!' Any offence he would reward with a drill detention. 'Come back tonight for an hour!' Drill detention consisted largely of running round and round, to the rap of the Sergeant's cane against his knee. 'Pick 'em up! Never mind your bloomers! You should smoke less, Stench!' Stench's real name, as he knew very well, was Stent. One evening, as darkness fell, the pounding detainees, the sweating Stenches, could take no more. Booing wildly, they broke their penitential circle and fled through the school gates. It was a famous scandal. Masters moved among us next day, conducting their investigations. There were canings, sullen mass apologies. The Sergeant was moved strangely by it all. He instructed the offenders, re-assembled for what was to be the most appalling drill detention in history, in the making of a catapult. 'Boys will be boys. Boy's natural weapon . . . What's Stench sniggering at?'

I began that first year as the bright infant: the best Barley Road had to offer, near-immaculate in Arithmetic and English. I was ten out of ten embodied. But Queen's had no resemblance at all to Barley Road. It wasn't simply that Arithmetic, by some sleight of mind beyond me, became Mathematics. It wasn't only that from sitting in a shared desk, I found myself with a desk of my own. (Though those desks did seem most powerfully to determine our behaviour. They could be turned, in so many ways, into rowdy extensions of ourselves. You could convert them into a form of transport, in which you travelled the room, making a move whenever a master's eye was elsewhere. In Haddock's class this was the matter we actually studied. While Haddock groaned away about Geography, a subject that seemed to fill him with private horror, we gave our attention to the movement of desks. In quest of popularity and admiration, I was a greater risk-taker than any. My aim was to traverse the entire room in the course of a lesson. Even Haddock felt bound to notice migrations of such audacity. I think he came to hate me.) It was not, this huge difference between elementary school and grammar school, any single item: it was a bewildering mass of them. It was the beginning of the social wrench that was to become more painful as time went on; the alienation from old friends, old quarters of the town . . . from our own parents. It was the scorn for the former furniture of our lives on which the existence of Queen's rested. It was the determination of the masters to convert us into 'gentlemen'. We were called gentlemen on some sort of hypnotic principle. After ten thousand repetitions we should become gentlemen through sheer numbness, as it were. 'Gentlemen!' the Head would cry, entering a noisy classroom. He defined the quality of a gentleman by colourful negatives. That is, he would pick on certain behaviour as that of 'guttersnipes'. 'There are *guttersnipes* among us . . .' One was a guttersnipe, a hooligan, a noisy little ruffian, undergoing a scowling conversion into a gentleman. The school scowled at us. It forbade us ever, in the most informal circumstances, to make public appearances without cap and tie. It was fierce about the angle at which caps were worn. I hated the squareness with which one was required to place the cap on one's head. I liked an oblique effect, the peak rakishly twisted. It was the angle at which the maritime heroes in the *Wizard* wore their caps. I was aware of being deplored for the way I wore not only my cap, but my socks. Socks pulled up were the mark of the dull boy, I believed. My socks were always about my ankles. In these matters, the school's outlook coincided with my father's. I was always being wrenched into conformity . . .

It was the prefects. They lived in a little archaic room of their own, at the back of the Old Hall. Gowned creatures, they would suddenly emerge from their Tudor burrow and move among us, detecting error. No cap, or cap improperly tilted. Too noisy; or suspiciously silent. Full prefects had black strips dangling from their gowns that were weighted with shot, to keep them hanging trimly. These were used to sting offenders. But it wasn't so much the detail of their punitiveness; it was again this overwhelming sense that we were being policed, and by such arbitrary heroes (oh, so awfully we admired them, from Foremost (E. J.) to Hindmost (J. C. S.)!), into gentlemanliness.

There was also the plain barbarism of life in those exhausted buildings, Tudor and Victorian. Under the perfunctory Gothic of the nineteenth century additions there were cellars, unused, formidably dark. They were known collectively as the lion's den, and small boys were driven down into them and had their trousers removed. The agony, in that blackness, of crouching in your underpants, wondering if you would have time, before the next lesson began, to collect your trousers from the dusty tangle at the entrance. In the changers, more Gothic dungeons, you could be basined or racked. Basining meant having your head held under water; racking meant having your arms ferociously threaded through the bars of radiators, and then, very slowly, wrenched. Or you were made to squeeze your way through the space between a hut, which had been temporary since the Great War, and a wall of the main building. You didn't have to be a claustrophobe to feel utter terror of this dark suffocating passage, thirty or forty feet of it, only just navigable by the slimmest, with boys waiting at either end to send you back again.

The trivial, eternal cruelty of schoolboys? But there was so much of it; for small or unpopular boys the morning and afternoon breaks were agonies—if not agonies of torture, then agonies of the expectation of it. My first absurd feeling about the school, that its Tudor air, its turrets and whipping post, its stone roses and half-false, half-real antiquity, spoke of beheadings, hangings and drawings and quarterings, seemed not so absurd as time went on . . . I grew wilder and odder

90

and more and more intent on my role as the clown of the class. The answer to a setting so mysteriously menacing—what were they trying to make of us?—was silliness.

Obvious enough, that silliness, to everyone. My report at the end of the year had a comment in red ink from the Head. 'This boy's behaviour,' he observed, 'is that of a silly child, and must improve'.

How could I explain that to my father?

Mother sent me with that report to meet him from work; she was not going to have the explosion under the family roof. I remember walking, so slowly, along the road to the bus-stop, genuinely unable to develop any speed, for I was carrying a heart turned to lead. There was this heavy lump of metal in my breast, and I could barely walk at all. And when my father got off the bus, his *Daily Express* the usual flattened oblong under his arm, we instantly met a neighbour, and my father was so light-hearted, so inappropriately jolly. My heart grew heavier still. How, when the neighbour left us with some final jocularity, to switch my father from such good humour to . . . ? No word for what I'd have to switch him to! Usually I'd take the newspaper from him, looking forward to the cross-word, the serial, *Beachcomber*. What an odd part of my pleasure it was, to be reading what had been made grubby, polished, so thoroughly used, by father's own reading on buses and over his lunchtime sandwiches! The *ironed* nature of the newspaper, when he'd done with it—its forming always that meticulous oblong—spoke to me of him; seemed the very essence of my father. That evening he handed me the paper, since I hadn't the spirit to take it for myself; and the *Daily Express*, too, was made of lead . . .

'You're just wasting your time! If this is how you're going on, you'll have to leave that school! You seem to be behaving like some bloody baby! If you think I'm going to put up with this sort of thing, you're mistaken!'

The summer evening uselessly being beautiful all round us. An acquaintance looking up from hoeing his garden, calling out: 'Lovely weather!' My father scowling at him, as if all the world had a bad report. Then he saw that other comment, Haddock's own: 'He might get somewhere if he didn't think it his duty to amuse his classmates'.

'Christ!' said my father. 'I'm not sure you're all there! What have you gone—stark raving mad?'

He had a gift for monumental anger. It would occupy itself now, for days, with the food served up to him, the growth of the plants in his garden, any opinion any of us had on anything whatever; he would certainly make one of his great sweeps through the house, simply tearing up or throwing away anything that was not in what, for father, was its proper place. All that giggling in the classroom—that fooling that was designed to win some sort of status for myself, as a daring idiot—all that was now, and it seemed with unfair irrelevance, bound to lead to one of father's most melodramatic exhibitions of gloom and anger. Poor Mum! It didn't help much, sending me to meet him, ensuring that the explosion took place out of doors. Father wasn't a man for single explosions!

Oh, I know what lay behind the school's behaviour. The dread of ruffianliness! The desire that we should be known for our politeness, respectability, good conduct! It admitted, all that intensity of intention, no feeling for the untidiness of boyhood . . . the sheer disturbance of being a boy! It tried too hard, too grimly. Its aim, for us, of 'gentlemanliness' was so arid, and it took no measure of the actual conversion that was involved for many of us. We were first generation grammar school children; and given the cruel reality of class divisions in pre-war Britain, that meant that we had stepped from one world to another, perfectly different. To interpret shrewdly and with good humour between those two worlds—that might have been an aim for such a school. But there was no interpretation. The two worlds scowled at each other, inside us . . .

My father's world scowled at mine.

There was the matter of booklists. At the end of every term you were given a booklist for the next term. On the first day you must bring money to pay for your new books. There was an arrangement by which you could buy certain books secondhand from the school's stock. I loved new books, and hated old ones. Sometimes I chose to buy new rather than old. But whatever I did, as often as not the booklist was the cause of an appalling row over breakfast, that first day. 'How do you think I can afford this!' It must have been a real problem for my father, finding that money. I was aware only that (such

92

guilty secrets aside as I might have about choosing new rather than old) I could do nothing about it. 'Dick, he's got to have the money!' 'It's beyond me, why they always have to have more books and then more books. Do they think I'm made of money?' I would struggle with the tearful desire to laugh at the notion that the school thought of my father in such terms; or indeed thought much about him at all. How far apart they were! . . . 'But that's the list, dad! That's the list we were given!' Shouts. Tears. Alas, alas . . .

There was also the matter of the umbrella. When it rained, my father thought it was sensible for me to take an umbrella to school. I did not know how to convince him that no boy dared appear with such an object. 'Bloody foolish! Get yourself soaked, and your mother has to nurse you! And that cap— a few more rain storms and you won't be able to wear it!' 'Dad, I *can't* take an umbrella!' 'Don't understand it! Never will understand it!' Shouts. Tears . . .

And paradoxically, alongside my state of disturbance—in this matter of being converted, I was responding so sulkily to treatment—I had developed a perverse pride in my status as a grammar school boy. I was bucked to be wearing that cap with its crown and roses and its purple ribbons. I made much, in my talk with Reggie Oliver, of the school's great age. It was as if I dated back myself to 1584.

'In the early days, Reg, that's in the sixteenth century, you had to talk Latin all day. Even among yourselves. Someone went round with a little stick and gave it to any boy he caught talking English. Then *he* had to find another one talking English. The boy who had the stick at the end of the day was whipped.' (Haddock had told us this one afternoon when he seemed to be overwhelmed by his curious hatred of Geography.)

'Barmy,' said Reggie, and aimed a blow at my upper arm, by way of reproof.

'No, honestly. And they had beer for lunch then. Ale.'

'You'd believe anything.'

My grammar school talk made Reggie uncomfortable. He'd resort to older, surer topics.

'Belly Bennett's in the film at the Regal.'

It was an old joke of ours, to pretend that this was how you spoke the name of Belle Bennett.

93

'Not Adolf-y Men-jew?'

Now that I learned French I was tempted to be superior about the pronunciation of Adolphe Menjou's name—but in abrasive moments like this one, he was a safe joke too.

But this companionable badinage was losing its magic. Secretly I was beginning to be impatient with Reggie's simple jests. They had about them no trace of rose and crown. And no doubt about it—Reggie's dismissal of the school's antiquity was galling. It was like his references, of which he was rapidly making one of his steady jokes, to the masters' gowns. 'Like old women! Frocks!'

The gowns still, at bottom, made me unhappy—with their black, rustling severity. They symbolised the remoteness of these men who taught us. It was like being instructed by sinister surgeons. But at the same time—my, how proud I was to be subjected to such discomfort . . . often, dread!

'It shows they've got degrees.'

'That's not all they've got,' said Reggie. The feebleness of the retort did not make it less infuriating.

The punches we had for so long affectionately aimed at each other's upper arms began to hurt.

2

We went there, I imagine, every third or fourth Sunday for years; to the great grey complex of fortresses, as they always seemed to me, that formed the mental hospital where my grandmother had been a patient for nearly a quarter of a century. This was the asylum they always made the jokes about at school: 'He came from there,' a boy would say of another, and I enjoyed the joke somehow, without ever quite matching the place of the joke with the place I knew so well. When they laughed about it, I saw the stock asylum they saw, full of comic lunatics, and not the long sloping corridors, the locked gates, at the heart of which, those Sundays, we found my small, blank-eyed grandmother.

I suppose my mother took me for company. Not, timid woman though she was, that she was scared of the hospital. She had grown used to it. She knew the man at the gate, to whom she presented her pass; she knew most of the nurses who, at one time or another, led us down those corridors and unlocked those great gates from the jangle of keys on a waistband. I liked our visits because my mother knew so many of the people there; it was curiously nice to be known at all in a place so formidable. There was at the back of my mind an idea that all this ceremony, this being taken through the web of corridors and having unlocked for us what was normally locked, was a kind of honour. It was an honour paid to my small, bothered mother, and indirectly to my grandmother. They took such pains to bring us together.

I liked, too, the glimpses we had into great laundries, full of chattering mob-capped women and immense wicker baskets. Then there were the patients we met, in their grey hospital clothes, walking very close to the walls, their faces waxy, their eyes so often blank. My mother knew them, or thought she should know them, all; and 'Hallo, my dear' and 'Nice to see you' she would be saying as we went along—sometimes evoking no response at all, sometimes a sweet empty smile, sometimes an astonished gape. My mother was always worriedly warm, anxious never to be thought the tiniest bit unfriendly; and so, behind the jangling keys, we would make our way deeper and deeper into the building, until at last we came to where granny was.

Sometimes she was in bed. Suddenly, behind a last gate locked and re-locked, we would find ourselves between a double row of beds, simple iron beds with pale grey blankets; and there, pale grey herself, my grandmother would be lying— propped up for the occasion, her small lost face lighting up as we came. It was never a great light, never the great easy change of face with which other people, people not in the hospital, greeted their friends. This was a timid brightening, a little look of recognition and gladness beneath which one was aware of an enormous emptiness. Impossible, I now know, even to guess how great that emptiness was. For over twenty years my grandmother had known nothing of life outside this

95

hospital; it was clear that she remembered little of life before she came, and her knowledge of life inside was discontinuous, flickering, always uncertain. My mother was always saying, 'But, *of course*, dear, you remember . . . *of course* you know . . .' And my grandmother would assent, the little bright area on the surface would assent; but you could never know how much she knew.

The times when she was in bed were the most uncertain— for when she was there it meant she was poorly, that she was further than usual from the world; and on those occasions there were long blanks when she would stare, without discontent, without disquiet, in front of her. Then my mother would busy herself talking to my Aunt Lily, pausing only every now and then to pat her mother's inattentive hand.

My aunt had gone into the hospital with her mother a quarter of a century before, because she was too young to be on her own and there was no one else to care for her. She had been taken in as a worker in the laundry. I never knew whether she had herself, congenitally, any weakness of mind that might have justified her being there . . . But there she had been, all her youth, knowing little if anything about the world outside; a simple woman who talked to my mother in a curiously conspiratorial manner, with a looking round before she spoke that was perhaps a mannerism you pick up if you live all your life in an institution. What struck me most about her when I was a child—I think *because* I was a child—was that my aunt had a notion of herself as 'Lily', talked about herself as 'Lily', as if Lily were another being, of tremendous interest to her. She pitied Lily, 'poor Lily'; and collected avidly all descriptions of her volunteered by other people. Say, as my mother would, given her habit of precipitate frankness, 'You don't look too well, Lily', and my aunt would positively snatch at the remark, make a kind of musical round out of it. 'Lily's not too well, oh poor Lily's not too well, she doesn't look too well, Lily's not too well . . .' her whiskered face grinning. 'How are you then, Teddy?'

I was a little afraid of her whiskers, her apparent view of herself as her own puppet—and her poor grasp of time. That last had led her to present me for my twelfth birthday with a wooden horse, quite small but still a wooden horse, on wheels.

Our second year at Queen's seemed largely to reinforce the discoveries of the first. For example, that Latin was beyond us. I'd say now it was beyond us because Ratty Rogers, who taught us, was simply . . . ratty. He was methodically irate. It was all declensions and conjugations and grammatical laws . . . like learning the rules of a complex game that we barely ever played. Oh, there was a little, dull, restricted play. Balbus built his bloody wall; the sailors rowed their ships out to sea, and back again. Caius went to the Senate and made as good a speech as he could, bearing in mind that he had to avoid the third conjugation, which we'd not yet reached. Ratty groaned at everything we did. He had known boys in the first year, he said, who could do better. The first year were all paying pupils, pink-cheeked—a nest of little expensive mice, we thought them. It was awful to suppose that they could do better than we did, in the school's third year—but we became dulled to the awfulness of it. 'The trouble with you lot . . .' Ratty would say even before the lesson began—as he bustled into the room, bundled up in his old torn gown. 'We did this in Bell Part One . . .' Our approach to the ablative absolute was beyond his powers of belief. 'Write it out a hundred times . . .' Ratty started from a position of pessimism : boys—that is, any actual boys in a classroom—had a natural incapacity for Latin. At best they represented new taxes on his credulity—how could anyone fail so weirdly to recall the gender of anything whatever?

Maths was worse. Stiff took us for this—Stiff Chignell, thin and spiky. He took that mystery, algebra, and darkened it. Somewhere in the midst of his confusing expositions was the secret meaning of this use of x and y. It was only when I was in the second year, mooning about a field one evening, that I suddenly saw what algebra was all about. It was more like religious conversion than intellectual discovery. The clouds opened—there was a blinding light. Next day Stiff put the clouds back. I was ignorant again.

I remember the deepening chagrin of discovering that all these subjects were turning into guilty obscurities. At Barley Road I had marched from understanding to understanding. Here I was sidling from puzzlement to puzzlement. Even English began to elude me . . . Haddock had taken us in the first year. We did an enormous amount of parsing. I hated

97

that form of tinkering with uninteresting sentences. At times, what with English and Latin and French, we seemed to be trapped in a jungle in which endless towering predicates, shutting out the sky with their foliage of objects, direct and indirect, were overgrown with subjects and extensions of the subject. Haddock varied this with poems from the *Lyra Heroica*. These we had to learn and recite; Haddock would mark the recitations. He marked us, on the whole, for our shyness or boldness of performance. Boldness was known as 'expression.' Shyness was often punished with a hundred lines. Haddock was a kindly man, but poetry seemed to fill him with a deeper rage even than Geography. He was on the whole so despondent about the commerce between, in particular, ballads and boys that, even now, *Sir Patrick Spens* has for me a grievous quality quite extraneous to its content.

But Rubber Wrightson, who taught us in our second year, was even less euphoric about English. He took us, in a succession of dreadful terms, through *Twelfth Night* and *As You Like It* and *The Rivals*. It was years before I could make the simplest head or tail of these plays. This was a result partly of Rubber's deafness. It seemed to make him generally uncertain about the continuity of things; so that, working drearily through the texts, we were able to introduce a degree of excitement by turning over two pages at a time, without his noticing. Perhaps he too was unable to follow the story line. His passion was footnotes. I think he found the text an interruption of those notes. It was fairly easy, when we were doing *The Rivals*, to persuade him to fill the blackboard with drawings of different sorts of wig. He had this great interest in wigs. As far as we knew, *The Rivals* was a play about the art of the perruquier.

Oh, the sadness of it all, I think now; our strange young lives so uneasily failing to mesh with the lives of our teachers. It's the sorrow of all teaching, I sometimes think—since it's really a confrontation of mortals with immortals. We were indolent with immortality. We were here for ever. Even Withers. He was the most powerful member of the form—powerful in his idiocy : a paying pupil who was, so to speak, in that plus-foured fifth form long before he reached it. I remember with amazement how much of the secret, immortal life of III B—that is, its life out of sight of the masters—was dominated by Withers and his strange, ugly fooling. He would dance in front of us, his trousers pulled up to reveal his sock suspenders and his haggard, blackly hairy legs. It was like being entertained by some coarse and witless Pan. We were obliged to laugh and applaud—Withers, and one or two cronies, filled us with puzzled fear. If they didn't like you, they'd bring a little electrical machine of theirs to bear—it gave you a shock. Their pleasure was to unbutton your fly-front and to apply the shock to your genitals. At other times, they'd simply grab at your midriff. For most of our time in III B, any sudden movement on the part of anyone whatever would lead to a quick, defensive response and a protective doubling up. It became so much a habit that I can only wonder that I've not carried it into adult life.

It was a nasty form—a nasty year. Our last year, as it happened, on the old school site: a new school was being built for us, in the middle of our playing field at the other end of the town. Those buildings, I believe, Victorian and Elizabethan mixed, stimulated something—I can't say medieval but historically backward, perhaps—in our boyish natures. About this time I was reading the novels of Harrison Ainsworth; and when I came to his *Guy Fawkes*, I knew what I was reminded of by the woodcut showing the conspirators round a table, sharp-faced, tall-hatted: it was the prefects' little house. You couldn't help becoming Gothic in that setting. It was in III B that one day I picked a quarrel with my gentle friend, Peter Bunce—alleging, as I remember, that he had looked over my shoulder when I was filling in my diary—such an offence!—and I piled into him; and poor Peter, the softest fellow, threw up helpless hands and then even more helplessly lowered his head, and I beat him all round the room until he burst into tears. I hated myself, and was ten feet tall with triumph. There was someone even *I* could hurt, and whose fear I could command.

You had various orders of friends. Some, like Peter Bunce in my case, were friends because you sat next to each other in class. Some were friends for reasons of local geography. That was so with me and Ralph Hobson. He was the only acquaintance I had who lived in one of the big houses in the avenues. Ralph's domestic arrangements amazed me: that is to say, his father had run away. Mr Hobson was in Australia, and though the official story was that he was absent on what had turned out to be an astoundingly long visit, a great irritation to all concerned but associated with business projects that in the end would raise the Hobsons far above us all, nevertheless Ralph told me bluntly that his father could not abide his mother. And though I had little aptitude for disliking people, and certainly not the mothers of friends, still I could see Mr Hobson's point. Mrs Hobson was consistently sad—she sat about being discouraging about any matter that might be broached—and, like Ralph, she smelled strongly of a heterodox type of soap. Ralph said it was a health soap. This strengthened a feeling I'd been given by the Hygiene lessons we'd received from Miss Thrift at Barley Road : health was admirable, but the response to it of any of the senses was likely to be . . . Well, the pinched nose with which I walked about the Hobson house, without actually pinching my nose, was an example.

Ralph had more comics than anyone I knew, and he kept them in a trunk on a landing. Of these he was willing to lend me quantities carefully measured out by himself; the payment being one that puzzled me. I had to submit to a beating on the bottom with a hairbrush. I saw this as a tiresome condition of obtaining comics, but my greed for them was great, and I submitted. It's the flagellation of the nostrils I remember, for all this activity stirred up the smell of soap.

In all ways Ralph sought power over me through my lust for his comics. Even when I'd paid up, as it were, he was capricious about the number he'd lend me. In my anxiety I became quite fawning, assuring him that my father would be pleased because comics kept me quiet. It was not true : my father was already expressing uneasiness about the tendency of literature to glue me to my chair for hours on end. On one occasion Ralph left me alone with the trunk and to what I had already been given I added a trembling extra handful : but when he returned he knew about it, and was very scornful, taking back even more than I'd added . . .

I'd escape from the house singing—stinging too, I suppose, though I've no recollection of that; glad to be free of the obscurely depressing intensity of the moments in Ralph's bedroom, the atmosphere of mysterious hygiene, Ralph's flushed severity as to the number of comics I might have. He would take back half a comic at the last moment, as if obeying a set of scales only he could see.

Still, as payment for literature, it did seem a bargain.

One of the charges brought by the neighbours against my father was that after a hard day in the garden he remained insolently debonair. 'The worst of it,' one of them told me years later, 'was that he'd be out there, at eight o'clock in the morning, clearly having had a complete, relaxed breakfast; and he would choose to work in immaculate white flannels. His hair would be laid flat and shining on his head. He would dig with his usual thoroughness—two spits deep, every weed extricated to the last fragment of a root. At five o'clock in the afternoon precisely he would stop. His flannels would be as white as they were when he began : not a hair would be out of place . . . I hated him.'

My father and immaculacy!

'Up you go and change into something decent,' he'd say as I crept downstairs on a Sunday in shabby comfort. 'You're not lounging about all day like that. To look at you, people would think we hadn't two ha'pennies to rub together.'

It seemed to my father very important that we should demonstrate our ability to rub two ha'pennies together. (It occurs to me that that might at times have been about the summit of my mother's capacity, if she'd been inclined to such an idle use of the money in her purse.) He also believed that, at a pinch, one should be able to use one's shoes as a mirror. 'He cares what he looks like. You could see your face in his shoes.'

Left to myself, I was inclined to allow my shoes to lose all power of reflection. In them nothing was visible but their own coat of dust or mud. 'You're not walking about like that,' he'd cry. 'Go and polish them. My father would have flung us across the room if he'd found us wearing shoes in that state.'

So behind my father and his passion for polish stood *his* father—with a similar passion? My grandfather, according to these tales, was a man who backed his demand for the spick-and-span with various kinds of violence. Throwing his sons across the room was merely a basic technique. He would also, at Sunday dinner, strike them across the knuckles with the back of a carving knife (no one said it was the back, but I could not believe it to be the front) if any of them spoke out of turn or giggled. My father would speak of such disciplinary methods as if they represented a degree of admirable strictness compared with which his own conduct towards his children was softly permissive.

'My father would have tanned our arses and sent us to bed for less.'

'Oh Dick!'

What I could never understand were my father's reasons for adopting a less severe approach. Why was I not thrown across the room? . . . There was of course another way of looking at it. It lay in asking whether my father's attitude to family discipline was *in fact* milder than my grandfather's.

Take, for example, giggling at meals.

It always happened when my father was in a bad mood. Indeed, it happened often *because* he was in a bad mood. He would come in from the garden, bitter with Mr Folkestone for a remark unwisely made ('Think you can trust Mr Baldwin?'), a plant allowed to grow through a fence into my father's territory. It might be a bitterness for which there was no immediate or obvious cause: he would suddenly be charged with a malignancy that had its roots in . . . heaven knew what annoyance during the Whitehall week, inflamed by the Sunday discovery that for a son he had a giggler with an aversion for shoe polish . . .

It was my mother, usually, on whom his glower had much the same effect as if he'd sat there wearing a funny hat. Anger might interfere (nothing else could) with his perfect gift for carving the joint. The knife would stray, crackling would fly: 'Blast!' he would growl. My mother's shoulders would shake. Anxiously—she was as worried as the rest of us by this weakness of hers—she'd attempt some soothing comment. It never soothed—she really wasn't good at this. 'A lovely tender bit of meat,' she might say. 'Mr Friday (she meant Mr Fereday, the butcher) said he'd never seen—' 'Bugger Mr Fereday!' My sister would laugh at the word 'bugger'; but she had a sort of immunity on these occasions. Mother would catch my eye. It was all that was needed. The little spark of laughter in her eye was enough to set going the forest-fire of my own amusement. Father would fling down fork and carver, strike the table with his fist. Plates would leap in the air. 'Get out! Get out!

Get out in the bloody kitchen and wait for your dinner!' 'Oh Dick, don't!' And there I'd be, once more, standing forlornly between the gas cooker and the draining board, at once aflame with laughter and glum at what had happened; which would lead always, nearly always, to the most miserable sort of Sunday afternoon and evening.

Then there was nothing to do but make our contrition very plain indeed—and after years of practice, we were very good at doing that. If we succeeded, the Sunday evening walk was saved.

To go walking on Sunday evenings was unspeakable delight. And this despite the often angry preliminaries. Again my shoes would be found wanting in polish, my tie would have wandered out of true. There was violent tugging and brushing and my mother would join in with her handkerchief, wetting it with her spittle and scrubbing at smuts on my face. There would be the familiar sweet-sour smell of mother's spit, abhorrent and reassuring. I would wriggle. 'For God's sake stand still,' my father would shout. 'And put your cap on straight.'

We'd rush to the door, my sister and I. We had, from earlier days, a formula for that. 'Bags I'm door-opener'.

'If you don't quieten down we'll not go at all.'

And then across the fields.

For Betty and me it was picking buttercups, ripping the red seed off grasses and throwing it at each other. Then back to our parents' sober orbit.

'I don't know what Folkestone thinks he's doing. He calls it pruning. Murder, I call it. You don't prune a young apple tree like that.'

'No, dear.'

'That boy's been walking in cow's muck. Rub your shoes in the grass, for God's sake. And look where you're going.'

The familiar fields. Their marvellous familiarity. A fallen tree to scamper over. The stream to pore into—ah, the little hitches and stitches of water, round stones and twigs.

'Mind your shoes. You'll wear all the leather off, doing that. Now walk quietly.'

A couple vanishing into bushes—his arm round her waist, her wincing plumpness. Their excitement becoming mysteriously, disconsolately, my own. What did they do in the bushes?

At some point, always, a new house, half-built. To my father, a magnet. He loved exploring houses that were incomplete, and we loved him doing it. It gave me an intense thrill to hear him criticising the way something had been done, disparaging the plastering perhaps; and there was a feeling of importance when he sought our approval of his opinion that a room was too small, or a window ill-advised. 'I say! What a silly place to put the sink!' I remember the smell, heady to me, of new wood and plaster, and the whole curious excitement of being inside this skeleton of what, later, would be a home, fleshed with furniture. But for most of these houses we had a glorious contempt, and not much of an opinion of those who would consent to live in them.

However bad a day it had been, father would come out of a half-built house glowing with the happiness of, usually, thinking very little of it. Then with luck Sunday would coast home pleasantly. But one mistake—tread on his toe, fail to prevent yourself from kicking a cowpat, upset your sister with one shower of grass seed too many—and you were ruined.

'That bloody boy! Wait till I get you home . . .'

My sister was, poor girl, anything I liked to make her, by way of support for my fantasies. So when I opened a library in my bedroom, she was its sole user : she was allowed to borrow the *Holy Bible* (on her fiction ticket) and Dean Stanley's *Life of Dr Arnold* (on her non-fiction ticket) for a fortnight; and suffered staggering imaginary fines when they came back a day late. When I wrote plays, performed on the landing, she was cast as one and all of the very large number of minor characters who were wives, lovers, servants and enemies of the major character : whom she did not, ever, play. When I set up a telephone between our bedrooms, she was allowed to be the amazed audience for my calls, which were, always, transatlantic. When I began keeping a diary I insisted she should do the same; but I did not care to leave its composition to her— I dictated to her each evening her daily musings. At one time I had a passion for holding trials. I was always the judge. My sister was a long line of felons, faced with a great variety of charges. Including, I remember, persistent adultery. I thought it was criminally putting water in the milk.

As for milk itself, I now remember, we had it skimmed.

104

There was a dairy at the bottom of the road; and the skimmed milk was served out of a vast yellow bowl, a cross between a punchbowl and a chamber pot. You took a jug. The honour of doing this was often struggled for by my sister and me during the school holidays. It was an event. Going up the town with Mum, as a surviving diary reminds me, was an event. It was an event studded with the names of shopkeepers; they come back to me now, a fine roll of names smelling of cheese, bacon, bananas, leather, newsprint . . . Chant and Knapman, Charrington, Garner, Locket & Co; Janes & Adams; Hopping & Hunt; Friday and Stanley, White & Wyatt, Hentall and Howard, Snoad & Cooper; Amos Wills and Mrs Channer. Mrs Channer had a toyshop, but it called itself, most beautifully, a fancy repository . . . Shovelling up shit from the road when a horse had gone by was an event : steaming buns of dung. And so was running out to buy ice creams from the man with his tricycle, Walls or Eldorado. Oddly, ice cream was another thing that placed you socially. It was posh, in our view, to have a tub, which cost twopence. Our mark was the Snofrute, a triangular stick of appallingly cold water ice, which cost a ha'penny.

And going up the library—that was the phrase—was a daily event. 'I have just finished my library book,' says that extant diary for August 1932. 'It was rather sad, but interesting. Dinner—Kidney and peas.' Often I wrote the story out, my style as a summariser influenced by my reading of film magazines. 'It centres round Jem Blake, the descendant of a well-known and respected country family. He is a scapegrace, and cannot keep clear of betting. He learns a lesson when he unconsciously steals some money of his mother's . . .' And so on. Over the years, I wonder about that business of being a thief whilst apparently in a coma. What *did* I mean? . . . My hunger for books was so great that at one time I joined a penny library in the town. My first and only borrowing was of a novel by Remarque—the sequel to *All Quiet on the Western Front* : *The Way Back*. My father read it; which led to a sort of literary courtmartial. It was thanks to his angry questioning that I know the book includes the phrase : 'They pissed silver in the moonlight.' I had failed to note it in my own rather baffled reading.

For Art we had Granddad: a sad figure, tall and thin and white-haired, whose occupancy of part of the hut, which had been temporary since 1916, turned that thin-walled structure into a drum. What it drummed out was the pure relief of boys who found themselves, for once, in nerveless hands. Granddad had no ability whatever to keep children in order. His view of art was academic in the extreme: week after week he set before us arrangements of cubes and cones and pyramids, and invited us to engage in the exciting venture of rendering these naïve, dead forms in all the veracity of substance and shadow. We were to hatch and cross-hatch. Outlines were to be rendered either with amazing sharpness or with shadowy ambiguity. For the first we must have pencils of a certain kind meticulously sharpened. For the other there must be softer lead, as meticulously blunted. The sharpening and unsharpening of pencils was the chief activity of those lessons. Granddad was the most marvellous pencil-sharpener I have ever known. He was perfectly happy to work on our pencils, and we formed around his desk rumbustious queues. 'Oh, mine now, Granddad!' He was very deaf and would smile at these importunities. Granddad was so vulnerable that we were divided by his existence into two groups: those who enjoyed tormenting him, without a second thought, and those whose enjoyment was shot through with guilt. We all knew that Granddad was regarded by the rest of the staff as a liability. The Head would appear among us with unnatural regularity; masters using other parts of the hut would wander in, unconvincingly intent on conversation with the old man. It was part of the excitement of Art: that anyone might come in at any moment and distribute, with the air of someone doing something quite else, horrid muttered punishments. The Head came in once when Fido Philips was crawling about the floor being, in intoxicated accord with his nickname, a dog. 'What do you think you're doing, Philips?' the Head demanded, in that roar of his that might have cowed a lion. But such was the delirium of being in Granddad's class that it did not cow the dog that Fido was so vividly being. 'Bow wow wow!' said Fido—and made a dash for the Head before sanity intervened and brought him slowly, amazedly, to his feet. Fido was beaten, rather spectacularly, and the rest of us were given a hundred lines each. Granddad smiled through it all, not quite catching on.

Peter Bunce and I were keen on art. We were of that group that was uneasy about our treatment of Granddad. From time to time Peter and I persuaded Granddad to allow us to tackle somewhat freer themes: we were much drawn to rural sentimentalities, to sketches of ponds overhung with funereal willows, or mildly motheaten cottages. If it was guilt that drove us to offer Granddad these gloomy inventions of ours, the result was an increase of shame; for he took us very seriously indeed. In my second year I entered for the school Art prize: and elected to copy a sketch from a book I'd borrowed from the public library. By doing so I broke all the rules. The work was supposed to be original. I remember now the loving unease with which I set about my plagiarism—an unease partly due to the fact that however I tried, the scene (pond, willows, milkmaid) that I was cribbing from was perfectly squared off in the book, but in my version tilted sadly towards the bottom left-hand corner of the paper. Everything was curled and tilting, including the milkmaid. I confess now that I did not deserve the *proxime accessit* that I was awarded for this anxiously dishonest work. But the consequences were curious. I found that I could not bring the milkmaid to life. Not only did she tilt—she was also strangely wooden. When I discussed this with Peter Bunce, we came to the rather excited conclusion that it was because I was not at home with the female form. Odd—it seems a sophisticated insight for a twelve-year-old, but I saw that my difficulty with her figure lay partly in my sheer ignorance of the way it was constructed. Egged on by Peter, I confessed my problem to Granddad. And he—to my amazement, and shock, and excitement—gave me, with the strong suggestion that I should keep it to myself, a sheet of photographs of a naked woman—taken from many angles and in many postures, so that one could see, for example, what happened to her breasts when she raised her arms or lowered them. Alas! it was altogether too thrilling to keep to myself. I showed it around, and chuckled with the rest at the idea of Granddad's simplicity in giving such a thing to a mere boy . . .

And guilt mounted. To make up for such crimes, Peter and I became more and more attentive to the old man. And one day he invited us to visit him, to come to his house—he would give us, he said, it was the least he could do for pupils so enthusiastic, an old easel he no longer needed. We could take it out and draw in the open air . . .

It was one of the saddest houses I have ever entered: neglected, in a neglected garden. Granddad was a widower . . . On every wall, large canvases: all quite horribly gloomy. Typical subject: a London bridge, in fog, and a young woman leaning on the parapet, staring down into the water. Her plain intent: suicide. These, Granddad informed us quite cheerfully, were paintings he had submitted to the Royal Academy: this in this year, that in that—he remembered the years clearly. No, he had never had one accepted. Would we let him offer us some lemonade?

Peter and I running through the streets, glad to escape, sadly, jubilantly relieved, with the enormous easel held between us—a great, gaunt, ridiculous easel, such as we knew we'd never dare to take out in public, once we'd got the thing home. My father chopped it up for various uses. As for Granddad, he did not survive the removal of the school to its new site . . .

3

To look at, the new school was extremely stolid Tudor pastiche. That's to say, it had modest crenellations, and windows with stone mullions; there was the faintest touch of Hampton Court, and at each end there were short covered walks, which were vaguely cloistral. In effect, it was a rather boring oblong. All this I see with the eye of hindsight. At the time I thought it splendid for being so large and for making such an effort to look unlike any old school.

I had a friend who was new, too: Ray Bolton. He lived close at hand, in a house backing on to our own. For years I'd disliked Ray: he was among those who'd mocked me for not caring to climb trees. He was dark and agile and belonged to an altogether uncongenial cluster of boys. Then, suddenly, he turned into someone else. We began to play together in the fields. But it was not play, in the familiar sense. We did not dam the streams, or light fires in the joints of dead trees. Instead we lay in the long summer grass and talked. It was, for the first time for both of us, *talk* as a form of play. Ray set out for me his entire family history. I set out, for him, mine. We talked, haltingly, of girls; for both of us, remote creatures, rather more exotic than Red Indians. Ray was a reader, but he never remembered title or author of any book he read. He thought an interest in such details was the mark of the sort of person for whom the general title was Professor. That was what, with friendly scorn, he called me. I slowly persuaded him away from this view of things. One day he acknowledged the existence of Agatha Christie and decided that he could, without effeminacy, be aware that he had read her novel, *The Man in the Brown Suit*. 'I'm getting as bad as you,' he grumbled, but with evident pleasure. We rolled about a little in the grass. Intellectual embarrassment could still be dealt with by tussles of the kind.

The Boltons had no car, but they had a garage. It had been put up by Mr Bolton himself when the Boltons were talking of having a car, and was not much more than a garden shed; but it was spoken of as the garage, and that was enough for my father. He was more elaborately biting about it than about any other feature of the Boltons' home. At times he would call my mother to his side. 'Look, dear! He's going into his *garage*!' He would experiment with various pronunciations of this word, in a manner which was clearly to be taken as satirical. '*Ay'm goin' into may gar-ahge!*' This was quite wild, for there was no touch of that sort of preciosity in Mr Bolton's voice. But often enough my father seemed to express, for those of his enemies he was able to watch from his windows, a particular order of playful and even affectionate hatred. So my friend's father, having entered his garage, might leave it again, pushing his lawn mower. 'Oh,' my father would cry, beginning to caper a little in his delight, 'just see what a lovely lawn mower I've got! That's it! Push it up and down! Let's hear how it sounds! . . . Oh dear, he's having to oil it! Annie!' —for my mother would have supposed she was free to slip away again—'Here! Quick! We're oiling our beautiful lawn mower, which we've taken out of our wonderful garage!'

Then his mood would change: 'They make me sick! Who does he think he's impressing? I hope he doesn't think he's impressing me!' A short bark of a laugh. 'No better than anyone else. If he spent a little more time just telling that wife of his to keep her big mouth shut—'

'Dick!'—from my mother, who was not unfond of Mrs Bolton.

'—or keeping that boy of his tidy!'

A scowl from me: all that, at this time, I was ready to offer by way of protest.

The trouble was that once my father had established such an antipathy, so easily and accidentally rooted, he was able to graft on to it any allegation whatever, the worst-supported insinuations. One day I discovered that Ray Bolton was now held to be a bad moral influence. 'Thinks of nothing but girls,' said my father. Had he ever seen Ray with a girl? I thought it unlikely that the accusation had such roots as that. If Ray had ever secured the attention of a young woman even for thirty seconds, he would have rushed round to tell me. There would have been endless walking and talking to analyse and digest the event. It was more likely that my father took it that any son of Mr Bolton *must* be morally loose. He might, through this stricture on Ray, have been expressing a fear that I should myself become so morally loose as to think of girls. I certainly understood that in the case of a Bolton, thinking of *nothing but* girls would be much the same order of crime as I would commit myself if I thought of girls *among other things* . . .

The time came when my father discovered that I was masturbating. Not that it can really have been a sudden discovery. There must have been signs of it enough from my eleventh year onwards. I had long played curious games with myself in bed. The basic form of these games had been one of violent rejection by a lover, and then of violent reconciliation with her. Or with *him*—for sometimes I was myself a male and sometimes a female. In perhaps the commonest form of the game I was married, and my wife and I had appallingly quarrelled and gone sulkily to bed, far apart, smouldering; and then, swept by sudden reckless reversals of feeling, vast tides of

110

tenderness, we'd let the tiniest touch occur, heel on heel, tip
of toe on tip of toe, and brushing of hips, and then full and . . .
This next bit was a seizure and paroxysm of love, the heart
going off like bomb after bomb in the frail house of the body
. . . A variation embodied a childish understanding of the
excitements of being sexually afraid—of being menaced with
rape . . . I'd be, usually, a slender, white-bodied, delicate,
shivering princess (the rank was important), fallen into the
clutches of an Arab prince, a sheikh, some handsome barbarian
of the kind, and he'd strip my pyjamas from me—and I'd be
him too, of course, with scratching and bruising fingers—and
he'd run his armies of hands over my appalled flesh, and . . .
And, doing this once, he allowed one of his armies to mount a
particular assault, according to some new and startling strategy
. . . and the result had me sitting up in bed, horrified, and
turning on the light and not, at once, daring to look . . . I
thought I'd broken myself. I'd been most unluckily clumsy
and this delicate and useful part of myself had simply cracked
up under treatment for which anyone else would have known
it was not designed. I had long realised that I was inept with
machinery of any kind. I had always overwound clockwork
motors. I had simply overwound this part of myself, which
any fool but me would have known might (given the technical
possibility of it) have sported a small plaque saying : 'Danger.
Do not touch *for the sake of it.*' I had touched it most prodigiously for the sake of doing so. Or I'd allowed the sheikh
in my drama, that bawdy Arab, in running his dusky fingers
down my body, to pay special attention to the very heart
of my clockwork, and the damned fellow had overwound
me! . . .

I'd spoken of it next day to Peter Bunce—had tremblingly
whispered of it rather; half-boastful, half in the manner of one
doomed. Peter had been unappalled. It had not yet happened
to him, he said; but acting on information variously received,
he had for some time been engaged in a sequence of experi-
ments and was hopeful of an interesting outcome in the very
near future. He didn't precisely contradict my fear of being
smashed and ruined, for I couldn't bring myself to express
such a hideous idea; but clearly he didn't think it a ruinous
experience. Others seemed to have survived it. So I allowed it
to happen again. I did so particularly because the easing of my

dread permitted me to concentrate on the incredible pleasure that the amazing act had induced. There'd been this thick welling, every slow pulse in it a delicious outrage. The most exquisite anaesthesia had numbed the entire surface of my body, and had turned my bowels to ice veined with ecstasies. In quite splendid places—the root of my spine, for example—there had been delectable explosions . . .

My father took official cognisance of this development when Mr Argyll wrote to say that I was having difficulty in getting round the running track. I can't think why Argyll should have done this. Perhaps—the thought strikes me—I was made spectacularly short-winded by my self-pleasurings, and even a sensible man like Argyll was alarmed by such panting, such stumbling, such bolting of eyes . . . But I could not have forgotten such decrepitude in myself, so young. The truth must be that Argyll detected some special fatigue and puzzling weakness in me and simply thought I needed a medical check-up. And perhaps, for my father, Argyll's note sparked off a long unease. He certainly became very choleric, and ordered me to put on my cap and coat at once and accompany him to the doctor's.

On the way he made several short indignant speeches. A boy of my age, he said. Ridiculous. I should be interested in other things. I should go to sleep when I went to bed. What did I think a bed was for? He couldn't understand it. A quick review of the family on both sides failed to suggest any explanation of such unpleasant precocity. What made me think he enjoyed receiving such letters from one of my teachers? Had I no respect for my mother, who could not fail here and there to come across evidence of my depravity? What made me think that a mother wished to have her attention drawn to such a thing? Had I no respect or shame? Had I no interest in being healthy? Did I realise where it might lead? Had I considered my responsibility, not only to my parents but to my sister?

As we approached the door of the doctor's surgery he murmured: 'That young Bolton . . .'

It was a curious affair, that visit to the doctor. I was given a very quick examination: tongue, chest, a tap on the knee, perhaps: I can't remember. Then I was dismissed; but the doctor asked my father to stay. I sat waiting for what seemed a long time. Then my father emerged, looking grim. On the way home he confined himself to the occasional groan: 'A boy of your age . . .!' Since I was on my way to being fourteen, I cannot imagine at what age my father thought it would be all right for me to abuse myself. I didn't like to ask about this. Indeed, I didn't dare to say anything. I had no wish to discuss what I felt was my most private business, made abominably public: my SIN, as I called it in the diary I had just begun to keep. And it hardly seemed the moment to broach some quite extraneous theme.

But under the grumblings my father seemed a little crestfallen; and I now imagine that the doctor might have spoken for me.

Really, it happens with all boys. He's healthy enough in himself. Shortness of breath . . . well, perhaps he's one of those boys who don't believe in propelling themselves at great speeds round running tracks. Really, you shouldn't worry. And if I may say so, I shouldn't worry him. I think you might be making him rather alarmed about himself.

As indeed my father was. It was another addition to that gross state of alarm into which everything seemed intent on plunging me. I could smell the evil in myself, at times. It had the odour of the school gym, of gym shoes, of shorts and singlets shut up too long in kitbags. The sour smell of all our bodies, which hung in my nostrils, causing a kind of deeply despondent excitement. It was a thing of dread, this tang of flesh and bitter taste of sweaty desire. It was ludicrous too: coming down as it did to the humiliating comedy of those numerous sets of genitals . . . Though there were some in whose case the ludicrous made way before such a vague glow of . . . grace, was it? shapeliness? pleasure of colouring? Young X and young Y: one short with rounded limbs, the other long and slim . . . But my! It was all so very dangerous: for round the edge of this phantasmagoria of flesh, as round the edge of the playing field, or the changing room bath, patrolled the grown ups, sharply watching, ready and indeed eager to detect any deviancy, to pounce, shame, penalise. The Head had said in his account of the architecture of our new school that one of the reasons why we had changing rooms and showers was so that we might become accustomed to one another's bodies. The idea seemed to be that such sensible accustomedness would, in all but the rotten of character, bring about a grown-up indifference to the alarming excitement of—ugh !—all those limbs, joints, pieces of physical punctuation . . . And that was the point where my alarm grew monumental : because it was quite clear that no amount of accustomedness had the slightest effect on my lascivious fevers. The more I saw of X, the more I wanted to see of him, and the more depraved the manner in which he entered my dreams, by day or night.

There was little hope for me, I felt. Sensuality was simply a screening device, and it sorted me out with certainty among the rotters . . . A sixth former was expelled for *getting a girl in the family way*. A useful member of the First XV too, which showed that the highest qualifications could not preserve one from disgrace. It was like a distant but precise prospect of a coast towards which I was undeflectably drifting.

My lusts were exhausting enough : the fears and guilts that were added to them were appalling extra fatigues. It occurs to me now that it might have been burdens like these, invisible to good games masters like Argyll, that made it difficult for me to get round the running track.

As for my father, the effect of the incident was narrowed to the phrase : '*You go to bed to go to sleep.*' He would come into my room suddenly and pronounce it. Curiously, if I was half asleep it had the quality of a benediction : what was intended to warn, was found soothing.

And my father had distinctly decided that my depravity had been taught to me by Ray Bolton. I wonder now if he thought that it had been passed on to Ray, again as a piece of explicit instruction, by Mr Bolton. It could be expected from a man who boasted of a garage.

I could not exactly be forbidden to consort with Ray. Even my father must have seen that he could not base such a firm edict on a suspicion so vague. But he frowned when he saw us together; would urge me at times to widen the circle of my friends. And stationing himself at a window, he would wax more and more satirical and sarcastic about what he could see of the Boltons' domestic arrangements.

Not that I really understood what wickedness was, even when it was thrust upon me. There was a curious gulf between *idea* and *fact*. The fact retained its innocence long after the idea had grown quite corrupt. There was for example my brief, dreamlike relationship with Jack Forest.

Jack, for reasons I did not understand until much later (despite the evidence that fell, so to speak, into my lap), was widely known as Mary. He was a distinguished middle-school sportsman and not at all my kind of boy. But we sat together in physics; and it was in this lesson that he submitted to me the idea that I might touch him in a private fashion. It was a lesson in which I was glad of alternatives to what was officially going on. I was hopeless at physics. It could not be dissolved into vagueness and individuality. It demanded exactness. So I was pleased to be offered this diversion, of Jack's devising.

It was hard going, if you weren't to attract attention. But Jack returned the compliment, and once whispered sternly, as if testing some vital branch of knowledge: 'What would happen if I went on doing this?' I knew the answer, of course, but found myself unwilling to utter it.

Jack, I now think, was infinitely more aware than I was of the danger of this proceeding. I was inclined to be carried away—to attempt to burrow deeper into his alarmed warmness. Jack would hiss: 'Be careful. You fool. We'd get into *terrible* trouble if we were caught.' His anxiety only increased my interest.

Jack proposed we go walking, though I knew that was a euphemism, across the fields of an evening. But mine wasn't the sort of house—I didn't know how to tell him this—where you could say: 'I'm going out to see a friend.' Going out to see Ray Bolton, for all the shadow he was under, or any of three or four familiar names—that was all right, given that I was never out too long at a time. But any novelty would lead to instant grilling. 'Oh—who's that?' 'He's called Jack Forest, Dad. He's in our form.' 'What's wrong with your dear little friend at the back, then?' 'Nothing, Dad. I—' 'What sort of chap is this . . . what's his name?' The very name, one would begin to feel, reeked of rottenness. My father's imagination would have created at once a monster of depravity—if not some crafty pseudonym for a girl. The beginning of the rot. Wandering about the streets with unknowns. 'I'd rather you stuck to friends we know . . .' It wasn't on. I mumbled excuses. Jack grew scornful. Physics relapsed into plain physics . . .

One day that term a special assembly was announced at an unusual hour. Prefects were taciturn, masters withdrawn. There was, when we were all gathered, a great and puzzling speech. Vague hints at moral rot. Mostly there was decency, most boys were content to be boys according to some accepted definition; they got on soberly with their studies and their healthy games. But there were patches of mould. There were unspecified vilenesses. Two boys in particular were creators of corruption, and might become carriers if dramatic punishment were not imposed. This was the moment for it. Alas.

The two boys were named. We were surprised: quite un-villainous names. They were ordered to the platform. These boys, we were told, had been caught fooling about in the lavatories. I remember attempting to focus the wickedness involved. 'Fooling about' was the broadest description of everyday over-liveliness. The lavatories? Had they been tinkering with the plumbing? Then something happened that was straight out of my Victorian school stories. The caretaker was summoned, and each boy in turn was hoisted upon his back, there to be tremendously flogged. We dispersed—most of us, I now think, quite baffled.

It was much later that I understood that poor ordinary X and unfortunate quiet-mannered Y had been punished in this scarring fashion for the same experimental pleasures I'd been involved in with Jack Forest. Years later I trembled with anger at the thought of it.

For being a natural schoolboy, naturally inquisitive, for engaging in an immemorial and natural order of sexual rehearsal: gross public humiliation.

Some instinct prevented me from mentioning the incident at home. No need to provide my father with extra fuel for his belief that I was never an inch away from that complex of turpitudes, about which no one ever came out into the open . . .

4

My father now had hopes of promotion. For years he had followed one of his own desperate prescriptions for advancement. You studied the tastes of your superiors and imitated them. This had led him into playing tennis. Though he looked splendid in whites, I don't think it was his game. But the out-of-office jovialities it involved gave him presentiments of an improvement in his position. He discussed them endlessly. He was losing games with regularity to the baleful Ching and submitting to defeats by Maclagen that must surely induce, in that former enemy, feelings of affection. The temperature of life at home rose and fell according to the luck of the tennis court. My mother was anxious on his behalf, but did not enjoy being a lawn tennis widow. He joined other clubs and societies at the office. He was often late home. And he began now to invite me to help him with his files. 'Good exercise for you,' he'd say. 'See what you make of drafting an answer to this letter.' My prose style was gaudy and ambitious. I liked huge adjectives. There was no room for them in these official exchanges. Now, I weep a little for what lay behind those cries— it's what they surely were—for help. His own official style was halting and awkward—the strict meanings of words, I think, dissolved at the point of his pen, he was never sure that he was using them correctly. I was sulky and wretched under his demands: I knew I was no civil servant. 'Don't they teach you to write a decent letter?' he'd growl.

But oh, how different he was on holiday! A new man took over: someone given to playing cricket on the sand, flying kites, working slot machines on the pier. I think I was never happier than when he was pouring pennies into the slot machines. Such recklessness with those coins, usually so clung

117

to! I guess now that this was the essence of the holiday to him too: this annual disrespect for the penny. He wore flannels and an open-necked shirt; he courted the sun, which he adored. In the evenings we walked to a pub, and my sister and I waited outside with tonic waters: a blissful ritual. All the birds in the world squeezed out their songs around us. The pub sign blossomed over its door, a very flower! And near at hand, so near at hand, was the incredible sea.

I have never lost my sense of the incredibility of the sea. The world turned suddenly to this whispering liquidity. Nothing splendid; it was always the North Sea, cut into careful sections by the green and drunken groynes. The first step on to the beach was almost more beautiful than one could quite bear. The shingle making its hard sounds of readjustment to one's steps, the polished fragments of shell! The great seaside sky! And the gulls! A row of them would sit on the weed-green posts of a groyne, with the waves sometimes rising so high the gulls had to leap into the air and then back, as if the water had been a skipping rope. I noticed how, when a gull came down to a post already occupied, the resident bird was forced to rise and look for another. Musical groynes.

And then the walk in the town.

How we loved the seaside town, its foolish shops, its bustle of persons as liberated as ourselves. Such staring in windows! Talk so deliciously trivial! Clacton or Littlehampton or Felixstowe yawned about us, stretched its lazy arms! We bought evening newspapers and talked about the cricket results. Hammond, another century! Hammond scoring centuries was a dimension of ourselves; it made my father bigger, browner, more athletic, as if he were, in some quite measurable fraction, Hammond himself! The sun slid down and we stood to watch it. The dusk gathered and we had no intention of going indoors. An enormous acceptance of outdoorness possessed us. Dad told his jokes. They were sometimes rude. He informed us of the man in the cinema who found a pair of knickers on the floor and tapped on the shoulder of the girl in front. 'Are these your knickers?' 'No, mine are in my handbag.' All barriers were down: my father was telling disgraceful jokes! Back at home only a few weeks before, he'd discovered a copy of a magazine, *Razzle*. There had been a grim scene. He'd asked me to explain one of the jokes. A boy and girl, cycling.

He wore long shorts, she wore short shorts. They came to a wood, laid their bicycles down. Then they came back: he wore short shorts, she wore long shorts. What was the point? my father asked, agitatedly. I explained the point. He was very angry. 'You've got other things to do than read disgusting papers like this.' And now he was telling jokes that would have made *Razzle* blush . . .

Silly Clacton! Felixstowe daft with pleasure! Dad, annually daft, marvellously inconsistent!

Sometimes it was inland—at a spa. Great-Aunt Alma was buried there. There were old friends of our great-aunts, spinster sisters, who lived there in a tiny house I loved, full of bad Victorian novels and wax flowers under glass. I'd been there once, alone for a week with my father's Aunt Ada; she'd taken me to the cemetery for her annual conference with her dead sister. We stood beside the grave and Ada talked to Alma. Family news, entirely. 'Teddy's with me, dear. That's Dick's boy. Oh, bad news about Jack. He's left Muriel. Do you remember Muriel, dear? I don't think you ever liked her. But I'm afraid Jack has behaved very badly. Well, they say she asked for it—but all the same . . .' It was a bit like reading one of those bad Victorian novels—even in talking to the dead, great-aunt Ada was clearly only skirting the story . . .

In this gentle spa the chief delights were the concerts given in the band stand in the public gardens. Dad and I, sharing a programme. The Queen's Own Cameron Highlanders. Our interest, over the week, in the personality of this bandsman or that. It might be a matter of a trumpeter's fine knees. Dad and I would agree that we had never seen such knees. Or it was a moustache; or the tartan hauteur of the conductor.

And there was music we loved together. An encore once, called *Baby's Sweetheart*. It involved all those kilted musical heroes in whistling. We whistled the tune ourselves for months afterwards.

Such love, alas, such love—Dad and I united in our passion for a banal tune. It was the closest we ever came. In time music was to be among the causes of our terrible disunity.

Great-Aunt Ada was immensely tall: her height and erectness had always been a matter of pride in the family. She came of a little mountain-range of sisters; Dolly, Alma, Emily, Ada, all spikes of women with the strong family face. It was a point in my favour, on days when I was able to acquire such points, that I showed signs of being like Aunt Ada in this respect.

She had once been personal maid to a mysterious Lady Parsons: mysterious to me, that is, since as a child I did not understand why she should be known as 'Lady'. Since Lady Parsons was connected with my family, however remotely, I did not associate her with the fabulous world of Lords and Ladies. Rather I imagined that the usage reflected some special reason she must have for stressing her female condition. She featured often, and reverently, in Aunt Ada's conversation. 'Dear Lady Parsons would not have cared for *that*', was the common phrase. To me, through the years, Lady Parsons gained in definition, but lost none of her mystery, by virtue of the events, developments and ideas for which Aunt Ada claimed she would not have cared. They covered a wide sweep of social and political change, as well as a fairly coherent body of smaller matters; if my hair was ever a little long, for example, she would not have cared for that, nor for my treading on Aunt Ada's feet. As a child, I had trodden often on my great-aunt's feet, which were long and slow. Aunt Ada would generalise such vexations ('Nowadays young people have no thought for others') and then would elevate the complaint above all possible controversy by invoking her dead employer ('Poor Lady Parsons would *not* have cared for that').

My father had his own way of speaking of Lady Parsons. 'Gave Aunt Ada all those little trinkets. Bits of jewellery, too. Pity. The old lady has no use for them. Probably doesn't realise their value.' My father had his eye on some of these oddments. Several little pots he was sure were Wedgwood; some fragments of ivory and a locket or two. There was a nervous impression that the moment Aunt Ada died an uncle or so might swoop on her rooms and strip them bare. My father was perpetually on the mark for the sharp sprint that would be required when this happened.

Aunt Ada added her mite to the moral debate that seemed to consume so much of life. For a great many years, in her view, history had been dominated by the urge of women to take off more and more clothes, and of men to be less and less disinclined to take advantage of this brazenness. The women, she thought, were to blame. Men would be decent enough if given the opportunity; or rather, if shielded from the temptation to be otherwise. Most murders she ascribed to the mounting immodesty of women. The police would have far less to do if women were compelled by law to wear an ample minimum of clothes.

I sat with her once on the seafront at Hastings. It was in the heyday of beach pyjamas—as I remember them, a remarkably decent garment. But to Aunt Ada's taste they embodied the great cultural disaster of the time : they publicly emphasised the fact, which ought never to be acknowledged, that women had legs. As these harmless ladies walked past, each was subject to Aunt Ada's doomsday gaze; each to her energetic cry of 'Brazen hussy!'

My grandmother said : 'That boy! He always sits there with *that face* when I come. He never welcomes me.' And then she cried, as she easily did.

But I thought of her now only as the cause of weeping and wailing, angers and despairs. It was that endless question of her maintenance. The Guardians were angry, because the agreed contributions from her sons were never to be relied upon. My father tried to hold the family to their promises. So did Uncle George, splendid and rarely seen. But for the family gift for regarding any arrangement whatever as the fluid material for infinite contention and contradiction, this was the perfect occasion. To my father's anxieties about his career in the civil service, his perpetual doubt of my moral stamina, was added the everlasting ingenuity of the reasons why 'this brother of mine' or this other should not make those contributions that the Guardians exacted.

It came, at last, to a court case. The Barton police court was the setting. All, all were charged with failing to contribute to their mother's support. It was a famous moment in our history. All hope that it would pass quietly, a dry note in the court records of no interest to the local press, was lost when Uncle Jack entered the witness box. His sense of the dramatic, even in such a group, was remarkable. 'You are turning,' he cried, 'decent citizens into Bolsheviks.'

It was made for a headline in the *Barton Record*.

I remember, on my way to afternoon school, meeting my father and Uncle George returning from the court. They already had a letter written, and handed it to me to deliver at the *Record* offices. It was a plea for silence about the case. A sad private matter, they said. Unfair on those who had always kept up their payments . . . The *Record* was, predictably, unmoved.

But my father had his promotion. His worst fear, that the *Barton Record* was the favourite reading of Ching, Aston and Maclagen, turned out to be false.

5

I was in the fifth year now. Life had become denser, step by step. Ray and I walked in the fields, lay by streams that tittered distantly as we talked. The summer was a great breeding-place of loose ideas, desires even looser. Alliteration had given me a new name: people called me Bert. Ray and I were both being nudged further and further away from the world of physics and chemistry and maths. Our friends seemed indeed to be sorting themselves out, in terms the school provided: Science and Arts. The scientists struck us as being—this was the image for it—perambulant spanners. They saw life as being infinitely capable of being bolted and unbolted. Ray and I were aware simply of being vague and soulful, and sorry for any bolt that came within our romantically clumsy ken.

We did, briefly, attempt to be of the sterner world. We began running in the holidays. Both were, in fact, enemies of cross-country running. But we'd show them. Or rather, we'd not show them. We'd run secretly—would give ourselves the very curious pleasure of conforming, without seeking the least credit for it. Perhaps it was a very cunning way of not conforming at all. We ran across the fields that normally formed our simple debating chamber. Returning home, I'd take out my newly-started diary and describe the run in adjectival passages even muddier than the fields we'd raced through.

'No sibilant insects,' I'd note, using non-athlete's language, 'rose from the green entity of the pond.'

I had written an essay on 'Leisure' which began: 'Living like the lilies—languorous, lax, with a limp leather volume in lazy hands . . .' It was twenty pages long, and much of it derived from a dictionary of my own invention: I used words with reckless affection for their sound. 'Verbal flatulence', it was later called by the best English teacher I ever had. 'Good work, marred by the choice of words, which is sometimes ludicrous.' I believed that people 'divulged' into rooms. Reporting to my diary about a conversation with a master, I told it that 'he disintegrated a book from the pile at his elbow.' Anything secretly done was 'surreptious'; any excitement led at once to 'exhil*ia*ration'. In History I tried to make up for my ignorance of facts by verbal capering. This filled Sandy Spring, our History master, with a sad, dry amusement. We were doing the eighteenth century. Swift, he said, was 'a sort of super-Blishen.' I was delighted by this, and even more pleased when, smilingly weary, he called me 'Your Brainyship.' (The class at this moment burst into 'outroarious laughter'). I observed, as a fourteen-year-old sage, that life in Lower Five was becoming positively exciting ('exhiliarating'). 'Some elixir must be passing its ever diminishing waters into the eagerly churning millstones of our brains, sharpening the pulse and enlivening the power of thought . . .'

Part of this new excitement was sexual. The East Barton boys all had girl friends. This involved a most intricate exchange of letters, in which each seemed to act as postman for another. So Dick Mallet's letters came to him by way of Tom Ginger, who was supplied by Hugh Partridge. It was the convention that these letters should be displayed in class, kissed and pressed to bosoms. With no gift at all for this game, I began to feel it was one in which I must join. Ray had the same inclination. He now laid claim, anyway, to splendid experiences at a holiday camp. Every night, he said, a different girl: long walks along the darkening promenade. Perhaps it was not merely a matter of walking; he was interestingly vague about that. Limits were, however, indicated: 'I shan't rest,' he once said, 'until I get my prick into a girl.' It was the most impressively dreadful statement I'd ever heard, and left me quite awestruck. We formed a society with twenty-one rules. The evidence that, despite Ray's raw remark, we were drawn to literature rather than life lay in the almost erotic satisfaction with which we composed and re-composed those rules. The business of the society—known with curious frankness as The Virgins—was to make a list of desirable girls encountered in the street. Each was given a number and a description ('Face brilliant. Golden hair'). We had disputes about these descriptions; when Ray wanted No. 23 to be listed as 'West Indian lovely' I made great display of my scorn; *that* didn't account for her at all. He agreed sulkily, after a long conference, to change it to 'Portuguese-Indian lovely'. It was all, ethnically, guesswork. Our enemies—that is, those who got to hear of our society, and mocked at it—were to be subject to hideous punishment. My diary notes only one such incident. A small neighbour picked up a rumour—it can't have been difficult: Ray and I, at our most 'surreptious', patrolling the High Street with our notebooks, were not the most secret conspirators in the world. Our enemy called out at us as he passed. We sentenced him, says my diary, to 'a minor love-letter'. Literature, again. I guess we composed a *billet doux* for him, the work of some imaginary girl, and posted it in his letterbox. I have no idea how successful it was as a punishment.

But now life took over. Our scholarly interest in girls caught the attention of girls themselves. A small group from the convent made their interest plain. They did this by dogging us—by appearing so often round corners, coming at significant moments out of side-streets, that we could not doubt their purpose. Or rather, it was the purpose of one of them. No. 17 ('Face rather square. Nice hair'), she was attended by three handmaidens, whose business in life was clearly to promote her welfare as a wanton. ('Wanton' was my word for her, almost at once. Never did anyone set out to philander from such a puritanical base.) There were thrilling pursuits and evasions, one of the most exciting involving us in an amazing tour of Woolworth's before, one foggy night, the handmaidens vanished, and we were face to face with No. 17. It was a street corner ('standing on street corners', my father always said scathingly of my friends), and we were under a lamp-post ('under lamp-posts', he always added). We exchanged insults

124

and what my diary called 'bandinage'. There was a bad moment when she asked if we played Rugger for a school team. 'I often come and watch, but I don't think I've seen you,' she said. 'She is one of *those*, Ray,' I cried. 'I thought she was one of *those*,' said Ray. But it seemed to be a sphere in which ungracious exchanges were as effective as gracious ones. We were bound, it seemed, engaged, committed; our excitement was enormous.

Alas, there were features of the erotic life of which Ray and I had no understanding whatever. Especially of a fairly basic one : that the arithmetic of love is one to one. It never occurred to me that if there was to be any sort of progress, either Ray or I must vanish, just as No. 17's handmaidens had done. I'm not sure if it occurred to Ray. As it happened, it became clear that I was the chosen one. But I could not imagine going anywhere or doing anything—at any rate, of this importance—without him. As for him, now that I was in the position of Caliph (the very parish church growing minarets, those evenings), he saw himself in the position of Vizier. It was no more than his duty to stay at my side and give counsel and encouragement . . . There were further meetings, giggling encounters under lamp posts, and we were always together. Then I had a note slipped into my hand. 'Dear Ted,' it ran, 'Are you going out tonight if so I am. Meet me at the usual place.'

I handed over this note immediately, and speechlessly, to my consultant. 'I'll call round for you,' he said. I did not heed him. 'A false conditional!' I raged. 'What's up?' said Ray. 'Don't you see,' I stormed, 'that her coming out does *not* depend on my coming out. What she means is that she is coming out anyway, and that if I am coming out too, we can meet.' 'I really don't see—' said Ray. 'The "if", man,' I bellowed. 'The "if" is false.' 'Sometimes,' said the loyal Ray, 'I find you hard to make out.'

Over the years I apologise to No. 17, victim of my priggishness and that of my absurd shadow. Worse followed. Like some chief of secret police, I made a dossier on her. And at our few subsequent meetings, under dismayed lamp-posts, I charged her, not merely with illiteracy, but also with having had former affairs; much as if, appearing on a football field, I had accused some opponent of having played before.

Our last meeting was in the nature of a surly seminar. The pupil concluded it with a most spirited use of her school hat, a domed object which she would carry, when we met, by its elastic. She'd swing it, or it would leap at her side like some comic pet. Parting from me that last time, she put that monstrous hat through a manoeuvre that was pure contempt . . .

Ah, but it wasn't comical at all, close-up—that absurd childish wooing—in my case particularly, spectacularly absurd, since I had this priggish approach to almost everything. How awful it was! As though any other natural human appetite—the desire to eat perhaps—had become clogged with pruderies and shames. '*Hunched* over a table,' my father would have said, 'gobbling down *food*!' . . . Early on in the affair, my mother had passed unseen, as Ray and I and No. 17 and her school hat leaping on its elastic were exchanging our amorous discourtesies in the late afternoon street. She was delighted. 'Caught you, caught you!' she cried when I got home. She told my father. And he, by her report, was merely amused. 'Dad was a sport,' says my diary, 'and only said that he himself would have done it; he was touched by the similarity between my hair and his when he was my age.' But this sentimental mood quickly changed as other sightings were reported. 'This can stop,' he said. 'Slinking about the streets'. It didn't describe our exciteable obviousness, mine and Ray's, as lover and lover's assistant. Another of his appalling verbs.

'I have', I groaned in that handwriting that was certainly becoming smaller, more secret, 'too strong a desire for the human body.' My panic grew when we went, at Christmas, to see the Crazy Gang at the London Palladium. A great occasion which I described in detail, turn by turn. 'Below us lay the stage, the curving boxes towering downwards'—another of *my* appalling verbs—'to the distant stalls.' Item No. 8 was called 'Under the Sea': a girl did a fan dance. 'Her attendants closed in upon her. Loosed her gauzy dress. As the dress fell over her bosom she waved a fan before her. The other behind. The lights mellowed, almost faded, but shone, ghostly dull, upon her naked figure. She danced, a dance that brought my heart thudding hard against my chest. At each step she changed the whirling feathers before and behind. Her naked body caught at my straining nerves. I became a wreck.

126

The music, the dancing figure, the fluttering fans, filled my mind with an almost wicked exaltation . . . It made me madly sex-conscious. It taught me that I must beware. It taught me that I am dangerous to myself . . . I *must* beware.'

Alas. A sad plight for Prince Mihailovitch-Mdvani-Poniatowski-Tukachevsky to find himself in.

For some time, with the aid of an ancient Whitaker's Almanac, I had enrolled myself among the British peers. I had very much fancied myself as the Marquess of Abergavenny— the existing holder of the title being easily displaced by way of a fantasy of noble intrigue. When the truth came out, I elected to remain in the Fifth Form at Queen's. 'Please go on calling me Bert'. My shift from the British to the Russian aristocracy was a consequence of the fame, that year, of a brilliant member of the English Rugby team, Prince Obolensky. As a Prince I could have been reconciled even to my position in 'B' game's scrum. But I was greedy; a single princely title was not enough. That useful device, the hyphen, enabled me to accumulate titles. It was this Prince with the enormous name who was so horrified by his interest in the Crazy Gang's fan dancer.

There were circumstances in which my own name was enough. When it came, for example, to my having composed the Rhapsody in Blue, carelessly attributed to Gershwin. I wrote, around that time, a great deal of music, including the entire works of Eric Coates. My friends in the boxes at the Queen's Hall. 'Did Bert really write that?' But he did, he did. Sitting in my box, I smiled across at them, with terrible modesty. Tomorrow we should be struggling with the Aeneid, Book II. Tonight I was among the great infant prodigies of musical history.

Music amazed me. But I was still much of my father's opinion when it came, say, to Bach. I thought there was one word for what Bach had written: it was 'cantata'. The word 'cantata' was an enormous, disgusted joke, at home.

Then, by way of Williams, Ray and I received tickets for an amateur concert in London. We went to it with trembling suspicion. Simply to go to London after dark, unaccompanied, was a new and fearful experience. Ray and I were sombrely aware of prostitutes; and that evening we fancied we saw them around us in menacing thousands. We approached

London and that concert altogether as if it had been Babylon, and we went through the city like members of some juvenile Watch Committee, thrilled and disapproving.

We thought little of the concert hall, a university lecture room. It seemed to us inferior to the church hall at home. The orchestra, as it assembled, had us in fits of tolerant smothered laughter. Even the musical instruments seemed to us quite broadly funny. That we should all sit quietly in rows facing these people while they sawed and puffed away struck us as a crowning example of metropolitan immorality and folly.

And even when the concert was under way, and we had already, for ever and ever, been made slaves to this new order of music, our suburban philistinism struggled for expression. In the pizzicato movement of Tchaikovsky's Fourth Symphony, Ray nudged me and whispered 'Banjo team!'; and the chairs shook under us. And when the romantic thunders and wails of the last movement shook our souls instead, each of us decided at first to say nothing about it to the other. It was an aberration: nothing that time and the familiar walls of home could not cure.

It was only shyly, as we hummed and roared our way back to Barton through a Babylon transfigured, that we admitted to each other that things could never be the same. Where were Henry Hall and the BBC Dance Orchestra now? Where, indeed, was Eric Coates? We'd gone to that concert grubby ducklings, and we had left it grubby swans.

It complicated life considerably. We discovered almost at once that music of this staggering character was performed regularly on the wireless, on Wednesday afternoons, by the Bournemouth Municipal Orchestra. There was the problem that those afternoons were set aside for games. Bad weather became, for us, good weather. We'd watch the sky every Wednesday morning, desperately. Mere showeriness wouldn't do; it had to be quite brutally wet, to persuade those in charge of games that even their anti-musical sadism, as we saw it, could not justify their requiring us to turn up.

It happened, and often enough. To the sorrow, I guess, of Ray's mother: it was at his house that we listened to the wireless. Her dislike of classical music was great. But Mrs Bolton had a wide if shallow sympathy with adolescence. She

128

liked the idea that Ray and I were flirting, or furtively smoking. She treated us as if we were two lovable pimply clowns; she clearly enjoyed it when she came in suddenly and we stopped talking, red-faced. 'Don't you blush easily!' she'd say. She was very nearly, I sometimes thought, *rude* in what she said to us—or in what was implied by what she said. As when she told me that on a remarkably cold night Ray had been sleeping, she'd caught him at it, without his pyjamas. 'Naked!' she said. A round, jolly woman, she gave to a word like 'naked' a mischievous, strangely thrilling resonance. Altogether she loved us, and her love was big enough to embrace wet Wednesday afternoons, and the Bournemouth Municipal Orchestra. But she was not to be relied upon if Mr Bolton was about. In that respect, she was like my mother: puzzlingly inclined to be disloyal, as between husband and son. Once when Mr Bolton happened to be in the house and he came in to switch off the set during a soprano aria with a cry of 'Bloody canary!', Mrs Bolton stood in the doorway, nodding with awful neutrality.

But there it was—on Wednesdays kind enough to be inclement, we'd sit in the Boltons' front room, eyes closed, being with the music as we should never quite be with it again: I mean, physically possessed by it, our spines keyboards, our hands weaving a beat like some intricate invisible fretwork.

About this time, to the incubus of my new-found passion for classical music I added the burden of atheism.

For many years, Sunday School had been part of the pattern of life. I'd been, if not a pillar, at least some quite serviceable brick in the edifice of local Methodism. It always seemed, Sunday School, like some almost deliberate parody of day school. There were, for example, lessons. At a point in the afternoon we made circles of our chairs round our teachers and were told stories, with hints of the meanings that lay behind them. Most teachers looked vigorous as to the stories, and nervous as to the meanings. Our attention fell to pieces when narrative declined—and how our mentors sought to conceal the change of tone!—into moralising. 'Now,' we'd be told, with a brightening of some earnest face, 'do a drawing. Draw anything you like as long as it's a drawing of something in that story.' Among us, for years, we had Sid Burgess, who always put God into his drawings, and always gave God a top hat. There were teachers who smiled and let it go. 'God looks very happy, Sidney.' 'Yer,' Sidney would say. His nearest approach to religion was in his feelings about his scarcely believable collection of cigarette cards. Other teachers would foolishly try to put him right in respect of holy dress. 'God wouldn't actually wear a hat like that, Sidney.' Sidney would respond with some dreadful word. I never knew a teacher to make an issue of that. They would redden and hurry on to some impeccable piece of crayoning—mine, perhaps. Sunday School succeeded in making me oddly allergic, for years, to Middle Eastern dress. But I could draw it well enough . . .

It was difficult to know why some boys, like Sidney, attended Sunday School. On the whole, there seemed among us to be a level of satanic resistance to piety and well-meaningness perhaps uncharacteristic of the population as a whole. I rather guess many children were sent as my sister and I were sent. It was part of general respectability, my father thought, to go to Sunday School; but it did also guarantee him and my mother a quiet, and perhaps fairly profane, Sunday afternoon of their own.

Our early teachers were women. I fell in love with one of these. Even as a small boy, I felt there was a charming conflict between her evident goodness and the marvellous roundedness of her bosom. There was a Sunday School sports once, boys and girls running, and I discovered, being on one side of the course, that when Miss on the other side eagerly leaned forward to watch a race I could see deep into her corsage, and verify the debatable notion that the bosom even of a Sunday School teacher divided into two . . . When we passed into the care of men teachers it was a sign that childish things (ha!) were being put aside. That, at any rate, was the theory. For a long time we were with young Mr Webb, who was far weaker than any woman teacher we'd ever known. These older classes had to be taken into side-rooms for their lessons, which had ceased to have any strong element of narrative. Poor Mr Webb! He visibly paled as, Sid Burgess at our head, we made for the torture chamber in which he was to strengthen our grip on the good life. After a time he gave up the attempt to teach us, and as we entered our private room would throw himself at once upon his knees and frantically pray to God to forgive us for the mysterious evil that was in us. Sometimes, I am very sorry to say, we would sink to our own knees and offer up scandalous parodies of his prayers . . .

It was partly because of the shame of such things that I became a Crusader. You could be one if you went to a private school or what was judged to be an equivalent. You wore a tiny badge, and met on Sundays to—there is only one phrase for it—ejaculate religiously. You shouted rather jolly affirmations, to aggressive tunes. One of our leaders was an expert on railways. His addresses were full of images drawn from this interest of his; anyone who'd become temporarily unfit for the main line of faith went into the sheds for a spiritual oiling and greasing. He took us on outings to this London terminus and that and, never managing to feel quite secular enough, we were admitted to the footplates of famous locomotives. That was marvellous : if the general drift of belief held to by these kindly absurd people turns out to be valid, I shall insist on arriving in heaven in just that position, looking along the great line of one of those endless boilers, green and gold . . .

After a time it seemed to me that I was an atheist. I wrote to say as much to another of our leaders. 'I say,' he said when next we met, 'you *are* a *young fellow!*' I replied with what I took to be a rather powerful poem setting out my position. 'You do go it, don't you?' he wrote in a letter. 'But you can only appreciate the beauty of the stained glass when you are *inside* the cathedral'. It struck me that this was a vulnerable metaphor. On the same lines, surely, you could argue that you could appreciate the misery of a cell only when you were *inside* the prison. 'My goodness, you do take the wind out of a fellow's sails,' he said. It was not going to be one of the great exchanges on the topic. It must have been rather awful, having this young prig butting at you, so insistently. He changed the subject, that is what I now think he did, by taking me out in his sports car and talking about books. He was a great admirer of Hugh Walpole. I enjoyed those rides in his MG, open to the evening air; we often touched sixty m.p.h., which in those days was the speed at which heroes drove. Religion, and the revolt from it, seemed to be landing me up in fast-moving vehicles of one sort or another : an odd effect. I was still, at this time, confiding in my father. He was rather impressed by

my stand, but also rather uneasy. To be vaguely religious . . .
well yes, it *was* an aspect of respectability. 'You've got other
things to think of,' he said, meaning Maths and Geography,
without which you couldn't get into the Civil Service.

6

It was the School Certificate that faced us now : another form
of moral screening, as it felt. Douglas Hayward would get
through because he had always bound his textbooks with
brown paper. They were horrible to Douglas, because of that
tidiness of his; and because he always asked for homework
when a master had forgotten to give it. They poured ink into
his desk, all over those beautiful books. But he would have the
laugh of us all now, except that he was not given to laughter
. . . My old, dear, dull friend Peter Bunce would triumph :
rewarded for his trudging steadiness. The scientists would win
through, because there were knowable answers to the questions they were asked, and because they were people who made
a point of knowing things. I doubted if I would get through in
maths. I was the world's worst authority on those law-ridden
figures, the square and the circle. The parallelogram was never
what I thought its splendid name entitled it to be. Trigon-
ometry was about foolish forms of measurement : instead of
simply running a tape measure over a building, you stood at a
distance and imagined it as being at the centre of a mass of
angles . . . in my hands, a mess and maze of angles. I thought
I might manage English. Better if I were being examined in
some subject that might be called Chaotic General Excitement
—or others, invented in growing defiance of my father, called
Anti-Maths and Anti-Geography. Or Disordered Reading. I was
ready for any question about a magazine called *Everybody's*,
which Dad brought home weekly, or Hardy's *The Trumpet-
Major*, or the diaries of Sir Walter Scott, which were the

inspiration of my own breathless journals; or the novels of Ian Hay, which I read with pleasure and then was lofty about ('A very ordinary potpourri of balderdash . . .')

Well, English, yes . . .

Now I had passed gratefully, for English, into the care of a Welshman, Williams. He was a tiny man, some childish illness had left him small, reared on music and poetry, with an Oxford voice that at moments of excitement became a Welsh one. We measured his disciplinary temper by his slide into sing-song. He had the best of qualifications for teaching English—a great feeling for words and for what they could do. He taught English, in the first place, by speaking it richly: off the point, very often off the point, but always with vivacity. With him we never reached the end of a set book. There was so much to halt us, mischievously, on the way. *Julius Caesar* was the first Shakespeare we did with him. Williams, who had a useful trick of amazement, was struck by the similarity between Julius Caesar and . . . No, he mustn't go into that; he mustn't suggest . . . Oh, sir, tell us! It was, by twinkling indirections he made it clear, a distinguished colleague of his own he had in mind. And if it came to that, what about Cassius? The worthy Brutus? Some of the school prefects . . . Williams covering his face with a lace of fingers, in mock horror. We were deep in sedition before he gave one of his grave, entrancing starts. 'We must get on! We must put these disgraceful thoughts behind us!' *Julius Caesar*, as we did it with Williams, was about Barton on its single hill as much as it was about Rome on her seven. It brimmed with occasions for the reference from literature to life. So Stuart Brand, our most advanced sensualist, guffawed when Cassius declared his love for Brutus. Williams at once up in arms! How debased the word had become in our time! Every crooner made his meaningless affirmation of love. Every shoddy product of Hollywood claimed to be concerned with love. Had we any longer any idea what the word meant? Was it understood even—especially—by those who could be seen any night in suspiciously sticky attitudes in Barton Lane? Stuart Brand growled in his seat in the back row . . . We acted the play—not the commonest approach, then, to the study of set books. Jimmy Dawson, playing Caesar, carefully hitched up his flannels

133

before crashing to the floor, assassinated. We'd meet Williams sometimes on the way to school. 'I've been thinking of those speeches. "On such a full sea are we now afloat And we must take the current as it serves Or lose our ventures . . ." It's splendid stuff, isn't it?' What he had was eagerness. Where so much teaching was dry and essentially pessimistic, to be touched by his often electric energy and commitment was to pass, as pupils, from winter to spring.

It was common, then, to deplore American usages. At Queen's, 'Oh yeah' and 'O.K.' were virtually punishable utterances. Williams would have none of it. He'd been, he told us, the night before to the local fleapit to see a film starring Mae West. Ah yes! said Williams—there must be a pause for guffaws. We guffawed liberally . . . She'd been standing, in one scene, at a bar, a Russian at her elbow; and had turned to him and growled: 'Cigarette me, Cossack!' What liveliness! What invention! And didn't it remind us . . . no, we'd perhaps not yet read *Antony and Cleopatra*. But there was a moment in Shakespeare's play when the Egyptian queen, after she'd been triumphed over by Octavius Caesar, turned to her handmaidens: 'He words me, girls, he words me . . .' Was it not the same strong, inventive usage—an excited disrespect for formal syntax? Williams had a phrase for scholarship: it was, he would say, controlled excitement . . . He also had this gift for the careful abandonment of control. So now, those witty fingers shielding his face: 'You'd better keep this to yourself.' Sense of conspiracy. We were all conspirators, in Williams' class. The enemy was dullness. Williams never said so. It was implicit in his sparkling approach to anything that came up . . .

He was the first man to invite us to exercise our own judgement about poetry. A set book that year was *Poems of Today*, a selection of modern poetry—as it had been in 1922, when the book was compiled—by a committee of the English Association. The prefatory note said:

For the choice and arrangement of the poems, the war necessarily provides the starting point. The moods of war are shown, occasionally as they have been realised in the first crude shock of actual encounter, but more often as they have been deepened and stabilised in the impassioned memories of the poet. From the war, men's minds have turned to

England, sometimes with pride in her past, sometimes with doubt for her future, but never with despair. The poets have paid tribute to the hold upon them of school and college and home, of green countryside and rolling downland, of heroic memories and well-loved associations. The poetry of nature shows a strength of local feeling that escapes from the limits of provincial sentiment by its unassuming but deep-rooted sincerity. With the love of nature is found a sympathy with animals half-humorous, half tender. The sense of fellowship and the love of life are the more marked because of the events that have threatened both, but love between man and woman is a less distinctive note in the poetry of today . . .'

How like some kind of school report that was! 'Tends to pride and doubt, but never despairs.' 'Poetry of Nature. Strong in local feeling—I'm glad to see he has escaped the limits of provincial sentiment. Unassuming but sincere.' 'Love between man and woman. Seems to have lost interest in this subject.'

The first thing Williams asked us to do was to set down our honest opinion of a poem by Lucy Whitmell, called *Christ in Flanders*. It began :

> We had forgotten You, or very nearly—
>   You did not seem to touch us nearly—
> Of course we thought about You now and then;
>   Especially in time of trouble—
> We knew that you were good in time of trouble—
>   But we are very ordinary men.

Lord, I was moved by all that! I wrote a glowing commendation of Miss Whitmell's touching gloss on the Great War. The margin of my copy of *Poems of Today* contains a note of my instant reaction: 'In times of crisis,' it says, in agitated young pencil, 'these men awaken to a sense of want—the want of moral support, an indefinable striving towards the key to the great secret—who is God?' Ah! Williams went with us over that poem very gently, very gently. He tested the rhythms. Now that it was brought to our attention, we tried to characterise that rhythm, and decided a word for it might be 'complacent', and that it was perhaps like bouncing up and down on the back of a horse, if you couldn't ride a horse at all

135

well . . . There was a discussion that culminated in Williams' question : 'Is Miss Whitmell perhaps rather familiar with God?' *Coy* familiarity—the phrases rushed in. I have a note, at the foot of the poem, of the startled general opinion we came to, at the end of all that discussion, tidied into what I recognise as our master's language: 'Miss Whitmell, with limited intellectual equipment, has essayed the hazardous task of treating a sacred subject in a manner of colloquial familiarity . . .'

The crises in our lives take many forms, and some hardly add up to dramatic scenes . . . Alas, at this time I was being wrenched out of childhood by my father's furious sweeps through the house, destroying whatever he regarded as rubbish; which included many papers, magazines, almost any loose literary matter. But the gentle, witty war of Williams v Lucy Whitmell (Upper Five X intervening) was as decisive, for me. Williams saw clearly the importance of cultivating judgement in us. He saw clearly the need to bring our attention to bear on the words, the rhythm of a poem—to take us out along a line of thinking and then suddenly to leave us there, having to look out for ourselves . . .

Williams was one of those rare teachers who hasten maturity in their pupils . . .

It was as we turned into the straight for the School Certificate—only straight wasn't the word—that Williams changed the entire texture of life for me by proposing that I take part in the school play. And not any old part. The play was a latter-day account of one of England's more neurotic kings; the part was that of the king himself. The effect was much as though I'd been offered the actual English crown. It was the apotheosis, quite unlooked for, of those toyings of mine with aristocratic names for myself. What price Prince Mihailovitch-Etcetera now! Once again I saw my friends in boxes, being proud and incredulous. It was a straight canter to glory.

Not, as it turned out, any more straight than the approach to School Certificate. One matter at once arising was that of my aitches. A king without aspirates was not on. Williams gave me amused exercises. Pause, he said, and take a breath. At first it led to mammoth 'esitations—hesitations. Then it came. I walked about with my lips parted, ever ready. And the delirium began. It was nothing less: a delirium of conceit, and genuine excitement; and then of being taken over by that introspective king—as seen by the play's author, anachronistically perhaps. A species, in this rendering, of modern aesthete and pacifist; a man cursed with a premature appetite for being, as it were, a royal director of the National Trust, combined with the Tate Gallery and the Design Centre . . . Only too readily did I assume this role.

And interfering with that sense of the canter to fame was the feeling I had about the queen, a doomed lady. The part was played by Willy Henderson. Willy was small and dark, a pleasant, sensible scientist. Willy's delight was in motorcars and cricket. As, to my eyes, he turned steadily into the queen, wistfully sympathetic towards her husband's passion for silks and tapestries, so he became more obstinately a small practical schoolboy with an actual leaning towards the discussion of what you could do with an Austin Seven. My emotions built up into a storm : in that wild inner weather, reality and dream were alternate gusts. The irreconcilability of things was at its worst during rehearsals. I made a passionate avowal; Willy, under his breath, murmured 'Nuts!' A noble member of my court (actually Stuart Brand, making good histrionic use of his fatal profile) informed me that he was marrying the daughter of an enemy; Willy muttered 'Crikey!' I staggered about the school, trying to hold these disparities together. I examined my face in mirrors, rehearsing every morning the placement of hands required to mask my newly-arrived pimples. I wondered, against the vast sobriety of the evidence, if Willy felt the same about me.

And Williams was in trouble, too. The school, suddenly successful at sports at a national level, was launched on a policy of squeezing every ounce of athletic possibility out of every boy not actually disabled. Drama was under a cloud. It was held to over-excite everyone who took part—it made inroads on lessons, and interfered with the ready use of the school hall. Boys who should have been doing science were building scenery. And drama was—the feeling was very strong—precious : it was very much the most arrogant manifestation of the spirit of those (boys and masters) who belonged to the Arts side of things. Williams confided in me that a games master had called him 'Moonshine.' 'I congratulated him on the use of the term.' Between Moonshine and his colleague the cast of the play were the rope at which they strained in their tug-of-war. At times, over the dead body of one, we were rehearsing; at other times, over the dead body of the other, we were trotting round the track ('Five circuits at moderate pace and a final circuit full out.') It was one of several dramas too many, that term. The victory went to Moonshine, but not without resort to the loftiest of tribunals.

To my father it could only have seemed that the swollen-headedness for which he had already attacked me ('That boy's getting beyond himself') had been given the opportunity to become . . . oh, whatever it would be if the swollen head burst.

Looking back, I see this school play as the turning point in my relations with my father. It was a precipitant only, I guess, but it did speed everything up; in my diary, the writing changed within a few months from a round childish script to a tiny, cramped, secret hand—modelled on Williams' own which, he once told me, was itself influenced by Greek lettering. To my father, for a long time to come, Williams was the villain of the piece: he had taken over the fatherly role. It was he who began to direct me once I'd slipped past the obstacle of School Certificate—five credits, one even in maths, and disgraced only in Latin—towards the idea of an Oxford scholarship. It was he who took my literary ambitions seriously. I was now, as my father saw it, in the thrall of the intellectuals. Nothing worse could happen to a son of his.

'Intellectual' was a terrible term, on my father's lips. He had blundered into such persons in the Civil Service. They were those who'd been to certain schools, possibly to university; they were the beneficiaries of quite facile promotion, my father believed, because of their qualifications—their, as he used savagely to stress, *paper* qualifications. They were men of paper. 'Ask your intellectual,' he would say, 'to clean an inkpot, and he will make a mess of it.' It was curiously his measure of the ineffectuality of intellectuals. They would score low on the Inkpot Quotient. They were also not to be relied upon to polish their shoes, or generally to achieve personal tidiness. My father began to superintend my appearance with fanatical touchiness. 'You'll go and get your hair done.' I now associated short hair with philistinism. I would glare at my father's own hair—allowed, I thought, hardly to be hair at all; a thin oiled cap on his brisk head. I would sit and look at his hair and rage inwardly. It was a symbol of his crisp dismissal of everything mildly romantic, dishevelled. It was part of what I was beginning to see as his terrible narrow certainty. It was part of his refusal of every subtlety. 'No such thing as a conscience in this world. Get that into your head, and you'll be all right.' The King of England in me quivered with impotent undelivered royal gestures, and the boy I actually was would screw his face up with distaste. 'And don't make a face like that whenever I talk to you. I'm your father. I can say what I like to you without your making a face about it.' Alas. He could assert that this was so; but there was now nothing either of us could do to make it so . . .

At weekends I would dress in old flannels. 'You're not lounging about all day in those!' Those terrible verbs of his again. I was lounging, I was slouching, I was mooching about. He began to use a more brutal phrase for any part of my behaviour that struck him as being—another angry word—highbrow. 'Come over all *girlish*, eh?' Shoes themselves became a focus of his furies. 'When did they last see a bit of polish?' He began to address me obliquely, through my mother. 'Have you seen anything like that boy?' 'Oh Dick—it's Sunday—leave him alone.' 'What's Sunday got to do with it?' Mother unable to frame an answer to this. In her long-besieged tolerance, with her appetite for the happiness of those she loved, mother knew very well what Sunday had to do with it. But she also knew that my father's view of Sunday was unlike her own. Sunday was when you should be spectacularly spick-and-span; it was a day peculiarly threatened by casualness, and therefore a day when sartorial vigilance was specially called for. Sunday came to be a day my mother dreaded . . .

And there was I, hunched (another of my father's words) over my diary, and writing with increased freedom about my feelings for Willy Henderson. I recorded, in helpless detail, every occasion when, in gym or changing room, I caught sight of him half or totally disrobed. I set down my fantasies: of, for example, encounters between us in the local fields. He ran towards me, clad in a fashion that would certainly have caused comment among those who exercised their dogs in those decent meadows: a vest only. I had given up trying to invent realistic settings for these fantasies. Willy came to me in the fields wearing only a vest. That was that. I or the wind—inter-

139

changeable forces—blew the vest over his head. I imagined, in a torrent of breathlessly chosen words, the encounter between myself and this eccentrically naked schoolmate. 'I am mad! I am become a sex maniac!' I would inform my diary at intervals. 'Now this record becomes doubly dangerous!' This was an understatement. I was already uneasily aware that my father read my diary. 'Don't take it up with you,' he said one evening, when I was on my way to bed. 'I like a good read.' It was not a joke—I knew it was not a joke. Poor man! What sort of child did he begin to think he had produced? Not an intellectual merely, and someone who looked elsewhere for fatherhood; but a crazy deviant! He fought desperately for a hold on this crumbling son. Very well. The Head himself had interviewed him, and laid before him the prospect that I might aim at an Oxford scholarship. 'He's above-average material, you know. Of course, all over the place at the moment —these young moderns come under the most curious influences, I'm sure I need not spell this out to you—D. H. Lawrence, I believe, lately I've had reason to think he's been reading rather too much of that very much over-rated fellow . . . But distinctly promising. I think we can straighten him out.' My father was uneasily impressed. But the Civil Service remained his ambition for me. Safe, sensible. More than that: mother said, 'You're a disappointment to him, you know.' Mother's helpless frankness was often valuable. 'He looked forward to you being in the Civil Service, like him. He thought you'd come home together in the evening. Talk about things in the office.' 'With a bowler hat', I howled. 'He sees me in a bowler hat!' Mother unmoved by the hysterical note in my voice. 'You'd look nice in a bowler hat,' she said. He proposed a compromise. I would study, all right, for this absurd scholarship, but I would also study for entrance to the Civil Service. This meant keeping up my Geography and my Mathematics. I had no Geography. I had no Mathematics. Going into the sixth form meant for me, above all else, the abandonment of such subjects. But uneasily I agreed.

It didn't work. It simply wasn't going to work. My mother continued to play her own intolerable role—advocate and support for us both. So one evening, she talked about the Folkestones. Mrs Folkestone had been romancing, over the fence, about their only son, Jack.

'And she said, "My Jack was a dear boy—everything his father said was just right—and everything his mother said, too." ' Mother sighed—certainly, at that moment, unable to decide what effect all this would have on the balance of power inside her own family. Mother, surrounded by issues beyond her, acted on instinct—which often led her astray. 'Children aren't like that today.'

'No,' said my father. For him it was the perfect feed. 'If only they'd realise this—that there's no such thing as friendship in this world. It's all two for them and one for you. This boy here for instance—the sooner he realises that all his friends think two for the school and one for him . . . But you've got to let them find out for themselves.'

My father's most horrifying, most pitiable characteristic—this total rejection of the idea of real friendship. Rooted in temperament perhaps, in a dark temperament—but rooted also in the harsh world of Edwardian poverty, where disinterested friendship was indeed a rare luxury?

Quivering with rage, I said : 'Please speak about something you understand.'

'Look at all that work you do over there,' he said, pointing to my eternal armchair. 'Isn't that for Williams?'

'Williams'—I vibrated with anger close to tears—'is my friend and not my taskmaster . . . Oh—I know what you think . . . I know! . . . Oh damn!'

And my father: 'Oh—I know I'm a bloody fool—but I understand you better than Williams . . .'

To which, aware that my eyes were bolting out of my head, that I was crumpling the pages of the book I was reading, I could reply only : 'Ha!'

And years later I grieve for my intolerable father, having such a cuckoo in his nest!

I also know, years later, that every child is, to some extent, a cuckoo in the nest. Suddenly this dependent creature, who has admired and obeyed you, shoots insolently and (despite your experience of the biology of things) unexpectedly up; and becomes his own person. Almost by definition, the person he becomes is the opposite of the person you are. There he is, this overgrown thing, this swollen monster, flexing the unfamiliar muscles of his personality. The whole world is, all at once, dizzy: you do not know who is father, and who is son. Your instinct may be to drive this intruder, this multiple agent, out of the nest, out of your sight . . .

A feeling for the human comedy is all that will save you.

My father—(who was always leaving the company of some deeply wounded acquaintance, crying: 'They don't know when I'm being funny!')—my father had barely any comic sense at all . . .

7

And so I was in the sixth—and that, in a grammar school in the 1930s, felt like lordliness beyond belief. The sense of, as it were, aristocratic arrogance was strengthened by its being so much the development my father was opposed to. He would have had me already in the Civil Service. The nest was being swamped by the cuckoo in it. I should have been out in the world, sensible, bowler-hatted. Instead I was ensconced in my bloody armchair, its arm piled with books . . .

I wonder what the image is for my two calamitous years in the sixth form. 'Who would have guessed that life was such chaos?' my diary groans. It was chaos because, like any adolescent, I found myself suddenly on the fringes of the dense world of adult reality. More than anything I wanted now to . . . vaguely I thought of it as going to Oxford. That thought was an intoxication in itself, in 1935, as much as the idea of being in a sixth form. My father was always inventing new reasons why I should not go. His most outlandish was that my mother had kept me healthy till then; at Oxford my health would certainly fall to pieces. I should be an oaf with shoes unshined, and a sick oaf into the bargain.

Nothing mattered but reading and listening to music and going to the theatre—Williams had introduced us to the Old Vic—and the activity my father called my bloody scribbling.

But if I was to hope to go to Oxford, I must be sensibly diligent. To begin with, I must repair my Latin, the long damage of it. I now loved, helplessly, the sound of that language. 'Nox umida caelo precipitat, suadentque cadentia sidera somnos.' Ravishing! But there was no room in my deranged existence for the strict return I should have to make over the long and unromantic road of Latin grammar. I had no patience for study.

Sandy Spring, that gentle, vaguely weary historian who'd taught us until we reached the sixth, had droned at me again and again: 'Facts, facts, facts!' Into his teaching—into his long, half-private monologues, during which he'd lasso himself with a window cord, rocking on his heels, so that he seemed always on the verge of self-execution—he wove his scepticism about the relation between History and his pupils. 'The Prince Regent—a man who would interest you, Brand, if you were capable of being interested in anything—a dandy, Brand, with a passion for cravats . . .' Dandy Brand growling . . . As a variation on his performance with the window cord he would stand beside me and hammer home his points about, perhaps, a treaty—well, not hammer them home; tenderly beat them home—by flapping at my head with an exercise book. 'Facts, facts, facts!' I was now positively resistant to facts. Of what value were facts to Katherine Mansfield, W. B. Yeats, D. H. Lawrence? Of what value were facts to Chopin? To give up my dreaming, my cultivation of grand phrases, for the bare facts of History, for Latin grammar—even for the bones of literary history—not possible! My vagueness became a horror to myself. I could not now even complete an essay. We were taken for essay by the second master, Percy Chew, who was in charge of the sixth form; and would have us model ourselves on Charles Lamb. I wrote an inhibited paragraph or two, designed to anger him. From my reading I had derived the general idea that one should anger respectable people. Mild improprieties, based on passages from Aldous Huxley. Absurd paradoxes. Chew stormed in red ink: 'This is not an essay— it is a piece of gross impertinence . . .'

My father said: 'You don't seem to be keeping to your side of the bargain. I don't see you doing any maths or geography.' I was not doing any maths or geography. Odious subjects, appallingly dependent on facts. I was not doing anything that would have helped me to a Higher School Certificate—let alone a State scholarship. For two years I read novels, raged in my diary; cultivated a sort of higher ignorance, in a half-crazy reaction to the demands of father and sixth form master . . .

Percy Chew was among the most powerful exponents of the view that Queen's existed for the creation of gentlemen. 'Yesterday evening,' he would say, 'the school field—it was supposed to be a cricket match, you know, gentlemen—was like nothing so much as an elementary school asphalt yard when its children are out for a ten minutes break.' I can't think why he laid such a stress on the word 'asphalt'. Our own yards—though some of them were unenclosed, they were all called 'quads'—were of that material. It was something to do with a snobbery of surfacings . . . His most lurid invention in the style was directed at an outburst of enthusiasm at another game of cricket. 'You seemed to be cheering, gentlemen, like drunken Cockney flowergirls who'd just heard of Napoleon's downfall.'

The first Penguins had appeared ('Snap them up,' said Williams. 'They won't last. The English won't buy books bound in paper.') I was reading Aldous Huxley's *Crome Yellow*, André Maurois's life of Shelley, *Ariel*. 'Shelley,' said Percy Chew, 'utterly unprincipled, selfish . . . a piffling blackguard . . . bolshevising all over the world . . . a twopenny ha'penny character. He had no more merit than the weaklings in Russian plays who are always examining their own rather unlovely insides.' As for Huxley, he was 'superficial.' Very like Bernard Shaw, indeed: 'Shaw's learning is quite superficial. A slovenly thinker, gentlemen. '

He was given to saying things in threes and fours and fives. So the point about Shaw would be hammered home: 'Yes, a slovenly thinker, a slovenly thinker, a slovenly thinker.' He would sometimes begin a pronouncement with such a repetition. It was often so with one of his favourite phrases. 'If you don't take yourselves in hand, if you don't take yourselves in hand, if you don't take yourselves in hand . . .' Everyone filled with a sort of sluggish horror, waiting to know what the current consequence was of not taking ourselves in hand. He was noisy about all this: given to theatrical crescendoes . . . though one has to say, to equally dramatic diminuendoes. His voice, in any address to us, rose to the peaks, sank to the sea floor.

144

Oddly, 'noisy' was a word he applied to anyone he disapproved of. Shelley, Huxley, Shaw . . . all current politicians not in the Conservative Party were noisy. 'Fond,' he would say, pacing up and down the sixth form room as he pursued his unremitting monologue, 'of his own voice.'

To noisiness, as a mark of the sort of man we should aim at not becoming, he added the defect of envy. Another name for this was socialism. 'I see it all round me, gentlemen . . . young men going back on the creeds they were brought up to hold: not because they disbelieve them, but simply because they have been disappointed, and haven't enough forbearance or *backbone* to make the best of things.' Socialism was the elementary school asphalt yard of politics. Mr Chew did nothing so lacking in backbone as suggesting that boys of sixteen and seventeen ought to look hard, carefully and with critical concern at the whole range of human outlooks. The need to avoid noisiness and envy made all sorts of judgements—literary and philosophical as well as political—almost absurdly simple. 'I always think, gentlemen, of that passage in the scriptures that exhorts us to be thankful for that station to which God has called us . . . We can't all be at the top.'

'Unwilling,' he would add to his view of Shelley, Huxley, Shaw, 'to bow to a greater than himself.'

It was hard going, being in the shadow of a man so hostile to the very excitements that were burgeoning in some of us. For me, shadow upon shadow: it would have been enough to have been the victim of my father's disapproval. In fact, Chew did not disapprove of me at first. Oh, I was too emotional. It was another word for what he did not like. Odd for a teacher of adolescents to be so very down on the exhibition and exploration of feeling! But he was rather amused, to begin with, by my being so all over the place, so moody and exciteable—especially in my prose. It was what, he would tell me, could be expected of 'you moderns.' 'No sense of grammar. No control. No discipline. Free verse. Aldous Huxley. You read that really rather wretched fellow, do you? Do you? Do you?' He would laugh, genially. 'Take yourself in hand. You can do it. Signs of intelligence. Yes. Don't start thinking too highly of yourself. Another fault of you moderns. But distinct signs of intelligence.' It would make me nervous, as though I had pimples to add to my pimples.

'Don't think too highly of yourself.' I look back at the beleaguered child I was, and remember the miseries of guilt he suffered because everything that happened seemed to be thrusting him into a condition of helpless conceit. How could you listen to Beethoven or Chopin or Mozart, how could you read Lawrence or Huxley or Wells, without being charged with a sense of the wilful brilliance of the boldest human beings—and how, with that charge at work inside you, could you be as small and modest as your condition, as an obscure and self-consciously ineffective sixteen-year-old, suggested you should be? In my traffic since those days with adolescents of any kind I have remembered this curious agony : you have discovered the glory of being human, and are so inglorious.

Williams said anxiously : 'You mustn't, whatever you do, you *mustn't* think yourself superior to others. If you have discovered the excitement of thought, if you have become sensitive to the beauty of the world, that is your luck—not a mark of superiority.' Indeed. But when I expressed at home, in any way whatever, my feeling of the excitement of ideas or the amazing beauty of things, then I ran into my father's positive hatred of such emotions. He was actually *against* the practice of thought; he was actually *against* the appreciation of whatever might be regarded as beautiful. He had begun simply to watch my face, as I sat in the tiny living room we shared, and to comment on it irritably. 'You take life too seriously,' he would say. 'No—put that book down and listen to me. It won't hurt you to stop reading for a moment. What's the good of *thinking* about things? You never bloody well enjoy yourself. Take a tip from me. I make my mind a blank. It's the only thing to do. People talk to me about their ideas— that bloody man Ching, for instance—and I make my mind a blank. "Yes, no", I say. You want to try it. Carry on as you're going, and you'll be an old man by the time you're twenty.'

How, in the context, to feel anything but superior? How, in the context, to feel anything but miserable about it?

I was misusing my father's wireless set, as we still called it : making life intolerable with appalling music. 'What's that?' he groaned, finding me listening to Mozart. 'Sounds like someone being sick!' His tolerance was unreliable. He would come in and lower the sound to the vaguest whisper. 'I'm listening to that, Dad!' 'Whose wireless is it? Answer me that. No thought for your mother. Gives her a headache. Gives *me* the bellyache.' 'Oh, for goodness sake. It's music. It's . . .' How to say what—surely so gloriously, with such obvious glory—it was? 'You only listen to it because that bloody Williams tells you it's the sort of thing you should listen to. Tell me what's good about it!' 'Well, it's . . .' No! No words for what was good about it, given his immovable belief that it was a form of aural agony welcomed only by your damned intellectual, as part of his attempt to establish his superiority over ordinary decent people.

But the invitation to have my say, though deeply rhetorical, was untypical. From now on what drove me mad in discussion with him—no, it wasn't discussion; in being at the receiving end of his assertions—was that he was so positive always, about everything. The idea of the existence of other opinions was far beyond the bounds of his thinking. As I moved into a world of argument and counter-argument, of (as it seemed to me) civilised doubt and surmise and conjecture, so his lack of all uncertainty as to the truth of anything he might assert made me shake with horror. To the end of his life he could make me tremble with that brutal positiveness. Now he admitted no possibility of any other view whatever when he claimed that *no one* enjoyed classical music. No one *could* like it.

He was convinced it was all a pretence. In certain circles it was done to pretend enjoyment. Beating time to a symphony concert that was whispering away in a corner of the room, I would catch my father's eye. He would snort, and turn to my mother with one of his harsh laughs. 'We know how it goes, my dear. We show everybody we know how it goes. That's the important thing, you see'—his heavily ironical elucidatory tone—'to show you know how it goes. Hallo, he went wrong there! Oh dear! Good job it's only his ignorant parents who are watching.' I'd lose my temper, again and again. 'I am not showing anything. It's a pleasure to beat time to music. I hardly know I am doing it.' 'Hardly knows he's doing it, my dear.' His huge wink; then the snort; then the laugh. 'Well, I'm going into the garden until it's over. You can always put your fingers in your ears, my dear.' All of which would sometimes excite my mother into innocent satire of her own. 'I've seen them. There's a man with those big tin things and he bangs them together. And the conductor! Going mad!' Imitation of the conductor. 'Watch it, my dear. He'll burst into tears if you go on like that. He'll come over all girlish.'

Up to bedroom. ('He's going up to sulk!') Two pages of agonised resort to diary. At times I'd imagine how they'd suddenly appear in the living room: Sir Henry Wood, Sir Hamilton Harty, Sir Dan Godfrey. Indignant to a man . . . to a knight. 'Do you realise, sir, that music is among the main delights of all civilised persons! Suggest you apologise to this very sensitive son of yours.' My father's contrition. 'I didn't understand. What can I do to make it up to him?'

An attempt was made to shame unsporting boys in the fifth and sixth years by forming them into a Rambling Club. The idea was that the term 'rambling' would be felt to be so wet that even an opponent of Rugby football would shrink from it. In fact, most of us weeds rather liked the word. We liked it even more when we discovered that Jack was to be in charge.

Jack—his real name was Jackson—taught French; he was an awkward, bitter man. He wore defiantly cheap clothes— old sports coats and flannels usually. He talked about this sometimes in class. 'From Marks and Spencers,' he'd say, indicating his yellowing trousers. 'Marks and Spencers' was then a synonym for extreme cheapness. 'I hope it interests you that I pay as little for my trousers as I can . . . get 'em *off the peg*. You're probably appalled, aren't you? Most of you, I suppose, are little snobs. On the way to becoming bigger snobs. Eh?' He'd say such things with a sort of fierce amiability. Then he'd pick on some boy he particularly disliked and make a personal question of it. 'You're a little prig, aren't you, Hopkins?' Hopkins belonged to the Christian Union. 'You'll sneak off and pray for me, eh Hopkins?' It was taken as an eccentric form of joking. Hopkins thrived in the role of Jack's butt. 'I'll pray for you if it will help, sir.' A long stare from Jack. 'And persuade Mr Smith to pray for me, too?' Mr Smith ran the Christian Union, and Jack made no bones about his contempt for the man. 'Mr Smith making his holy way to the headmaster's *sanctum*,' he'd comment as his colleague's shape moved along the row of windows between classroom and corridor. I was often startled at the thought of such acid hostility towards boy or man, of which Jack made such an open thing. He hated the respectability of the school, the attempt to turn us into 'gentlemen'. He wore shabby clothes because the Head preferred his staff to wear dark suits. 'If I were the chief man, the Great Panjandrum, the master of all our destinies,' he said once, raking the class with his thinly smiling contempt, 'you'd sit there peeing in your bags.' We all laughed. Jack was in form that morning.

Because he lived near us, and I'd sometimes found myself walking beside him to school, there was a curious alliance between me and Jack. He admired the stories of Maupassant—those unmaskings of petty snobbery and hypocrisy, those stunning ironical twists of narrative. Once I'd fallen in beside him on the walk to school and, having read *The Necklace* the night before, had moved myself to talk of it, stumblingly but with excitement. Jack said, at length : 'You enjoyed it, didn't you? You admired it? It's an unhappy taste, you know. People who appreciate Maupassant's irony are likely to be unhappy people.' I was delighted to be admitted to the high society of the unhappy. For a long time after that I thought of myself, proudly, as one doomed to some kind of sardonic misery. There was no other literary bond between me and Jack. Mention another writer—Lawrence, Aldous Huxley, T. S. Eliot—and he would give a good-humoured grunt. 'You young fellows make a bit of an idol of T. S. Eliot, don't you? You like things to be obscure. Eh? Like crossword puzzles. Funny taste. You're a queer lot.'

To ramble with Jack on Wednesday afternoons was, as the authorities had failed to foresee, no disgrace but a delight. Maupassant would have smiled. And under Jack's own irony lay a feeling about the teaching of French that I remembered often when, years later, I became a teacher myself. He despised the bookish unreality of common practice. I think if I'd been taught Latin by someone with Jack's ideas about language, I might have been spared the grief it was in the sixth to respond with such incurably ignorant excitement to the music of Virgil . . .

I was at everybody's mercy. Wells made me a socialist, and I wrote with his impatient largeness; I was passionate with

Lawrence, paradoxical with Chesterton; uninformedly encyc-
lopaedic with Huxley; I was everybody's ape. I wrote poems
for the school magazine that alluded unmistakably to my feelings for Willy Henderson ('Passion, tamer of maddened metaphor . . .') and had them evasively rejected ('Hmm. Difficult.
Try something, ah, more lyrical. Masefield a good model.')
Meanwhile, the European situation shaped itself for war.
Williams introduced us to Henri Barbusse, Siegfried Sassoon,
Robert Graves. He also lent us his Left Book Club editions.
About this, I was clumsily innocent, not at all understanding that a book, whatever its source, could be under a
cloud. 'For God's sake,' Williams said, 'don't leave one of
these lying about in the sixth form room.' Slowly I understood
that Williams' own job might be at risk if he was known to
be lending this orange-coloured literature to boys. Williams was
a member of the local Labour Party. He took me to a meeting.
('Put your cap in your pocket'.) Life became conspiratorial.
I visited Williams in his lodgings; he played Chopin, read to
me from New Verse. At the door, saying goodnight at mid-
night, he lifted his landlord's hat from the hatstand: the
landlord, a sweet-natured dullard who was overawed by the
number of his tenant's books ('You're a deep man, Mr
Williams') was physically enormous, and the hat engulfed the
tiny Welsh face. How appalled Mr Chew would have been to
catch sight of his colleague at that moment! Ah, it was all a
conspiracy against the respectable! 'You needn't think, dear
boy,' said Williams, 'that I mean to be buried forever under
timetables and syllabuses.' Somewhere out there, unspeakable
emancipation offered itself. The business of preparing for
certificates and scholarships became more and more unreal.
I had no wish to be anything but a schoolboy—the alternative
was to be an insurance clerk or to sit for the Civil Service:
the very word 'office' was anathema to me. To be a schoolboy
was to remain in this world of confused kinds of loftiness and
fervour. But my head buzzed with unschoolboyish excitements,
ill-focused determinations. Life was a marvellously painful
skein of ideas and sensations, and there was no actual disposition of oneself that could accommodate it. With Ray
Bolton, a year behind me, I continued to walk the fields and
lanes: we were now devotees simply of different kinds of
weather. We would walk in storms because the leaves roared

on the trees, the rain was a rebel. But Ray was preparing to leave school, was making himself ready to accept the life of a clerk. 'But I'll still have my evenings and the holidays.' 'Oh Ray!' Meanwhile, the wind blew our hair into our eyes. We reflected with priggish pleasure that all the world's clerks at that moment were taking refuge in their houses. Such fear of weather we would never display . . .

About my own appetite for books my father was not as respectful as Williams' landlord about his tenant's. His attack on it was many-pronged. First there was the notion that when you could borrow books from a library there was no point in buying and retaining them. Second was the argument that books occupied valuable domestic space—to which there was a corollary: that books created dampness. At times he would sniff in the region of my bookcase; he'd take out a book and put his nose to it. Then he would open the book and would be triumphant when, as sometimes happened, a desiccated spider fell out. 'They're bloody graveyards,' he'd say. 'Ugh!' His most vehement objection was based on the idea that I hadn't read all the books I possessed. This led to rhetoric in which he accused me at one and the same time of reading too much ('Where do you think that will get you?') and reading too little ('You can't tell me you've read half these.'). To confuse the issue further, he was not above pointing to the existence of my books (but out of my hearing) as evidence of my being an unusual fellow. Mother would tell me: 'Your father's always saying to people: "Our house is full of books, y'know. Ted's a great reader." '

It was thanks to my mother that I had a bookcase at all. She'd bought it for one of my birthdays, and I secretly hated it for being of dark wood (the fashion among the discriminating, I knew, was for light woods) and for having glass doors. I detested the imprisonment of books behind glass. But I had never been able to speak of these dismays. Mother had spent anxious thought on the purchase—she never bought anything, however small, without it. Long before the bookcase arrived, it was acclaimed as a quite matchless piece of furniture, the very best Mr Craig at the shop could offer. Mother's lifelong illusion was that shopkeepers laboured to satisfy her wants in some fashion quite excruciatingly conscientious. 'For a charming lady like you, this is the piece,' she thought she had heard him say. 'I wouldn't sell you anything else. Nothing else would be good enough for a nice little woman like yourself . . . Yes, I think it's the very best I've ever had in the shop.' My sister, who accompanied mother on her many visits to Mr Craig, said the discussion was never quite of this nature. Mr Craig, she said, was a man of abrupt speech, displaying, if anything, a tart impatience with customers. He seemed also to take rather ill mother's confident naming of him as 'Mr Crepe.' She was always frightfully hit-and-miss with names. His attitude to her purchase of the bookcase was rather in the nature of : Take it or leave it. 'It's for my son. He's very clever and knows about these things,' Betty reported mother as saying. 'He's studying for his . . .' Her attempts to name the Higher School Certificate could be horrifying : it was a let-off when she allowed the idea to trail away, as in this case. 'Humph!' said Mr Craig. To my mother's understanding he meant (and she expanded his meaning accordingly, when reporting back at home) : 'Of course you have a clever son, I could have guessed it, and this is definitely the bookcase for a young man like that.'

Mr Chew, we suspected, had been reading philology the night before. Anyway, here he was, triumphantly rounding off some sudden seizure of a lecture by declaring : 'No one, gentlemen, can consider himself educated unless he has a grasp of the main language systems of the world.'

I didn't begin methodically to realise how outrageous it all was, all that snobbery and conservatism and academic display masquerading as education, until I met Ned. Ned was a scholarship boy from East Barton—he'd come to Queen's a year later than I had, but caught me up in the sixth. Ned was fatherless : his mother made a living as a charwoman. His essays, often read to us by Williams, had an epigrammatic tension and dry mastery of paradox that startled me, and made me feel more than ever hysterical, foolish, over-exciteable. He was a simple, dramatic socialist. I could not do anything so straightforward as to declare that the poor were exploited by the rich. My convictions, such as they were, existed at the heart of a filigree of dismally clever qualifications and reservations. After all, I had to be Bernard Shaw *and* W. B. Yeats *and* G. K.

Chesterton. I only knew, desperately, that everything was more complex than the most complex statement within my power . . . But Ned said his convinced things with trenchancy. He lived in a road near East Barton station . . . cramped and sooty terrace houses. 'What the children in my road need'— it is the first thing I remember him saying—'is not better playgrounds, but better gutters.' Whereupon he went off to play Rugger. Ned played games with the intelligence and self-discipline he brought to everything. My dislike of games, which I now equated with fascism, caused him the deepest amusement. 'You devote more energy to being a weed than I do to being a scrum-half,' he'd say.

About this time I began to learn the piano. Why did my father, so antagonistic to the kind of music I was now enjoying, invest in the upright that now stood, shining and encumbered, in our drawing room? It was, in the first place, a piece of furniture ('a nice piece of furniture', my father called it); then a photographic gallery; then a showplace for my mother's embroidered mats; then an indoor flower-garden; then a monument to my father's great skill as a polisher. 'N.B.', I would think as I fumbled with the keys, 'it is also used for musical purposes.'

On Monday evenings, Mrs Needle came to give me my piano lessons. Tall, always fur-coated, with a high colouring and a high voice, Mrs Needle fell short of my image of a music teacher. I had expected her to be part of my army against the philistines. But in almost all respects she seemed to be a thorough-going philistine herself. She was, I learned at the beginning of our acquaintance, in a sore state of dissatisfaction with her husband. How she had managed to marry a man who appeared to have an actual detestation of music, I could not imagine. 'It was a great mistake,' she would say cloudily, her spidery fingers running along the keyboard. 'Play the middle chord louder than the first or the third . . . Of course, he deceived me. He *pretended* to like music. You'd never have guessed when we were . . . *courting*.' She would laugh loudly when she used this word, as if, to hindsight, even this not very lively term was too romantic to apply to her pre-marital exchanges with Mr Needle. Then she would stare at me with her cloudy grey eyes, and smile in a manner I was always meaning to analyse in my diary. It was as if the lesson were a mere framework on which to hang her confessions of boredom and disillusionment and that other emotion, whatever it was, that swam when she smiled in those eyes that were at once misty and rather hard, like pebbles drying when you took them from the sea.

My aim, in the matter of the piano, was to play at once the major masterpieces. All Chopin, Mozart and Beethoven sonatas, great amounts of Liszt and Schumann, and a mixed bag of concertos. I did not run before I walked : I fairly tore along before I could even stand on my feet. It was the same weakness, and foolish order of aspiration, that lay behind my love of Virgil and refusal to grapple with him grammatically. Mrs Needle did not keep me under control. She was quite alarmingly indulgent . . .

A consequence of all this was that I borrowed scores from the school library. It was Ned's pleasure to catch me with several enormous volumes under my arm. '*One* would do,' he'd say. 'You can achieve the effect you want with a single volume. It would make the same impression.' I would be angry —but it was a different sort of anger from what I felt when under attack from other quarters. To be mocked by Ned was a wrathful delight. We were becoming a curious team—each other's comic, each other's feed.

And there were moments when our feelings simply chimed together. As when one day, after one of Chew's lessons, Ned called me over to the sixth form window. Outside, a fuchsia bush . . . tiny trembling blood-red bells . . .

'No wonder,' said Ned, 'Chew can stand it, with that to look at when he's busy boring us . . .'

There was a terrible moment when my father told me to shut my book, give him my attention, and answer the question : What did I mean to do with myself ? To this question I frankly had no answer, in everyday terms. I had lost all touch with the everyday. 'For God's sake,' cried my father, 'You've got to come down from the clouds. What are you going to do with your life ?'

'All I want to do,' I forced myself to reply, 'is to help to make the world a better place.'

'Oh,' he shouted. 'Oh, my God.' Then, 'Oh, *bugger* the world . . .'

My poor father ! I hate, still, *his* hatred of any generous,

154

any *soppy* idea, his anti-soppiness—which, let me be fair to the child I was, was also antagonism towards anything whatever that exceeded the bounds of a rigorous concern for Number One. But I try to re-feel that old scene through his emotions, and understand how he came to that . . . curiously superb cry: 'Oh, *bugger* the world!'

A worse moment came one night when I was writing in my diary. My mother had gone to bed; but he sat on. Of late I had drifted into the habit of writing my diary as if it were a novel. Using the third person of my own affairs reassured me of their normality.

'They lay in the grass, dry and hot under their bare skin. The world was in flames about them. He laid his head carefully on a pillow of hand and shut his eyes on the sun. The flames shot through his lids and were diffused into a liquid red . . .'

Curious—my father still there. The newspaper in his hands —but was he really reading it? An explosion of pages turning, one after another. The newspaper surely being used to express . . . impatience?

'Close to the ground you heard the dry, shuffling music of the cricket, and in the air the song of the birds became emphatic and heavy. He experienced one of those lapses of time-consciousness, when the normalities of the day lose all significance, and you inhabit a clockless infinity.'

A deep sigh: a glare at his watch. And a curious sense that my mother, upstairs, was not sleeping, but was listening. The house seemed to be listening. It was as if the house, too, was rustling a newspaper with angry impatience. What was it all about?

'Near him was Ned's head, silently bent over a book. Hawkes hummed monotonously, breaking now and then into some statement—'

My father bounced on the chair and groaned.

'—too coherent to accord with the occasion. There was a swish of grasses—'

'Put that bloody book away,' my father shouted. 'Put that bloody book and that bloody pen away and get up to bed!'

'But—' I said.

'Every night. You think you can do what you like. The light on all night. Think I can afford that? Unnatural!'

'What do you—?'

'You're not like anybody else! Mad! *I* fix the time for bed in this house. I'm not having you up to all hours—bloody scribbling. Come on, put it away! Get up those stairs!'

I found myself trembling. I was shivering from head to foot. There were black squares in my head: now standing upright, now on their corners. Hundreds of wild words streamed to my tongue, but none could be spoken. I wanted simply to scream.

'Are you moving? Are you going to do what you're bloody told?' My father was on his feet now, coming towards me, his eyes bulging. 'Do you want me to carry you up?'

A tiny corner of my mind became clear to me; I found I could speak. 'But look. What *am* I doing wrong? I'm just writing. I want to get this writing done. What's wrong with that?'

'What's bloody wrong with you—that's the question. Bloody writing! You can't do anything else. You can't do anything except sit there writing in that bloody silly book. If it's not writing, it's reading. Where the hell's that going to get you? But you get up those stairs! You go to bed when I tell you!'

'But tell me what's wrong with writing! Tell me—'

'I'll tell you.' To my horror, my father was squaring up, like some old-fashioned boxer. One leg was advanced, his fists were rotating. It was the playground invitation to a fight. Now my father began to dance, little sparring steps back and forth. He was shouting at the top of his voice. 'Come on! Take your glasses off! I'll show you!'

'God!' I cried. 'This is mad! What are you doing? This is madness!'

My father darted a blow at my chest. '*You*'re mad! Scribbling away in that bloody book!' Another blow. 'Writing things about me and your mother! I've read it! Like some bloody idiot, writing and reading the whole time!' A fist landed in the air an inch from my stomach, retreated, wound itself up, came again and dabbed three times, swiftly, at the air below my chin. 'All you're good for! Sitting on your bloody arse, scribbling!'

Now there was a sound as of some demented dressing gown descending the stairs. A stumble, a groan. And suddenly my mother was in the room, her greying hair flying. She threw herself at me, a little hurricane of flannel. Amazed, I found her fists beating at my chest. Then she kicked me. Distinctly, she kicked me.

'Your poor father!' she shrieked. 'Causing him such worry! You worry us to death! The neighbours! Not like other boys!' She was crying, helplessly. My father, I managed to notice, was still gyrating, his fists whirling. I backed away, towards the door. My mother was still beating me. 'Your father's good to you! Your father's so good to you!' she was crying. 'Bring him to his grave! Make him ill!'

'Oh my God! my God!' I cried; and turned and fled.

Up the stairs—I was running, I was going I knew not where, into blackness, into an agony of wild and horrible laughter. They were below me now, shouting, weeping; and as I reached the turn in the stairs, I heard my father's voice raised in an immense bellow that filled the house:

'*Rank insubordination!*'

This final touch of farce was too much. The Army term, snatched out of the air—this fragment of King's Regulations or whatever it was, summoned by my frothing father to clinch his hatred of literary pursuits . . . The situation exploded in my head; no rational action was suited to it, and with a cry of despair I fell down the stairs, backwards, aware of floating, of falling with hysterical harmlessness. Then I lay on the hall floor, uninjured, disembodied, and from somewhere hands were coming, this shell of my body was being tugged upright, and I could hear a voice shouting, above the sound of wild weeping:

'He bloody well *is* mad!'

Perhaps, when the exam came, I *was* mad. I had no hope of success. Little of my reading, even in English, had been to the point. Oh yes, I would read *The Spanish Tragedy* with due regard to probable context questions, I would certainly go through Virgil and Ovid with cribs, I would undoubtedly make myself once and for all a master of European history, 1789-1914 . . . at any moment: when I had finished *Eyeless in Gaza*, read Katherine Mansfield's short stories . . . oh, and then her diaries . . . when I had run through, that's to say tottered through, this volume of Schubert borrowed from the library . . . I would work when I'd written in my diary about the very interesting agony of not working.

I turned up at school for a vital Latin exam in the afternoon: it had taken place in the morning.

'Of course,' said Chew, not ungentle. 'Not unexpected, I'm sorry to say. You moderns. Well, there it is. To be frank, had thought of late that your chances of getting a schol. were dwindling. Lack, one's sorry to have to say it, of application. Afraid your people may be cut up. Eh?'

What my father said, shaking pepper over his dinner, was indirectly said, to my mother. 'Well, he'll have to face facts now. It'll do him good. You don't want to worry about him, my dear. He can go off to the library in the morning—advertisement columns of the *Morning Post* . . . No more mucking about.'

And what my mother said was: 'Yes, he'll have to do that. Have to shake himself out of it.'

What I said was: 'I'll die before I work in an office!'

Which led to my father putting his knife and fork down sharply on the plate. It had always been a signal for his most memorable furies: that rap of metal on china. He said, not turning round, but throwing the words over his shoulder: 'If you think you can bloody well sit there ('Dick! Dick!') and read your bloody books for ever and ever at my expense, then you can think again. You're no different from anyone else. I've had enough of your thinking you're different . . . and all those masters at that bloody school encouraging you. You've had your chance, and you've chucked it away. So it's a bloody office for you, like any other ('Dick! Dick!') bloody lad of your age. And the sooner the better. The sooner you're under the eye of some head clerk who can show you what a day's bloody hard work is, the better.'

PART FOUR

1

What it actually came to is that Mrs Needle found me a job on a local newspaper in Crawley Hill, where she lived, two or three suburbs distant from Barton. She urged me to be sensible. It would be a kind of writing, surely? I was rather surly about that. I suspected the *Crawley Hill Standard* might not be the most suitable medium for my sort of prose, which was fulminatory, or of the character of a rather brief firework display: a handful of rocketing phrases, preferably with erotic undertones . . .

I was welcomed when I followed up my letter of application by F. R. Gibson, who owned the paper. He also owned two stationer's shops in different parts of the local shopping street, the Crawley Hill Circus. Perhaps because his name in that form was so familiar on the front of his shops, he was never known outside the office as anything but F. R. Gibson. Inside, for economy's sake, he was known as F. R. He was extremely deaf and amazingly noisy. At that first meeting he berated me for failing to date the letter I'd written him. He asked me to consider the question: Could he, if he had ever written letters without dates on them, have built those great shops in the Circus, and got to own this important newspaper? He glared at me so long at this point that I tried to patch together some answer to his question, worse than any I'd been faced with in the Higher School Certificate; but he seized me by the wrist— his way, I found, with everyone, even the most fragile mayoress, was to lay hold of some loose part of the body and drag his victim with him, for he rarely stood still—and tugged me, stunned, into the editorial office.

I have never forgotten my first glimpse of a printing press, on the way. It was the eve of publication, I guess, for the presses were running. Through grimy windows, I caught sight of machinery; paper was being sucked through it as through some satanic wringer. Part of the machine seemed to have arms, which rose to catch sheets of paper and then, with a macabre groan, let them fall into heaps on a moving tray, which shuffled them into the shadows as if removing them from human sight for ever. Staring down at the machine was a tall, very thin man who, as we passed, turned and made a quite startling face. On thinking over rapidly what I'd seen, I concluded the man had no teeth : but in fact his face had collapsed as if not his teeth alone, but all the bones had been removed.

'Charlie!' F. R. Gibson roared. 'Machinist! Been with me twenty years! Complete rotter!'

'Eh?'

'Swine,' F.R. shouted, impatiently. 'See Trout first!' He burst through the main door of the newspaper office and threw open the door of an inner room. 'Mr Trout!' he cried. 'New young 'un for you! Grammar school an' all that! Start him on Monday!' The proprietor then briskly ransacked the desks in the office, throwing open drawers, glancing at letters in one of them that had a romantically private appearance, sniffing at apples he discovered in another. 'All these young men. Depend on me for a living,' he cried, and vanished.

Mr Trout was small, so dapper that even the baldness on the top of his head seemed carefully chosen. He asked if I had a nose for news. I thought for a wild moment that he had an actual configuration of the nose in mind; but before I could reply he swept on. It wasn't a nine-to-five job. I couldn't rely on having my evenings free. This he said as though it accorded with some vital principle of his to deprive people of their evenings. Well, he said dismissively, Monday then.

Leaving the office, astounded to discover that this was the way the world wagged (shouldn't there be references, the inspection of my School Certificate?) I cried : 'Good morning.' Then, aware that I'd hit on the wrong time of day, I cried : 'Good evening.'

'Good afternoon,' said Mr Trout, accurately.

I was, as I told my diary, a wage-slave. For ten shillings a week I'd sold myself to the sordidness of things.

My father was relieved that I was enrolled among the living,

162

but dismayed by the actual occupation I'd . . . well, you couldn't say chosen. That I'd submitted to being thrust into. He bought me, without consultation, a pork-pie hat; displaying an unexpected understanding that newspaper reporters did not wear bowlers. I kept it until I met Tess, who was everything in the form of a girl that my father feared I might meet. She threw my hat one evening into the Thames, from Waterloo Bridge.

I was, then, but in a very probationary way, a newspaper reporter. What at first it seemed to amount to was that I sat at one of those desks and attempted to rewrite the accounts of football matches sent in by the secretaries of local clubs. It was worse than composing essays for Mr Chew. The idea of writing, even of modestly re-writing, for print, even for modest print, robbed me of all nerve. I crept through the work, anxiously rewriting my rewriting. 'Done it yet?' Dobson kept asking.

Dobson was the senior of my two fellow-reporters. He had what I could only regard as a theatrical approach to the work. He never took off his hat in the office, but pushed it to the back of his head, as if to suggest that a reporter could never safely assume that he had come to stay. His ambition, as I quickly discovered, was to reach Fleet Street; and believing he would be acceptable there only if he'd taught himself to radiate a hideous kind of urgency, he brought to the placid events of Crawley Hill a precipitance that was unnerving. 'Getting through it,' I'd mutter. 'Speed essential,' Dobson would say. 'Get a move on, youngster.'

My other colleagues more than made up for Dobson's dash. Mr Trout rarely rose from his place at the typewriter. He covered important council meetings; the main police court, but only now and then; and an odd evening engagement. Otherwise he worked away stolidly at his weekly column, which was called *The Crawley Hill Jottings*. It was the work, so he signed himself, of The Jotter. I would sometimes stare at this penname, wondering how he could have brought himself to adopt it. It sounded as if he were confessing to some unhealthy habit. But that was perhaps not an unfair description of the Jottings themselves. They were like congealed gossip of a remarkably low level of interest. Mr Trout had occupied his chair for nearly thirty years, and he had lost touch with any sense of what was of moment even in the undramatic world of Crawley Hill. The Jottings were about tiny domestic events in the lives of aldermen and parsons; about local controversies, as Mr Trout thought them to be, that must have left even quite lively citizens sunk in apathy. Now and then the editor did, indeed, address himself to happenings in the larger world. The Jotter was a great tut-tutter. He wagged an occasional finger at monsters to whom he punctiliously referred as Herr Hitler and Signor Mussolini—but another finger, at the same time, in the interests of fairness, at Mr Stalin, Major Attlee, or the leaders of small states threatened by fascism. Mr Trout's view of affairs was that all would be well if only the leaders of nations would remember to be temperate, or would over- come their tendency momentarily to forget the other man's point of view. So he would in a marvellously muddled way set out what he thought might be the consequences of some rash act—it might be the rape of Czechoslovakia—and observe : 'Herr Hitler can hardly wish this to happen.' The dreadful events that led to the Second World War were all seen, in Mr Trout's Jottings, as inadvertencies on the part of men who would be saved from themselves if they would only enrol among Mr Trout's readers.

My third colleague was Desmond Wood, who had made a distinct mistake in becoming a reporter. If Dobson represented journalism as an activity based on frenzy, Desmond, of whom I became very fond, represented it as one based on almost total absent-mindedness. His real interest was quite unworldly —and not, one saw, capable of providing the basis for a living. He loved churches, and especially those very dull churches that in the nineteenth century replaced, everywhere, the charming buildings that had survived from centuries much earlier and much less self-important. Show Desmond a really banal church, alive only with the guilty memory of the edifice it had ousted, and he would glow with pleasure; and make additions to the meticulous notes he kept. Crawley Hill and the other suburbs we covered—for the *Standard* in its hundred years of existence had consumed a number of peripheral news-sheets—were full of such churches. Desmond was always tempted into stepping into them and adding to his notes, when he should have been at police stations, fire stations, jumble sales and other places where news was gathered. There was war between Dobson and Desmond Wood. 'For heaven's sake, man,' Dobson would cry. 'The *Standard* isn't an annual. It's a weekly. That fire happened three weeks ago!' I could never see that to be dilatory in recording the unfolding history of Crawley Hill was a crime. One chimney fire—it was usually a chimney fire—was much like another. Desmond's contributions to the paper were always forming the substance of angry disputes on Fridays, when the paper came out. They added to the dim pages of the *Standard* a quality of simple unpunctuality that I was alone in favouring . . .

Alas. At Queen's there had been a brief period when I'd discovered, to my chagrin, that I could run rather fast. For a time I'd been in danger of being an athlete. I had brought this phase to an end by manifesting, and I can't to this day be sure if it was genuine, a tendency to sensational cramp. Run once round the field and I would fall writhing to the ground, my leg muscles knotted. Now I discovered, once I'd broken through that shyness about print, that I was a reasonable newspaper reporter. There seemed to be no journalistic equivalent of cramp to fall back upon. The nearest I came to it was in my encounter with Tess, who led me into habits that almost brought about my dismissal from the *Standard* offices.

2

Women were among the early discoveries I made, once out of the monastic ambience of school. There was, to begin with, Daphne.

Daphne was F.R.'s secretary—so ripe that she seemed always about to burst out of her blouse. I was reminded of a fallen conker, still in its case, but with the case split, gaping. 'Mr B,' she called me, but in a manner that hardly turned me into

165

a senior. I never felt so young as when she addressed me : 'Mr B—how are you, then?' Her large eyes teased. But then her whole body, her entire presence, was a tease. 'How *are* you, Mr B?' Her leg stretched out, while she inspected her shoe. She always seemed to be inspecting parts of herself : sometimes, maddeningly interesting parts—the hem of her dress, often.

'Oh—bearing up, Daphne.' I was beginning to learn the language of such exchanges.

'You look very cheerful, Mr B.' It sounded, for some reason, as if she were making the most intimate appraisal of my condition. Then her hands going out to her typewriter—embracing the machine. Everything she did had the quality of an embrace. She transferred her attention to a pencil and I blushed.

'Tell me something, Mr B.'

Wild responses suggested themselves. Instead :

'Hmm—I'm off to a funeral in Cedar Grove.'

'Ugh!' And she tumbled laughing over the typewriter, her arms extended, her hair falling. Her blouse gaped, and her skirt was under the most delicious strain. I would fly out of the office, down the steps, into the Circus, driven by a feeling of indescribable success. Amazing triumph propelled me across to the bus stop. And it was only as I drew to a halt that I wondered what it was all about. I was bound for a funeral in Cedar Grove. What was there in that to have filled me with this sense of stupendous accomplishment?

I ran into Tess—I collided with her—at an evening meeting of the Crawley Hill League of Nations Union. In a tiny sober meeting she stood out, dark, mysterious, restless. She sat next to me, and was whisperingly satirical about the notes I was making. 'It's all talk,' she murmured. 'You're flattering them, writing it down.' 'I've got it all wrong, anyway,' I whispered back. Mr Trout had made it a condition of my employment that I should become a master of shorthand. I felt about that much as I'd felt about my father's insistence on Maths and Geography. No room for study ! From a single page of Pitmans I'd turn with wild relief to a hundred pages of Richard Jefferies. At the rate I was going, I should be a competent shorthand writer in a hundred years' time. 'Your writing,' Tess whispered, 'is an artist's. Oh, very interesting. I've never seen writing more *complex.*' I was in such a heaven as made the seventh heaven seem tedious. Here was the person I'd been hunting for—and luck had made her a *female* person. We were shushed by the platform. 'Don't let's stay,' said Tess. 'I don't know why I came. Oh yes, I do. It was to meet you.' Music by Chopin began to flood into my head. We crept out, my notes dreadfully incomplete, and she held my hand at once. We parted, hours later, with a kiss. I had never before kissed a girl. Suddenly her lips became enormous, filled the entire world, and I homed on to them. Given such magnification, how did I miss them? I missed them by inches: my lips landed close to her ear. I tried again, and was successful. I had never imagined that lips were so soft, so scented. 'Meet me,' said Tess with a peremptoriness that I found exquisite, 'tomorrow evening at the bus stop in the Circus.' That evening I was booked for a piano recital at St Andrews, Crawley Hill. I did not care. I was totally, finally, for ever in love.

My immediate notion, that we were on a brief glorious ascent to marriage—within a week it would all be sealed and assented to—did not survive the next day of introspection, consultation with my diary. Lately I had been reading Schopenhauer. From him I had derived the view that, as I put it only too explicitly on our second encounter, love was a device elaborated by nature to divert us from the maddening monotony of the procreative process. It seemed to me, as I remember, a view of things that I must present to Tess with sullen urgency. We walked up and down various hills leading to and from the Circus, and Tess was not as hospitable to my Schopenhauerian assertions as I had expected her to be. At one point, indeed, she threatened to leave me. 'Thinking has dried you up,' she declared; and for a moment vanished into the shadow of certain unforgettable trees. Then she returned. It was the pattern of our relationship, for a long time. 'Oh, you're ridiculous!' she cried, and took my hand and so adjusted the geometry of our bodies that I found myself again, and with much greater efficiency, locating and impacting her lips. 'Oh you *beast*!' I cried. Later Tess affirmed that this cry of mine, so unSchopenhauerian, was for her the turning point. Gauche, over-intellectual though I was, still there was hope for me. I was capable of amorous outcries, bypassing the intellect. Tess decided to hang on to me.

She was the daughter of a local councillor, and therefore, in theory, matter for Mr Trout's Jottings. She was employed, as it happened, by a distinguished theatrical photographer, in the West End of London. From the beginning she teased me—drove me, indeed, quite wild—by her accounts, never quite comprehensible, of life in the studio where she worked. There were these handsome fellows, oh actors and so forth, she mentioned names mildly famous, who, oh, I mustn't take this seriously, pinched her—no, groped towards her, in what I understood to be the characteristic darkness of the studio. 'I don't like him! Really, I don't like him!' I felt, her hand in mine, dreadfully uncertain as to how I should feel about *him*, and how I should take this . . . excited uncertainty of hers as to whether she'd been pinched, or groped towards, or not.

We wandered, night after night, through Crawley Hill and its neighbourhood, and I was divided quite neatly between the confident, accepted lover, and the chap who might be somewhere near the edge of a great group of actors and other fellows, all enormously knowledgeable as to the erotic uses that might be made of a photographic studio . . .

It meant that I missed, I failed to be present at, a number of evening engagements. Mr Trout was patiently angry. 'You know,' he said, 'you'll have to choose between business and pleasure.'

Dammit, I thought—imagining myself choosing business. To do that would be, very simply, to choose against the grain of all reasonable inclination. 'HERE LIES . . . WHO CHOSE BUSINESS RATHER THAN PLEASURE.' 'Katherine Mansfield, meet my young friend—one of pleasure's most sturdy opponents!' I thought of preferring an amateur rendition—ugh! Trout's favourite word!—of *Elijah* to the company of Tess, and to Tess's kisses. Horror rose within me.

'Oh, look—'

'We can't go on like this,' said Mr Trout. 'Can we?'

An accident of tone made his voice suggestive of actual indecision. 'Well, you see—' I began.

'If it goes on we'll have to part company. Now, be a sensible fellow. I think you show promise at this job. But we can't have a staff man who's not to be relied upon. Can we?'

Again the open tone. And Mr Trout positively smiled—at

any rate, his mouth was subject to an amiable seizure. 'Now I must get on. Lots to do. No time, you see, for this sort of thing. That's the point, you see?'

'Ah,' I said dismally, and found myself smiling. Disloyal face! 'Go and get yourself a coffee or something,' said Mr Trout, now tender. 'And let's have the court stuff by lunch time. Eh?'

He began to whistle—a generalised tune that so often came from him at awkward moments. I smiled, shrugged, became gloomy, smiled again—and went storming across to the tea shop in the Circus. How much easier if villains were one hundred per cent villainous! Damn Trout! Scorning his lustreless view of life, one felt one could hardly let the man down, with his damnable, illusory offer of fairmindedness . . .

So I became intermittently reliable. Trout had taken to me—there was no other way of interpreting his infernal lenience. In theory, I and my diary were in favour of my being dismissed, in disgrace. Then we'd run away to . . . we'd run away with Tess. But I tried to imagine, in practice, telling my mother, who would crumple, or my father, who would explode, that I had been found unworthy of a post that didn't even qualify for a bowler hat.

My diary, given to bursts of awkward honesty, informed me that I was glad of Trout's softness, and devoted two pages to a bitter self-portrait. Morally, it appeared, I'd forfeited Tess's attentions; and should probably limit myself to reading second-rate novelists . . .

3

But Mr Trout could be sharp enough, in those early months. I remember how unsympathetic he was on a day when I faced, for the first time, a certain truth about myself that made it difficult for me to be a comfortable journalist. I shrank from entering, notebook in hand, on a private scene.

That morning Mr Trout gave the telephone a final grunt;
then glared across the office. 'Old Craddock's dying,' he barked.
'God,' said Dobson. 'On a Wednesday morning!'
'Someone must get down there at once.'
'This police court stuff,' said Dobson severely, 'won't wait.'
He pushed his hat further off his forehead. 'That'll be a story
and a half—old Craddock! You'll have to send our young
friend.'
Our young friend froze. I had begun to write a poem:
'These who type their lives away . . .' 'What shall I do?' I
asked wretchedly.
'The Rev. Adam Craddock,' said Dobson, 'is the greatly
respected Vicar of St Luke's.'
'Yes, I know that.'
Dobson ignored me. 'He has been there for some forty
years, and his death will be a major event in the district. He's
a Canon of St Paul's. One of his sons is a writer of detective
thrillers, not totally unknown. Etcetera. Etcetera. He might
die before we put the paper to bed—'
Mr Trout groaned at the idea of a death so thoughtless.
'—or he might hang on for weeks. Meanwhile, we need to
know what is happening. So—'
'I go down and . . . ask about him,' I said, miserably. Damn
Dobson, with his heavy and ill-directed irony. He was perfectly
friendly when he wanted to be. But there was this need he
had to stress the almost unbearable strain and fever of newspaper life. From Monday to Friday it was Doomsday, every
week.
'Light dawns,' said Dobson, and attacked his typewriter.
'Knock at the door and say we want to know how he is,'
I mumbled. There was, clatteringly, no reply.
I was aware that I should get a bus to St Luke's. It was a
mile away. I ought to feel an excited professional urgency. But
I found myself walking, very slowly—horrified by my errand.
How could you—when a man was dying . . .? How could
you knock at his door and say: 'I'm from the *Standard*—can
you give me a paragraph on . . .'
I was tight inside at the thought of such a callous intrusion.
Surely it was callous? When someone you loved was dying,
did you wish to see some . . . trivial nosey-parker from the
local newspaper?

I was circling St Luke's—and the circles threatened to grow larger and larger. I made myself turn into a road at the end of which stood the pale spike of the church. The vicarage was next door. Here it was—the front gate, the silent drive . . .

I walked past . . . Then I was half a mile away, outside quite another religious gate. Here lived John Evans, the Baptist minister. Evans was young, lively—edited a parish magazine the *Standard* was always quoting, for its epigrams. Or, as I had sometimes thought, its pseudo-epigrams. 'God,' Evans had written recently, 'would be an unlikely owner of a motorcar.' Dobson had written this up under the headline: GOD NO MOTORIST, SAYS REV EVANS. Mr Trout had shaken his head over that: changed it to LOCAL MINISTER'S ATTACK ON MATERIALISM.

But a nice man, Evans . . . And there I was, knocking at his door, and then stuttering over a statement of my problem. What he said, gently, helped me then and throughout my three years in Crawley Hill. Of course, he said, hang on to your sensitiveness about being an intruder . . . but remember that, to take the present case, dear old Craddock really was an important member of the community—people really did need to have news of him—and his family truly did need, I'd find they were very eager, to inform the world of his illness through the *Standard*. So I must go along to the vicarage feeling that I was bound, courteously, of course, on a small mission of public importance . . .

Actually, the vicarage gave me the first sherry I'd ever drunk in my life . . .

It *was* hard, though, adjusting to the ambiguities of the reporter's position. Not more so anywhere than in the police courts. Especially Court No 3 in the town hall at West Green. On other days than court days it was a committee room for council work; and at one end was a row of cupboards where the councillors hung their coats. When the court was sitting, this amenity was used by magistrates and officials; and whenever Court No 3 ran on longer than its neighbours, its solemn proceedings were likely to be interrupted by shuffling and apologetic entries, low curses caused by the eccentricity of the cupboard doors (if not disastrously loose, then fatally stiff), and the tittering sound made when wire coathangers clash. I sometimes attempted to imagine myself being tried in Court

No 3. As time went on and I became more familiar with the range of small offences dealt with by the courts at Crawley Hill and West Green, I grew certain that I must, one day soon, appear in the dock. Impossible that I should for long be innocent of all of such a miscellany of possible misdemeanours. What would it be like to be on trial among those tiptoeing confusions? What would it be like to be tried by Major Plaice, doyen of the court?

The Major was a large, muddled man, who was always wrong about the date, the venue, the order and nature of the cases. He would address a witness with words intended for the defendant. He would pass sentence at the wrong moment, or of a severity beyond his powers. But his wits achieved sudden sharpness and cohesion when he saw an opportunity to make some stern pronouncement. 'In all my days on the bench . . .' he would begin. Never more disgusted. Too much of this sort of thing. Must stop. Utmost severity would be brought to bear. Far too much of it—far too much of it, these days.

Far too much careless driving, failure to pay the rates, failure to obtain a dog licence. Far, far too much theft, burglary, petty larceny. And infinitely far too much exposing one's person with intent to insult a female . . .

Of this last there was a case that led to my having a vision. The unhappy man in the dock had exhibited himself on a railway platform. Had feebly attempted to plead that it was a hot night—he was, perhaps in an unwise manner, refrigerating himself. 'We're not going to have any more of this, y'know,' Major Plaice had snapped, as if he were dealing, not with a permanent human weakness, but with some new-fangled vagary. 'This sort of thing has simply got to stop.'

. . . In place of the shrinking defendant, I seemed to see another occupant of the dock. Police evidence was being given : 'He refuses to give his real name : says he's one of the Seven Deadly Sins, your worship. Admits to being called Lust, but won't give his full name.'

In my vision, Major Plaice then leaned forward with a wild gleam in his eye. 'Well, Lust, we're determined to put an end to this sort of thing. Treat it with the utmost severity. There's been too much of it recently in this neighbourhood. From the evidence we've heard, my colleagues and I are convinced that you are one of the ringleaders. You will go to prison for twelve months—and I hope the Press will give this case the fullest publicity. We have made up our minds that disgusting conduct of the kind that has been described to us shall be stamped out. Next case—'

The next case—before my vision faded—was that of the defendant refusing to give any name but Greed. 'Now, look here, Greed,' Major Plaice had concluded, leaning forward on his indignant elbow . . .

Not all magistrates were as dotty as the Major, not all courts as ill-suited to their purpose as Court No 3. But there was much about police court reporting that I disliked. It was summed up, I think, by F. R. Gibson's statement of philosophy, made soon after I'd joined the paper. In a roar that served with him for intimate communication, 'We're in this to make money,' he told me, as if I had shown signs of believing that the *Standard* was a philanthropic venture. 'Now, take this story here.' A galley lay before him—an unmarried mother accused of stealing groceries valued at 5s 9d from a shop in the Circus. It was headed: 'LAVENDER DRIVE WOMAN IN DOCK.' 'See that headline! That'll be in this week's bill. OK? Why, young man? Why? What a silly question!' (I'd not asked it.) 'Because everyone in Lavender Drive will buy a copy! See? Every name sells a paper. Remember that! *Every name sells a paper!*'

It was a principle I tried not to observe. Dobson, inclined to regard me in general as a colleague of promise, thought I was nevertheless the weakest writer of headlines he'd ever met. 'Worse,' he once said with affable scorn, 'than Desmond Wood!'

I grew used, as the months wore on, to being manhandled by F. R. Gibson. When we met, on the Circus usually, I'd gird myself, draw together my bones, which seemed suddenly frail. The enormous hand would grip my arm, or F.R. would gather me crushingly to himself, and the usual shout would come:

'Well, what d'you know?'

The theory was that I should answer with a brisk résumé of the latest local news. But this I was never able to give, partly because F.R. disbelieved in my power to give it. The pattern of his attitude was fixed. Expectation, collapsing instantly into

173

disappointment. So the question was always followed by a second shout, this one melancholy.

'You don't know *anything*, do you!' he'd cry.

'I—'

But F.R. would hold me there, scarlet-faced among the shoppers, and groan: '*You don't know a single thing, do you!*'

It was partly why I tried the effect of growing a beard.

The first failure to shave found my father incredulous. 'You're not going to walk about like that?' I said: 'My great-grandfather had a beard, I think?' 'What's that got to do with it? That was when everybody had one.' 'George V was bearded.' My father missed the opportunity of asking why I, a republican, should wish to resemble a king. 'He was in the Navy,' he snorted. 'Bernard Shaw,' I said, rashly. My father groaned. 'What will they think at the *Standard*?' he asked. 'Do they want you looking like a . . . This is not Russia, you know.' 'Ah,' I said. 'You're really afraid I shall be taken for a communist.' 'I can tell you one thing,' said my father. 'Your mother's not going to be seen out with you if you walk about looking like some . . .' He rustled his newspaper furiously. 'Like some *tramp*.' 'A communist tramp with a touch of the Royal Navy,' I offered. 'Take the bloody thing off,' roared my father. 'Do something sensible for a change.'

But I persisted—even though my mother became quite tearful. It didn't suit me, she said. I asked her to wait till it was more than a superficial hairy grubbiness. 'You'll like it when it's down to my chest,' I said, hoping she might smile, however ruefully. But my mother asked me to imagine how she felt among her neighbours, knowing what they must be saying. 'But what can they be saying,' I demanded, 'about such an ordinary thing as a beard?' My mother hinted darkly that it would be added to other grounds for unfriendly comment. 'They think you're dreamy. Mrs Pitt said she was sorry for me, having such a dreamy chap on my hands.' 'I am not on your hands,' I snapped. 'How am I on your hands?' 'Feet in the clouds,' said my mother, ramming clichés together. 'Oh God,' I said, and ran to my diary.

Poor mother! This was the time when I grew most deeply

174

ashamed of her, for the remarkable irrelevances she introduced into conversation, for her failure ever quite to grasp an idiom. Shrinking from people who smelled, she complained of their 'body odeon.' Trouble with a gasfitting could be the problem of the 'pirate light.' She amazed (perhaps also titillated) her neighbours with talk of being plagued by 'daddy's long legs.' During the crisis of 1938, she confessed afterwards, we had all been 'quoting in our shoes.' At times she conflated phrases as they might hardly have seemed capable of conflation : 'She was,' she said of a neighbour defeated in some everyday exchange, 'squashed into a square peg.' Sweetly attentive to my appetites as she always was, she bought me from time to time a Penguin : hiding it behind her back as she announced the event, and, when it had been handed over, and I'd said I hadn't got it already, it was what I'd particularly wanted, crying : 'He hasn't got it, he hasn't got it!' However, she was always convinced that these estimable paperbacks were called Pin Wins. To the local bookshop she must have been known as the woman who came in for Pin Wins. It had become a favourite shop of hers, outside the core of her love among the shops, Mr Fereday's the butchers, Jackson's the grocers; as was also one she obstinately called the Ann Tick Shop. Or rather, since she often took the edges off things, wore away names she'd already had her curious dab at, the Ann Tick. 'The lady in the Ann Tick said . . .'

4

It was Ned, not I, who had gone into the Civil Service. No one at Queen's had seemed to put much effort into suggesting he should try for the university. He was already amusedly scornful of the way that, having been taken in as a clerical officer, a new entrant was pointed towards his future. Or, on the whole, was *not* pointed towards his future. No one, he complained, would be deterred from electing at once, at the age of seventeen or eighteen, to become, in spirit, a superannuated clerical officer. 'Oh, Bert, we're all so very elderly!'

My father detected these dissatisfactions in Ned—and the unease expressed by Ray Bolton and Peter Bunce when they visited us: both in insurance. 'All these young fellows,' he snorted, 'coming down here with long faces, because they've not been made managing directors before they've served a twelvemonth.' He tore into Ray once, for groaning about the sameness of his working days. 'You'll get used to it,' he said. 'We all have to get used to it. What do you expect? Dancing girls? It's that school you went to that's the trouble. Gave you young fellows the idea you were intellectuals. I'll tell you something. The intellectuals will never run this country. They couldn't run anything.' There was always, alas, a curious quality in his voice when he could make a speech like this, demolishing hopes or expectations: it paced, his voice, like a cat, stretched out for hunting. 'This country is run by a few men with experience. It's experience that counts. That's what you get from day after day in the office. You can call it dull, if you like—that's all right.' A favourite phrase: it meant that in his view it was quite monstrously *not* all right. 'They may not have brains—but they've got intelligence and commonsense. The intellectuals have *no* commonsense. Their trouble is they don't know how to deal with facts.' At the use of this word, for me such a sore one, I was betrayed into a snort of my own. 'Some people,' said my father, 'will find out how important facts are when it's much too late. What some people need is a good woman who'll knock some sense into them. But can you imagine your good woman wanting to take on some blasted intellectual?'

He knew about Tess. I suspected Mrs Needle of telling him. However described, Tess would not have qualified as a good woman, in my father's sense of the term. A good woman would have wanted to visit her young man's parents. As it happened, I spent much of my energy in thwarting Tess's curiosity, in this respect . . .

There seemed to be, at a conservative estimate, some twenty Tesses. The one I cared for most was the kissing Tess, the Tess breathless with pleasure when we met. I could measure the truth of the pleasure by my own. In the midst of the doubts, the puzzled disturbance I felt when she hinted at the nature of life in the studio, or in the Dukes Avenue mansion that was her home (Dukes Avenue! I evaded invitation to that daunting road as I withheld invitation to visit Barton from her)—in the midst of all that, I had no uncertainty about what united us: the word for it was love. Schopenhauer, I'd decided, had been talking through his—intellectually very handsome—hat . . .

Close to that best Tess was the other who would suddenly sigh and seize my hand and bring it round her body till it was cradling her breast. I was so dizzied by her giving me this right of intimate touch that the world slowed, my expectation of life increased ten-fold, and the notion that I might go further, be more generally intimate, became a perfectly leisurely notion . . . thrillingly patient . . . It was not, I now think, the effect that Tess intended.

There was also the bafflingly teasing Tess, who talked, and then strangely stopped talking, of her experiences in the photographer's studio. And there was the Tess who thought I was too gentle—oh hell, she seemed to be saying, it was this gentleness for which she loved me, and she really couldn't bear it—altogether too much of a good thing! Why didn't I boot my parents, and Mr Trout, and the whole of Barton, and Crawley Hill entire, out of my life—and so, of course, out of hers. 'Why don't we run away? Oh, let's run away! Give me one good reason why we shouldn't run away! We could find a cottage somewhere and wear what we liked and do what we liked and you need never wear a hat . . .' It was at a moment like this that she threw my pork-pie into the Thames. I told my father I'd left it on a coathook in a cafe. 'I bet you didn't tell your father what I did with your hat? Oh, Teddy—you're such a *coward* . . .'

There was a dreadful evening when I brought her together with Ned. Here was quite another Tess. This one was strangely playful, frivolous. As we stood to get off a bus, she bumped into me, sending me mildly cannoning into Ned. Ned half-turned and sighed in a dry, painfully patient way. It was like some terribly unsuccessful joke in a variety sketch. Worse: it was like a joke addressed at entirely the wrong audience. How could she have thought that Ned was to be amused by such bumpings and cannonings? Worse still: it was not the kind of thing she'd ever engaged in, when we were alone. That order of horseplay—it wasn't among our ways of amusing ourselves, was it? Uneasily I sensed that she had bumped into me, causing me to bump into Ned, as a sort of challenging communication with my friend. She was saying something to Ned. I remembered how at Barley Road there'd been a boy who used to punch out at me, whenever we passed. We'd hardly ever spoken—the punch sprang from some instinctive hostility, terrifying because so instant and convinced. There seemed just such an instinctive acceptance of enmity between Tess and Ned. Ned was being patient, that evening, for my sake; but I felt it would have been very easy for him simply to walk away, disgusted . . .

Disgusted? But how could disgust possibly arise between my best friend and the girl I loved?

To my father, almost all he read in the newspaper was designed to make him angry. The world behaved absurdly in order to provide him with the opportunity for scornful comment. 'Good God!' was his usual cry as he ran his eye over the headlines. 'Good God, they're at it again!' They were, in short, governing, stealing, murdering, engaging in scandal—being born and dying. 'They' were, I suppose, the human race. It was this persistence of theirs in doing what they seemed unable to avoid doing that filled my father with his daily irritation. I used to wonder what sort of front page, what sort of headlines, would give him satisfaction. A foolish surmise: because this anger with humanity *was* his satisfaction. It sent him off for the day filled with vital fury.

Mankind's only hope of being excused for an act of folly lay in that act being deplored by my mother. This was especially so in the field of the murder of a woman by a man. 'Dreadful thing,' she would say. 'That man. Cut her up.' 'What's that?' 'Nasty face.' 'Who's got a nasty face?' 'Oh, that man! You've read it.' 'How do I know what man you're talking about?' My father's invariable opening retort to any such expression of partisanship: a pedantic rejection of her vagueness. 'If you want me to know what you're talking about, you'll have to give him a name.' Mother was always at her most inexact in the matter of names. 'Oh, you know his name. Everyone's reading about it. It's all over the papers.' Given this sort of opening, my father would have argued for the innocence of Caligula himself.

At times, though, my mother would be filled with the opposite indignation: her view that men were at the root of everything vile would be replaced by a view far more natural to her, that women were the prime cause of human misery.

There was an evening when she felt the need to speak of this theory, having just read of a man accused of slaying his mistress.

'One day,' she proposed, 'men will get fed up with it. These women lead them on, and they ask for what they get. But it's the man who pays. The woman twists him round her . . .' She couldn't remember how the phrase continued. 'She *rouses* him. That's how it always happens.'

'Wait a minute,' said my father hotly. 'How do you know what happens? How do you know what happened in this case? . . . Six of one and half a dozen of the other.'

'He buried her in the garden,' said my mother, as if that answered his scruple.

'All right—he buried her in the garden. I don't care where he buried her.' Irritated, my father dashed hither and thither along the paths of argument. 'No woman's worth hanging for. I've no time for such things. I've better things to read about.'

My mother understood that she was being attacked merely for giving her attention to the case. 'You've got to take an interest', she said.

'*I* haven't got to be interested in it,' said my father. 'And I'm *not* interested in it. They can strangle anyone they like. They can bury them in Hyde Park, for all I care. Let them get on with it. They have to fill the papers with something.'

'Who are all these theys?' I murmured dangerously: and then was relieved to hear a knock at the front door. As my mother scurried to see who it was, my father groaned spectacularly. 'Who the hell's that?' he asked the uneasy room.

My mother returned with mixed cries of amazement and alarm. 'Teddy! It's Ned! Teddy will be glad to see you, Ned! Dick! Ned's come to see Ted! Ned!' Ned entered coolly amid these explosions of introduction and welcome, with their uneasy undertone. Visitors always bothered my mother, uncertain of the reception her husband would offer. Thus her

179

urgent repetitions of a visitor's name, designed to prepare and, if possible, reconcile my father.

He chose to be guardedly jocular. 'Hallo, there! . . . And how are you getting on at the office?'

I cringed. My father would certainly claim this occasion as his own. 'Hullo,' I said, helplessly, and Ned winked. 'I'm learning,' said Ned, 'to be a reasonable piece of blotting paper, I suppose.'

'Blotting paper? How do you mean?'

'I carry out instructions.'

'If you can do that efficiently,' said my father, 'you're well on the way to becoming a decent clerical officer. You know, it's surprising the number of young men who fancy they're too clever to act on instructions. Think themselves above it. I'm having trouble at the moment with a young fellow . . .'

I remembered a passage from Ned's last letter. 'As I walk, I disturb the superannuated dust. I feel official fingers at my throat. The other day, walking in Whitehall, I saw a nun. She was beautiful, in her flowing robes. I trembled to see such beauty in such a place.' I trembled myself, watching Ned's wryly attentive face. Now my father was well launched into a statement of the importance of understanding the *instructions* given by a *superior*. And acting on them, promptly. 'Your young man who can do that,' he said, 'can expect steady promotion. Within reasonable limits. He may have to wait patiently for . . . several years. He may have to study the, ah, tastes of the man above him. If your superior's interested in lawn tennis, it's good sense to take an interest in it yourself. It never does any harm. You've got to watch points . . . Patience. Prompt carrying out of instructions. Watching points. That's the way to get on, you'll find.'

I wanted to leap out of my chair, to halt my father with a scream. 'How dare you talk to Ned as if he were . . . some time-serving nonentity!' I wanted to cry. 'Can you imagine Ned pretending to be interested in lawn tennis because his bloody superior's interested in it?' But Ned was nodding— smiling. 'You certainly need a little cunning,' he was saying, 'if you don't want to stay in a rut.'

'I don't know about cunning,' said my father, clearly not displeased. 'But it's no good . . . acting simple.'

'Well, I'm struggling hard against my natural simplicity,'

said Ned; and turned to me. 'Are you having to do the same, in your newspaper office?'

I was appalled. Was Ned pulling my father's leg? How could he give his assent—with whatever revision of language—to any of my father's propositions? I made an unhappy face. 'Well—'

'Mrs Bates,' said my mother, 'says young people have it easy.'

I sank lower into my chair. What could Ned be making of this nonsense? How was he to know who Mrs Bates was? How was he to respond to this inconsequential secondhand assertion?

'What the devil,' said my father, 'does Mrs Bates know about it?'

'She's got two children.'

'So what? I've got two children. Thousands of people have got two children. What has that to do with anything at all?'

'I've come to the conclusion,' said Ned, easily, 'that it's best to do without children. Have you made up your mind about that sort of thing, Bert?'

I uttered a strangled cry of despair, disbelief—unspeakable chagrin. Ned said, with a grave smile: 'I think you ought to be addressing your mind to it, you know.'

'That'll be the day, when he addresses his mind to anything,' said my father . . .

A horrified half hour later, I walked at Ned's side away from the house. 'Oh my God,' I said.

'What's the matter?' said Ned. 'I thought you were . . . rather oppressed in there. You seemed to be in the dumps, for some reason. I rather like your father, you know. He's an amusing rogue. Your mother's a bit—what shall one say?—difficult to keep track of . . . But they could be worse. Don't you think so?'

I sank into a deeply gloomy silence, which lasted until Ned began to talk about the book he was currently reading.

I just didn't know—at home in my rage and humiliation, or in some group gathered by Ned at his home in East Barton—how people managed to talk. More—how they managed to say the right thing. At least, what they said always *sounded* right to me. In the jungle of possible speech they trod confident paths. I would sit, listening to the way one remark created another : forlornly noting how people chose, and at speed, to agree or disagree with what was said to them. The longer I sat listening, the more numbly certain I grew that this was an activity for which I had no gift at all. Sometimes I would prepare an interjection of my own—frame it, unframe it, polish and then suspiciously inspect and check it; tap its wheels and listen for hollowness that might lay me open to stinging rebuttal or, worst of all, a blank stare. But by the time I'd begun, nervously, to think of using it, the conversation would have passed on to other things. Then I'd be aware that I hadn't spoken for—oh, ten minutes, half an hour; then it seemed that any word from me would simply startle my companions. So I sank into silent, grimacing misery. 'I wish,' Ned said, 'you would suck your tie less, and talk a little more.' It was true, I discovered—I did positively insert my tie into my mouth, at times. Well, clearly I was a defective human being. It was obviously the natural thing to be able to talk spontaneously, to be carried on the flood of a conversation. I was some sort of monster. People must remark, when I'd gone : 'He never says a word! Queer fellow!' Ned had also hinted that, by his family and friends, this tie-sucking silence of mine was taken for a species of snootiness. 'Toffee-nosed' was a word that was used. Oh God! I was a toffee-nosed monster; and no one understood how painfully I longed to be a lively, unselfconscious talker. I dreamed of liberation—of making long, vivacious speeches, of positively capping the comments of others. Leaving Ned's home, I went back over the evening's talk, inserting my own contributions : intelligent, flexible, keenly phrased. I even considered fastening my tie down immovably with a tiepin—or several tiepins. But then I imagined my sardonic friend saying : 'I see you're going in for tiepins. It's the thin end of the suburban wedge, y'know.' And I'd never be able, on the spot, I'd *never* be able, unless given two or three pages of diary—and you couldn't *read* your conversational contributions out of your diary, though I had wildly thought of doing so—I'd never be able to work out a reply to *that*.

5

I was so often very shy, at first, whenever Tess and I came together. We were meeting in London now more often than in Crawley Hill.

As a setting for Tess and me, London seemed a bit much, really. I worried, at the back of my head, at the thought of all that achievement: the making of great roads, shops, theatres, galleries, parks . . . Oh, the world was too fantastic altogether, providing, for my visits to this elaborate city, great dramas of weather: storms of rain, amazing outbursts of sunshine. Everything seemed heroically large in London. I loved it—but no other place, not a battlefield or a volcanic crater, could have seemed so out of scale with my sense of myself.

I felt it most when I met Tess, on one of those evenings, under the portico of the National Gallery. She seemed at ease anywhere. Her movements—as she jumped from the bus on the other side of the road, then crossed to join me—were those of someone completely at home. The world was hers. She would smile as she came, which seemed to set the whole scene smiling, and I'd have this sense as of things happening outside all likely scale. Was she really—dark smiling head, heavy body, the very clothes she was wearing—mine? The possession was excessive. Too much, to be given in this way a whole human being—and a female one, into the bargain. I felt then like someone who has made a monstrously unwise purchase—has bought something too splendid and onerous for his way of life. A complete human being, now putting her hand in mine and dragging at me, as I stood there, half-paralysed by my sense of being inadequate.

'Wake up, Teddy! And look pleased to see me!'

I was stunned into sombre silence by the pleasure of seeing her.

'You've got your remote look. You don't like me much this evening, do you?'

How could we, so quickly, have reached this wretched and false proposition? The evening was thirty seconds old, and already the world had come to an end.

She'd have a tale to tell, of something observed on the way. Telling it, she'd break off to comment on a face in the crowd, the way someone was dressed. It was much of what I loved in her, this quick and laughing response to things, and the rapid changes of mood. Horrible not to know how to respond!

'It's going to be one of your talkative nights, Teddy!'

Deepening glumness as we moved among the fountains and the lions (she addressing the pigeons), crossed to the Admiralty Arch (she pulling me back from in front of a bus), exchanged the uproar of the square for the wide peace of the Mall. Again, such an absurdly grand avenue for us to walk in! Someone had built the War Office for us on the left, and others, monstrously overdoing it, had formed St James' Park as a place for us to dawdle through. And still I'd hardly said a word.

'You are grunting well tonight, Teddy. Why don't you smoke your pipe or something? Please don't stand on ceremony with me, sir, she said. Read your book if you want to. What are you reading now? Oh, Teddy!'

St James' Park receiving us—trees like mocking butlers. 'Miss Tess Grayson and Mr Grunt-and-Mumble'. Laburnum making yellow arches for our entry. And suddenly, her gentler mood.

'Dear Teddy—what's the matter?'

Then I wanted to cry—to tell her everything, at once, all that had been in my mind since we'd last met. I would do it! Yes, I would! Permitting no interruption, I would—

'Missed me?'

'Oh—!'

'Sometimes I don't know how I can bear to wait for the day to go. Sometimes—'

And then it was all right. Then we'd hold each other—and then silliness followed. The liberation, for the moment, seemed total. Laughter made a new world, of entirely proper scale, and it was all ease; all some extraordinary condition for which the only possible word was happiness. But so quickly it could be destroyed.

'What have you been doing today?'

And I would take it as if it were a quiz, some vital examination that I had to pass. The new chill of misery would make my answers stiff and priggish. And that happened because I was afraid it would happen.

'A funeral.'

'What? Don't mumble!'

'A funeral. Ugh! Why do people have to do that? Get it in the papers?'

What the Baptist minister had said about this, about going with my notebook to the houses of dying or dead, helped some of the time. It hadn't helped that day: there'd been the little front room, smelling of sorrow, and a bewildered woman with very red eyes. 'Yes, well, he was ever so well known round here.' Wringing her hands constantly inside her apron. Having to ask questions—his full name, his age, the jobs he'd done, the local organisations he'd—And she responding with such eagerness, in spurts of tearfulness and sudden dryness—at one point she'd even laughed, though I'd not been able to tell why. And this heavy, priggish feeling had come down upon me, surely it was priggish? This wonder that one could do this, that it could be done by this broken woman in the little room full of her husband's presence . . . And back at the office, Trout would ask: 'Got that death, then?'

All this I wanted to say to Tess, but fear that I would say it wrong made me leave out all that was really important, the woman's hands trembling and twining inside her apron, that unsteady alternation of tears and bright informativeness. And Tess said:

'You are so terribly superior! People *like* being in the papers!'

I hunched my shoulders and stared gloomily ahead, and Tess sighed and seized my hand and brought it to her breast.

'I do have to work hard to keep you cheerful, don't I?'

London the war had not yet stamped over! Such a demented geometry of roof and dome and spire! I thought the enormous accident of its composition could only be spoken of as perfect. Everything was perfect. Accident itself created perfection. It was a young feeling—amazed acceptance of the great world, suddenly discovered. Refusal to think it improveable!

Everything was perfect, and everything was breathtakingly related to everything else. A well-known concert pianist, for example, giving a recital at St Saviour's Church Hall, Crawley Park. Years before, it seemed, he'd been organist there. I trembled to see the great man walk on to the stage, real, touchable. He smiled, rather brusquely, in the direction of the audience; fiddled, frowning, with the piano stool; and then, for quite a long time, stared into the piano, as if making an inventory of its innards. Suddenly, driven into action by some invisible bully, he began to conjure, out of that beautiful object, the tumbling music of Schumann's *Etudes Symphoniques*. My heart melted, at once. Prospects of infinite, if very vague, happiness stretched before me. The music was Tess herself. Tess, running up to a knot of musical meaning, stayed a while to unravel the knot: then, free, ran away, to a tune that was . . . oh, was a sort of skipping, spinning, bright-eyed twisting and turning . . . and so down, down, to a gruffness, another matter of knots, a . . .

Going home, after one of those nights in London. As I walked from the bus, down the hill from Barton Church, there was the lightest of winds and an enormous moon. The trees seemed to be shrugging; there was the secret movement of a leaf—something like a sigh from inside a bush—

And the sky, enormously white and taut: as if it had only just been possible to pin its fabric down at the horizons.

Too much to see! Across the valley, something winked glassily, touched by moonlight . . .

My father came into the hall as I hung up my coat. 'What do you call this, then?'

'What do you mean?'

'What bloody hour of the night is this to come home?'

I could frame no answer, but shrugged helplessly, and turned towards the stairs.

'Hoi!—I want an explanation! When a boy of your age comes in halfway through the night, I want to know why. What have you been up to?'

Such a phrase! What was implied by being 'up to' something? I shook with despair and horror.

'I've been in London. I don't have to say. My own life—'

'It's not your own bloody life. You're still a child. I'm still responsible for you. And I can tell you something straightaway.

186

I'm not having a son of mine slinking about the streets with some slip of a girl—'

There was that burning flash inside me then, the rage that had no hope of expressing itself. Tess, so beautiful, so subtle— a slip of a girl! The man's delight in reducing anything fine to one of his disgusting phrases!

'I'll kill you!' I found myself shouting. 'I'll kill you! I'll kill you!'

The undertow of my life was plain hysteria, and I try to understand why this was so. Largely, I think, it sprang from my father's total, scathing and often raging scorn for everything I now unremarkably enjoyed and believed in. Much of what I read seemed an account of another form of life than my own —so different, it might have been on another planet. What could it be like to be of and among people who accepted litera- ture, music and the exchange of ideas as natural ingredients of existence? What could it be like *not* to be regarded as an idiot and airy poseur for embracing such things? ('He'll come to his senses, my dear!')

I could have left home? But I had no notion of how to flee. Forty years on, when the young are so mobile, it may be difficult to believe how *stuck* a nineteen-year-old could feel then. Ned wrote: 'Somehow—some time—I am sure we shall escape. Surely we two can do it. Meanwhile let us dream of islands. I live on dreams.' But when I thought of escape, I was smitten by what I saw as a craven sorrow for my parents. *Their* dreams were so apparent. They wanted me at hand, their visible son: the family circle, however groaningly, complete. I felt appallingly guilty for being the sort of son I was.

As a matter of habit, without discussion, after tea on Sundays chairs were drawn up round the table for cards. Oh, how I hated those games! I chafed against the loss of reading time. But I could not bring myself to ask to be counted out. When Tess said she could not understand this—her parents had long since ceased to count her *in* on anything—I replied with a quotation. 'Alas, though I agree in theory, My will, my will was born weary.' Nonsense! I now think. I was simply helplessly softhearted. It was what, years later, my father would tax me with: 'You're always so bloody tolerant!' Among my defects it was, I believe, for a warlike man of my father's stamp, even worse than my being an intellectual.

A cousin came visiting—a Cockney comic, in the style my father loved. He had an unforced gift for setting the table, and all else, in a roar; and I loved him, too. He removed my music from the piano, with music hall eyebrows raised—'Beeth Oven?' he cried, and 'Chopping?'—and played and sang the songs I remembered from the living room at Sutton Villas, when I was a child. All the uncles round the piano: 'One man went to mow' and 'Nine green bottles.' My father himself rendering his one and only piano piece: 'One finger one thumb kept moving . . .' Now, Billy caused my piano to yield up warm music of that kind, hammering happiness. My father sat singing, smiling, topping up the glass of beer that had been placed among the photos and the vases. The piano, unaccustomedly, shook. The house was, suddenly, amazingly content. I sat, trying to sing (oh my damned grammar school voice), and thinking, secretly desolate, that this was the son my father wished he'd had. This was the 'young life' he said the house was short of. It was all wrong. Why the devil couldn't he have the son he wanted? How could I have grown into such a hurt for him?

'This boy,' he said soon afterwards, 'misses all the best things in life.'

'Dick!'

'He's too high and mighty for ordinary little pleasures. I'm sorry for him . . . Nothing that ordinary people like. I'm really sorry for him.'

'Oh Dick!'

'No, my dear. Let him hear a few home truths. One day when he's missed all the best things in life he might remember what his ignorant old parents told him—'

'Don't worry,' I told my mother. 'I'm not here.'

'You're not all there, you mean,' said my father in a brisk parenthesis. 'You see, my dear, it's all that bloody school—that blasted *New Statesman*—'

'And the *London Mercury*,' I said.

'Cheap comments,' my father told the ceiling. 'Wisecracks. Sits about in his oldest clothes and talks like an old man. He's jumped twenty years, that boy. He'll have no young days to look back on.'

'Damn damn damn,' I cried, and rushed from the room.

'If you've got no answer, run away,' shouted my father.

'Oh Dick, not on a Saturday,' my mother cried : having, I had time to reflect in my rage, added the sacredness of Saturdays to her lifelong, hopeless invention of grounds for domestic peace . . .

It was a trap; and, like Ned, I could only dream. Hysterically . . .

In any case, athwart any attempt to imagine escape lay the certainty of war. The oddest sensation of those years was to feel so doubtlessly that soon things would explode, soon our world would be the world of H. G. Wells' *Shape of Things to Come*; and to be faced with the daily denial of this inevitability by so many kinds of authority. 'There will be no war this year or next,' my father's *Daily Express* proclaimed : a statement which seemed positively pessimistic alongside his own prophecies . . . or characteristic refusal to declare himself at all . . .

As the war came closer, my father grew more briskly contemptuous of any attempt to discuss what was happening. 'I've got one stock answer,' he told Mrs Pratt, from two doors up. 'It'll all blow over in a week. They can't argue then.'

'But surely,' said Mrs Pratt, 'it's very worrying, isn't it? I mean, things are quite nasty, aren't they? In the paper Major Attlee says—'

'Major Attlee!' My father barked his amazement at the utterance of this name. 'Who the devil's Major Attlee?' He laughed so long over this question that Mrs Pratt seemed to conclude that information was really being sought.

'Well, he's—'

'What does anyone know? They're all guessing. They have to say something. Does Hitler tell Major Attlee what he's got in mind?'

'Well—' Mrs Pratt was astonished. 'One can't help thinking—'

'*I* can help thinking,' said my father. 'Very easily. What do I want to think for? I've got better things to do.'

'But surely you've got ideas about it?'

'Look' said my father, unfolding and refolding a newspaper in order, perhaps, to provide an example of those better things he had to do. 'If people had fewer ideas and kept their own noses clean and got on with their work, we'd all be

189

better off. *Ideas*!' He transferred his scorn to the entire operation of the human intellect. 'Why should I bother to have ideas? Who would pay any attention to my ideas? Is Mr Chamberlain going to knock at the front door and ask what ideas I've got?'

'A charming picture,' I murmured.

My father glared at the pile of books on the arm of my chair. 'You know where ideas take you,' he said, as if the argument had come, at last, into port. 'Sitting around on your—'

'Dick!'

'Never going out. Scribbling in exercise books. Trying to score points over your elders.'

Mrs Pratt laughed nervously.

'I just thought you might have a point of view,' she said.

My father rose and made for the door.

'What I have at the moment,' he said, laughing with determined coarseness, 'is a—'

'Dick!'

'—strong desire for a Jimmy Riddle.'

6

If I had no clear idea of the manner and means—and destination—of my ultimate escape, it was Tess who, for the moment, was escape itself—the precarious, precious device that, when I was with her, floated me free from Barton and Crawley Hill. Her hand in mine, I murmured:

'Lay your sleeping head, my love,
Human on my faithless arm . . .'

'Oh,' said Tess. 'That's lovely. Who wrote that?'

'W. H. Auden,' I said. Then, truly floating, I chanted:

'Never mind, my darling. Nothing matters but sleep. Save you, and me, and sleep—all the rest will keep.'

'Auden?'

'No. Lawrence. There are so many lovely poems about . . . sleeping with someone. There's—'

That twist of her mouth that meant she was amused in some manner I could not fathom. 'You're full of other people's words, aren't you?'

It wasn't till later, brooding over my memory of the evening, that I was hurt by this. Now I said: 'Oh, other people's words . . . They become *our* words, don't they? I mean, isn't that what poetry is? I mean—'

Tess sighed. 'I love the way you're excited by words. You mustn't think I don't.'

'Oh,' I said. In my later brooding I wondered if I had not been complacent at this point. 'I don't see how one could really . . . grasp what one feels without the help of as many—'

Tess said: 'I'm not a poem.'

I was puzzled. But then she said: 'You haven't kissed me for at least ten minutes.' Gladly dutiful, I took the hint; and when I'd done, and we'd walked tipsily and in silence for some time, she told me, very business-like and practical, a story about some incident in her working day. Young Starbuck, she'd surely told me about *him*, a regular visitor to the studio, had—in the middle of a session—pinched her bottom. The studio had been busy and dark at the time—but she was fairly certain it was Starbuck. 'I slapped his face.'

'You did?'

'No. Of course I didn't. He'd have enjoyed that—don't you see? I didn't give him that pleasure.'

I was interested but felt substantially detached. Of course it must be difficult for Tess, from time to time, in a darkened studio. This Starbuck was evidently a . . . He was obviously a playboy, a superficial fellow. Fancy being in Tess's company and simply wanting to pinch her—

I found myself unready to think of any part of Tess in such gross terms as were suggested by the word 'bottom.'

Later, in my brooding, I felt uneasy. Were there signals Tess was making that I did not understand?

But the uncertainty was swept away in a flood of tenderness. If only we were together, in some bed, in some . . . cottage perhaps, and nothing mattered between us but ourselves, and sleep . . .

I had this total dread of failing to understand people. At times it has struck me that the roots of this might have lain in that early film-going experience: in those scenes when *he* left in the highest moral dudgeon, slamming the door or cruelly pricking the sides of his horse, while *she* flung herself against the door or onto the ground; the pianist in the pit wringing out of our withers the very last drops of . . . whatever is wrung out of withers. I couldn't bear the idea that I might have been guilty of some massive misapprehension of this kind. It gave all my serious relationships a quality of anxiety if not anguish; to which, I guess, my victims might well have preferred some plain manly breakdown of sympathy . . .

Daphne, in the office, was different. Dammit—why was Daphne different? A few hours after that exchange with Tess, there Daphne was, bending over the wastepaper basket. I believed she did this more often than was natural even for a secretary. There was a froth of underwear: the button securing her skirt at the back was under such strain that I half expected it to cry out. She turned and straightened up, her breasts amazingly active. 'Mr B!' she cried. I thought her voice was full of reproof. 'Good Lord,' I responded helplessly. 'I've mislaid an invoice,' she said; and I fled, not daring to examine the remark. For some reason, I had lost all power to understand what an invoice was.

There were times when I longed to be Tim Fish. He was the *Standard's* advertising manager. Tall and brash, he had a wide mouth through which laughter, usually very loud, burst in helpless floods. Sometimes the outer office rocked with noise: Tim's laughter, Daphne's high giggles, F. R. Gibson's shouted amazements. 'Got that half page from the draper's, then?' 'Look here,' Tim would guffaw. 'They need tickling. They need bringing round to it, see. Don't worry. I'm working on them.' Usually it was Daphne he seemed to be tickling. If F.R's broad back was turned, Tim might be diving for the zip on her jumper. 'Oh, *Mr Fish*!' 'Eh?' F.R. would roar. 'What's that?' 'Trouble with your typing, dear?' Tim would bellow, leaning over her shoulder and looking boldly down at the happy heaving of her breasts. 'That ad,' F.R. would shout. 'You want to get a grip on things. You don't want them to slip out of it.' 'Well, yes and no.' And Tim's laughter and Daphne's giggles would halt Mr Trout in his Jottings, in the office beyond. 'There are men trying to work in here,' he'd call. F.R. would slam the door open. 'What are *you* shouting about?' The two would glare at each other with the astonishment, never resolved, that was so characteristic of affairs under the *Standard's* roof. 'A madhouse,' Mr Trout would mumble. F.R's voice would gather unbelievable resonance. 'Got page five ready, then?'

I thought it was a gift: this ability, demonstrated by Tim Fish and Daphne, to take sex lightly. A magical and unimaginable gift! They must be so healthy and competent, to be able to ride those waves of lust and passionate inquisitiveness under which I came, so often, so close to being drowned. My amazement was capped when, one day, Tim Fish told me he was engaged.

'Well,' he said, 'my young lady is always at me to find a better job.' He'd come into the office at lunch and found me alone—with my bar of chocolate and my Penguin. It was my usual lunch those days: twopence for the chocolate, sixpence for the Penguin. This was the first conversation we'd ever had, face to face and with no one else present. I was surprised by the quiet way Tim talked, the absence of laughter and jokes. It seemed to me that I had a sobering, even a depressing effect on people. When I was the sole audience, the music hall stopped. 'I ought to look for something in Fleet Street, she says.' Tim made a face. 'I suppose I will, in the end. But I like a small place. I'm not very ambitious, really.'

'Your young lady?' Had I sounded too amazed?

'We've been engaged a couple of years now. Nice kid!' I tried to imagine myself talking to a near-stranger about Tess in terms of such detached and modest appreciation. 'A bit of a pusher, though. Oh, she's right, I guess. Chaps like me want a bit of a—a bit of a kick up the backside, now and then. I'll get round to it, in the end.'

I struggled with the desire to ask Tim how, being engaged, he could justify his activities with respect to Daphne, and especially to the zips that offered such . . . I thought, trembling, of those curiously easy entrances to the warm contents of

Daphne's skirts and blouses. How could you divide yourself into the legal man and the illegal . . . the promised and the forsworn?

'You're not going steady?' Tim asked. And when I shook my head—with Tess it was a going terribly unsteady, wasn't it?—Tim said: 'Won't be long, I imagine, in your case. You seem, if I may say so, a . . . sentimental sort of chap.'

He placed a hand, suddenly avuncular, on my shoulder, and then was gone, into the outer office. There was an expectant shriek from Daphne. Tim's helpless laughter. Then, for some time, a species of murmuring, which made me tremble with the certainty—as I attempted to resume my reading of George Moore—that Daphne's expectations were being totally realised.

'. . . and *The Church Gazette*,' said Dobson. 'We might as well add that title, you know. How Trout can give a column to that old bore Blossom, I don't know.'

It was true that much space in the *Standard* was taken up with the reporting of sermons. Trout attached great importance to parsons as spokesmen of the community. Weekly they attacked the human scene as if, I used to think, it had been some awfully diluted Sodom and Gomorrah. They were opposed to the latest fashions, the frivolity of youth, the defilement of the English language by American idioms. The Rev. Charles Blossom, Vicar of St Andrews, had been seized, on his latest appearance in the pulpit, by a diffuse rage directed at the cinema. The invention of film, he conceded, was a mark of human ingenuity and to be praised (if in a rather bothered fashion); but the use of film to spread disturbing notions about matrimony, and to glamorise crime, was deplorable. He was not given to filmgoing himself, but one couldn't help knowing about these things. Trout had headed the column: HOLLYWOOD BAD INFLUENCE, SAYS REV BLOSSOM. 'That'll bring Sam Goldwyn to his knees,' Dobson groaned.

There was one parson, however, who was not in Mr Trout's good books. The Rev. Adrian Rawson was, in a mixture of roles I never understood, both clergyman and journalist. Long, very thin, pitchblack in dress, he carried an umbrella that seemed to have no connection with the weather: its use was to mark the punctuation of his speeches. He came into the office with scraps of tenuous information, rarely related

194

to life in Crawley Hill; releasing them in a series of riddles.

'Guess,' he teased an irritated Mr Trout, 'who I ran into at the Club yesterday?' 'I'm sure I don't know,' snapped Mr Trout. 'A distinguished and provocative figure.' 'Oh yes.' 'I put a question to him. At once.' 'Who was it, then?' Mr Trout made the stem of his pipe seesaw alarmingly between his teeth. 'No less a person than Dr Buchman.' 'Dr Who?' 'Dr Buchman, my dear fellow.' 'I'm not with you.' Mr Trout began tearing up paper, savagely. 'The founder of the Oxford Group. The inventor of Moral Re-armament.' 'Oh—him!' 'I said'— here Rawson raised his umbrella to trace the quotation marks in the air—' "What, Dr Buchman, is your dynamic?" ' Mr Trout drew in irritated breath as the point of the umbrella sketched out the question mark close to his nose. '*What* was his *what*?' 'What was his *dynamic*!' Indicating the exclamation, Rawson struck the electric-light shade hanging over the editorial desk. 'Oh damn it!' growled Mr Trout. 'Do you know what he replied?' 'I haven't the faintest idea!' 'He said : "My dynamic is God!" A striking answer, don't you think?' 'I've got this column to finish before lunch,' said Mr Trout, returning with noisy emphasis to his typewriter.

Rawson seemed unaware of the bad temper caused by these intrusions. 'An excellent answer, don't you think, young man?' he now said, turning to me. 'I'm afraid I'm not . . . enthusiastic about the Oxford Group,' I mumbled. 'A rather memorable encounter,' said Rawson, smiling contentedly . . .

My own rage against weekly journalism continued to collect round Mr Trout's weekly column. 'The Jotter! The Old Hen would be more suitable,' I told my diary. 'How he scratches for items of unimportance in this mean old farmyard of Crawley Hill! And makes it an excuse never to do the most mildly irksome job of reporting!'

It was a fact that Mr Trout made a comfortable and virtually continuous occupation out of his column. Creating thick weather for himself with his pipe, he'd heap it together over the week; one stolid paragraph after another. Dobson said the Jottings were to the *Standard* as a ton of lead might be to a sailing dinghy. 'One day he'll send us to the bottom,' he grumbled.

Mr Trout seemed to become ever more polysyllabic. 'Crawley Hill citizens,' he'd begin, 'will have jubilated over

the intelligence that one of our most distinguished lumin-
aries . . .'

'These bloody words,' Mr Chubb would groan in the printing works, his tweezers hovering irascibly over a tray of type.
Chubb was the foreman, a man of sad disposition. For a
printer he was oddly hostile to words, at the best of times.
He'd slam them together, muttering to himself.

I spent a lot of time in the printery. It was like passing from
the genteel banalities of the saloon bar to the muscular
candours of the public bar. I had a special liking for one of
the linotype operators, Jim Hackett, bald, donnish—a sort of
down-to-earth don. Jim was a man of wit whose letters,
though I seemed to be the only person to know this, were the
most stylish ever to appear in our correspondence columns:
which they did under a pseudonym. Sitting, tapping gently
away in the arbour where his machine stood, he was always
ready with an amusing verbal antidote to any fatigue or fury
I felt. Return, perhaps, from a particularly painful funeral;
or from a long and depressing tour of the families of those
who'd been married at the weekend; or from the weekly
visit to the fire stations, or the police stations, or the many
vicarages and manses; or from police court, or the ratings
tribunal, or a flower show; and Jim was the man to take your
headache to. Among his other qualities, he knew the background to everything. He knew about F. R. Gibson and the
secretary before Daphne (F. R. Gibson!); he knew how Mr
Trout knew about F. R. Gibson and the secretary before
Daphne (a matter of keyholes—Mr Trout!); he knew about
Major Plaice, of the West Green Police Court, and Cr. Mrs
Dunstable. (Major Plaice! Cr. Mrs Dunstable!) I, always ready
to suppose that life was all foreground—for all my literary
sophistication and my growling diary, so anxious by temperament to think that people were as blameless as they presented
themselves—was constantly amazed by these conducted trips
that Jim took me on, behind the scenes. I see myself as constantly engaged, in that clicking little arbour of the linotype
(however animated the conversation, Jim's fingers were never
still), in the utterance of amazements. He! She! They! Mr
Dobson! Mr Chubb! The Rev. Adrian Rawson!

How astonishing the background always was!

Horribly, I'd find I was there myself—in the shady background of things.

'Saw you with your girl last night,' said F. R. Gibson.

'Oh.'

'Hiding in a doorway, you were. Didn't think you were like that. Thought you only read books. Eh?'

He wanted to be answered. I felt very foolish.

'Ah.'

'There he was, in a doorway,' said F.R., raising his voice for the sake of Mr Trout, who was frowning over his typewriter.

'In a doorway,' said Trout, looking up and nodding vacantly.

'With a girl,' said F.R.

'Oh,' said Trout. 'With a girl.' He pointed to me. 'Him?'

'I tell you,' said F.R. 'In a doorway, last night. With his girl. Dark hair.'

'Oh,' said Daphne at the door. 'Really. Mr B!'

'Yes, him,' said F.R., whirling round. 'In a doorway.'

'Ah,' I said.

'What was he *doing* in the doorway?' whispered Daphne, archly.

'Eh? Doing?' shouted F.R. 'Dark hair she had. Thought he only read books.'

'Only young once,' sighed Mr Trout, his frown hideously deepening.

'Oh, Mr Trout!' said Daphne, as if the editor had propounded some particularly disgraceful notion.

'Well, I saw you,' said F.R.

'Yes,' I said.

'She's got lots of blokes,' said F.R.

'Who *is* she?' asked Mr Trout, with sudden irritation.

'You know her. Thingummy's daughter. He's a big chap. Council. Regular order for visiting cards.'

'I know her?' asked Mr Trout.

'Nelson. Bilson. Grayson,' said F.R.

Mr Trout whistled. 'Oh, that young lady,' he said.

'Lots of young fellows,' said F.R. He turned to me. 'Didn't you know?'

I, at that moment, knew nothing. It wasn't happening, this torture by unfinished sentences. What were they talking about? *Who* were they talking about? If they were talking

197

about Tess, how dared they? Even by being part of their consciousness she was desecrated. They couldn't think of a pretty girl without supposing her to be vulgarly surrounded by suitors. What awful rubbish it all was! Why did I feel so weak?

I smiled feebly.

'Has a regular young chap. Very fond of him, I believe,' said F.R. 'Didn't you know? Want to be careful, young man.'

'Might be trouble,' said Daphne.

'I expect he knows what he's doing,' said Mr Trout. He wasn't interested; and the Jottings were being held up.

'Ah, well. I saw you. Watch out,' said F.R.

He rushed through the door and instantly rushed back. 'Big fellow. Her regular,' he said. He sketched out a blow in my direction. Mr Trout, not looking up from his machine, said : 'Starbuck's boy. String of garages. Starbuck's Motors.'

'Go on!' cried F.R. His fist hung suddenly in mid-air, its facetious gesture uncompleted. 'That lot? Money coming out of their ears . . . Didn't know it! My! my! *That's* who he is! Knew he was a big chap! Didn't know it was one of *them*!'

He turned his fist into an open hand, and let it fall on my shoulder. As usual, he expressed dismay by pretending total collapse. His big shoulders abandoned all pretence of shape. He sank his head. Even Mr Trout, though he did not look up, held his hands clear of the keys and stared at some point high on his manuscript. Then F.R. breathed : 'My! my!' very softly, very elegaically, squeezed my shoulder and slow-marched from the room.

Mr Trout was typing again. 'Done all the parsons yet?' he inquired, out of the frowning depths of his preoccupation. I didn't answer. From all participation in everyday life I was suddenly cut off as if by deep freezing. I went out of the room and was in the printery and moving towards the lavatory; and I had no sensation of contact with door or floor. From the limply clacking linotype, Jim Hackett looked up and raised his eyebrows; but I passed him and went into the lavatory and locked myself in.

I stared out of the window. North London lurched this way and that, a landscape out of control. It was as if my eye had lost all power of seeing horizontals. A bus changed gear over the roofs and beyond, in the Circus; and it sounded like Tess's

laughter. Like what might hideously lie within Tess's laughter
—a mocking ridicule . . .

Starbuck! Well, Starbuck was a common enough name . . .
But it wasn't, was it? . . . But then some people might accidentally be beset with Starbucks. Casual visitors to their
place of work, who pinched their bottoms; casual . . .

Jim Hackett outside the door. 'I say! When you groan, do
keep your voice down! It's causing Mr Chubb to feel more
depressed than ever!' Then, speaking lower: 'If you're in
trouble, old chap, why don't you come out and talk about it?'

7

Starbuck? How funny, said Tess. Her mother had been talking
about him, only the day before. Well, they did talk about him,
so boringly, from time to time. There was this ridiculous idea
that they ought to get married, because they'd known each
other all their lives. 'Our daddies are as thick as thieves. Pay
attention to that word "thieves". Oh, you wouldn't understand.
I'm so glad you don't understand. You see, if I married little
Georgie Starbuck . . .'

She laughed, and all the furniture of my mind was scattered.
When she talked like this, I didn't know where anything was
in my head.

'Fancy even listening to what they say about little Georgie
Starbuck.' The word 'little' seemed to fascinate her . . .
Suddenly she took my hand, brought it up to her mouth; and
bit the fleshy base of my thumb. 'Are you sorry?'

Oh yes. *That* was proof of her innocence, or rather of my
folly: it seemed quite amazing proof. Trout, F.R.,—even Jim
Hackett, who'd whistled a little when I told my story—all
shallow fools! The music began again in my head and I tucked
my astonished hand away, preparing to demonstrate my re-
pentance on any scale required.

199

My father's rage at my association with Tess, based partly, it seemed, on the principle that lovers should never meet after dusk, was always ready to break out. It did so once when Aunt Ada was on a visit.

The old lady had brought her little bottle of whisky with her; and now, having taken her nightcap, sat blatantly marking the level with, I noticed, an indelible pencil.

'At this time of the year, Dickie, the gentry will be going to Madeira.'

'I suppose so,' said my father, who was frowning over her head. I shut my eyes and saw the gentry taking off obediently at Aunt Ada's hint, in a small fleet: the ghost of Lady Parsons at their head.

'It's the Labour people that's the trouble now, Dickie, isn't it? They're rather against the Conservatives, aren't they?'

My father clearly preparing the phrases he would use when she'd gone to bed. 'The bloody nerve of that old lady . . .' But I knew the family habit of double-think would take over, changing the nature of my father's comments in mid-rage. 'You have to hand it to the old girl. Always been careful. Makes you wonder what she's got stowed away in that flat of hers . . . All our family have been the same. Characters, all of them.'

'This Hitler. He was only a housepainter, you know, Dickie. I've nothing against painters, but it isn't right, the way he's throwing his weight about.'

'That's true enough, Auntie. All noise, though.'

'I've got a Red living below me, Dickie. Well, I avoid him. Yes. He's a rank socialist . . . a rank socialist . . . Oh, I don't know what your grandfather would have thought. He never held with that sort of thing . . . And Lady Parsons would *not* have cared for it.'

'They're all noise, Auntie, all of them.'

'But don't you think, Dickie—?'

'I don't think, Auntie. Why should I? I've got other things to do.'

'Will you put my medicine away for me, Dickie . . . ? And what about Teddy, now? Someone said he was courting.'

'Courting?' My father laughed with noisy bitterness. 'That's an old-fashioned word, Auntie. It's not like when I and my brothers were young, you know. Or when you were young.

If I'd gone slinking round the streets with slips of girls . . .'

'I'm going to bed,' I said, marvelling at the operations of my father's censor. What fantasies of courteous, chaperoned wooing were about to be aired? 'Goodnight, Auntie.'

'I know what my father would have said if I'd come sneaking in at all hours of the night,' he said, raising his voice as if he were making music for me to climb the stairs to. Ah yes, music, I thought, as I heard my mother cry 'Shush, Dick!', Aunt Ada clear her throat to make way for some statement of Lady Parsons' disapproval, and my father's voice rise higher and higher in the key suggested by his sarcastic purposes.

There was an undeclared war between Mr Trout and Dobson in which, to my surprise, I was Mr Trout's supporter.

The editor had the illusion that Crawley Hill was a vastly more important area of the world than it really was; and that he knew far more about it than he actually did. And he was so eager to keep news from his rivals that he had come to regard the most trivial piece of information as an awful secret.

I grew friendly at one time with Dingle of the *Monmouth Park Gazette*, who was of my own age, had large round innocent eyes and a view of our occupation so comic, so tending to cause him to collapse with laughter, that often one knew only that . . . he thought everything extremely funny. That's to say, he would be seized by laughter, grabbed and bullied by it, and would lean against anything that offered, a lamp-post or a wall or, at worst, a passing stranger, and shake with helpless guffaws and giggles. A word or phrase would surface: 'old Temple' (that was *his* editor): 'the Rev. Dawson.' The Rev. Dawson had a habit, when we went to him for news of his parish, of the strangest elation combined with a belief that we needed quite elementary assistance with our note-making. 'Then,' he would cry, at dictation speed, 'the Rev. Dawson spent the rest of the morning among his mums! Buns and prayers, buns and prayers! The buns by Mrs Stokesley—that's l-e-y—and her noble helpers! The prayers by the Rev. Dawson.' He would pause for thought. 'The incumbent went on to address, two d's, two s's, the Youth Group. Subject, most deeply explored, most *deeply* explored, the Power of Prayer. Capital p, capital p. That was Wednesday. Don't forget the 'd' in Wednesday. On Thursday . . .'

Because Dingle and I together were capable of behaving very badly—that's to say, we made each other laugh in totally unsuitable circumstances, and especially in the Rev. Dawson's study at the vicarage—'You *are* lively fellows,' he'd say, and we'd feel dreadful—such a kindly man!—because of this, we rationed the number of occasions when we joined up to cover our common beat. But Mr Trout held that we should *never* work together. How could we hope for *exclusive* news if we were not exclusive? 'I say,' he'd complain. 'It's unethical, you know.' It was not the word for my working association with Dingle. 'Better say,' I once murmured, 'that it's a little bit childish.' 'Glad you see that,' said Mr Trout, gloomily. 'Life's not a joke, you know.' It wasn't; which was one reason for that appalling amusement in which Dingle and I were involved. Under his laughter Dingle, who was to die at Dunkirk, had a horrified feeling for the way the decade was marching towards unspeakable disaster.

But Mr Trout too—and though in my young way I raged against him as a dullard and a trivialiser, I knew this—was a kindly man. To Dobson, he was an anachronism. He damped down Dobson's more brutal headlines. He modified Dobson's more dramatic language. He did not care for the senior reporter's opening paragraphs in his news from the courts. These were often little vignettes : of some black-clad old lady trembling in the dock as she admitted to some aberration—theft from a shop, perhaps, the lapse of a personality crumbling in old age. She'd be there, in Dobson's words, a crude little portrait : her tears, her shivers. Mr Trout's instinct was against this personalising of a wretched report of a wretched event. He preferred a story to begin : 'At Crawley Hill Police Court on Friday, Mrs Ellen Smith, aged 67, pleaded guilty to stealing a tin of soup, valued at ninepence, from a shop in the Circus . . .' 'Boring!' Dobson would exclaim. 'She cried in the dock! That's where you begin! A human story! Life! Colour!' But Dobson, too, was more often kindly than not. There was—it seemed to me that it easily came about as a reporter's career developed—a dissociation between his private qualities, and his professional ones.

'Let's face it—we're newshawks,' Dobson would say. I did not think the term accounted for any of us. We did not sweep majestically down on a story; rather we were newsworms, slowly making holes in the vast lawn of news. Or news-moths, perhaps, champing away in some small corner of the immense woollen pullover of the news . . .

Mr Trout's great modesty was in respect of local drama or music. He was ill at ease with both. Forced to attend a concert, he would worry over the opening of his report. His usual solution was to consult his dictionary of quotations. There should be, he felt, something a little highflown to begin with. ' "If music be the food of love, play on" ', he once wrote. 'This was amply demonstrated at St Andrew's Hall on Thursday evening . . .'

One dangerous consequence was that he rarely gave proper editorial attention to the pieces I wrote about drama or music. I was once or twice in trouble for using phrases to which the amateur artists concerned, sometimes very justly, took exception. 'Mr Tring,' I wrote, 'in this performance of *Out, Brief Candle*, seemed to rely entirely on his moustache to suggest villainy.' That was fair comment: but it was not in the bland style expected of the *Standard*. There were letters to the editor. It was much worse when I wrote a report of a concert by a local orchestra. Amazed by the shapeless sounds they made, I suggested that these resembled someone's attempt to walk about without his bones. There were more letters to the editor, who said: 'I don't think this sort of thing does us any good. Just tone it down, old chap, will you?'

F. R. Gibson said: 'See they're writing to complain about this young man. Good. That's good, see. Draws attention.'

Which made Dobson swear under his breath.

Of course, I think now my father might have sensed that Tess was more than his unworldly fool of a son could manage . . .

The woods. Between the *Standard* office and Crawley Hill police court were these quite famous woods, which had been thinned and abbreviated and generally tidied until the word 'woods' seemed far too shaggy a term for them. Fifty years before one of England's most excitingly melancholy poets wrote about the thinning of those woods. He could now, he said, see from his window the red flannel petticoats drying on washing lines in the road on the further side. I was angry about all this, in my diary, as if it had been the work of my father and Mr Trout and F. R. Gibson and Percy Chew, pursuing a common campaign against foliage. But to walk through the woods, after police court, was the best experience I ever had in Crawley Hill. Especially after rain : when the water lying on the roof of leaves gradually dropped to the ground, a drawl of rain. Or when rain was actually falling, and the leaves gleamed with it, and bubbles popped up on the surface of puddles, like the floating rounded hats of drowning men . . .

Through the woods I raged, sometimes, taking the opportunity of their privacy to name the objects of my rage aloud. I remember about this time stumping along the paths, crying again and again 'Oh dammit father! dammit father!': and coming face to face with one of the most enchanting women I've ever seen only once. She was beautiful, dark, a gently proud face, and she was astonished; and I was horrified. And so we passed . . .

But I believe that, with my father, this business of Tess and me was largely a matter of respectability again. In yet another department of life I was thwarting his wish to have his offspring totally respectable. It was like my growing another beard, but this time to my waist.

I'd abandoned the first beard: too exhausting, one's very face being a political issue.

8

Politics was a curious rage inside, collecting to itself all my other rages. I went to see a man who'd come back, broken, from service in Spain with the International Brigade. He was young, very thin, and lay on a couch in a house on one of the local estates. He apologised for the sickly smell that came from his leg, intricately smashed, cased in a hard, grubby tube of dressing. Medical aid had been rough-and-ready, and he'd never use his leg again. It might have to come off. He talked with a stunned fierceness of those battlegrounds—so that he seemed still to be there. He *was* still there, he said—the days in that drab room in Crawley Hill had no reality. At night he woke from bombardments that were altogether out of control —the whole world turned to a whining of shells, the thump and cruel crash of shells landing. 'I think the world's gone mad,' he said.

Mr Trout fidgeted with my account of this visit. 'We don't want to make a hero of him,' he mumbled. 'I think he *is* a hero,' I said. 'They don't have to go,' said Mr Trout. I shrank from the piece I'd written, though it was warmly done and Mr Trout, in the end, barely altered it. ('Well, I suppose there are lots of people down on the estate who'll know the fellow,' he said, grudgingly.) It seemed deeply wrong that the nightmare among the orange groves should feed the torpid columns of the *Standard*.

Tess said : 'You'd never last a moment in Spain, my dear.' Then, when she saw the misery in my face : 'Oh, that's not an awful thing to say. Really it isn't. You'd be so . . . You'd break down at once. You couldn't stand it. You're not thick-skinned enough.' 'That chap wasn't thick-skinned,' I said, re-belliously. 'But Teddy—just to go there, he must have had something—Oh! He must have had something you haven't got. Now, don't sulk!' I wasn't sulking. Or I didn't think I was. I was simply dejected—trying to grapple with monstrous ideas about the relationship between one's beliefs and one's power to act on them.

Did life mean me simply to be a clown on the everlasting touchline of things? But how did one ever come to believe that one was *involved*?

In one of the accepted uses of the word, Hugh Cramm, a reporter on our rival, the *West Green Weekly*, was involved. He was a member of the Communist Party. That gave him, I saw, a curious confidence. When the rest of us talked politi-cally, Hugh smiled—a pleasant smile, but without humour. He was like an expert listening to amateurs talking naïvely about his specialism. He was always able to refer any point of discussion to some trim, rigid, impervious structure of doctrine. We others talked raggedly, trying to invent principles; his principles had long existed, complete, hard as rock—a range of mountain peaks. They were there, established, confirmed, their position fixed by massive exploration and map-making. Oh, the rest of us floundered about, trying to make some sort of political footing for ourselves, and he was absolutely in place, his whereabouts quite certain.

'I wish I could take the roof off the Kremlin and see and hear what's going on inside,' said Dingle, from the *Monmouth Park Gazette*.

'But how unnecessary,' said Hugh. 'Even if you won't read the literature that will answer your questions, you could work out for yourself exactly what must be in the Soviet mind.'

'Good Lord,' said Dingle. 'I'm not even sure that I'd like to be able to do that. If life ever became so mechanical . . .'

Hugh smiled, and turned his smile, as increasingly he seemed to do, on me.

'Someone of your seriousness . . .' he once told me. 'I think I know a man capable of commitment when I see him. I hope you're giving it proper thought. I'm sure you are.'

He invited me to tea. Hugh was living, with his newly-married wife, in one big room in a terrace of houses on one of the hills tumbling out of the Circus. 'Come and meet Olive and let's talk things over. Then we'll go down and see what's happening at headquarters.'

It was a tidy room—much like Hugh's mind, I thought; only such furniture as was necessary—no bric-à-brac at all—and a few shelves of what was plainly 'the literature.' The oddity was Olive. She was thin, nervous, exciteable. No tidiness there, of mind or appearance. She spoke with sudden excitements and glooms. 'Oh, Hughie, there's no tea, we've run out of tea, why is there no tea?' There were no fullstops in her talk—everything hung to everything else by commas, at the most. 'The tea, my dear,' said Hugh gently, 'is still in your shopping bag. Remember?' Her wildly bright eyes darkened. 'Why don't I ever remember such things? Why have I such an awful memory, Hughie?' Hugh shrugged, and I half-expected him to draw for an explanation on his habitual vocabulary—so much like huge building blocks, every statement a verbal fortress. 'In the shopping bag, dear'—for in her gloom she seemed to have forgotten what it was all about. From her thin sallow shoulders the straps of her dress seemed about to slip. I tried not to look at her small breasts, very visible as her dress made its constant attempt to fall away from her. 'Oh yes. In the shopping bag.' Her body, as she went from the room, had a loose, helplessly immodest obviousness, and I was dismayed by the wishes that formed within me. Were they wishes? They were the sketches of acts so possible that I seemed half to perform them : touching her where those candid limbs met, making myself as loose and spidery as she was and winding myself about her. She would look startled, if I did that, but would not resist me. Nothing about her body—which her dress tried uselessly to clothe—suggested resistance . . . She would submit to me, with a wild vagueness—talking, as she did so, of other things . . .

I did not understand myself in these matters at all—where was the patience I felt when I was with Tess?

Hugh was saying: 'I have to go and do my duty—selling the *Worker*. Sorry. Replacing a sick comrade. Be back in an hour. Sit and read. Olive will keep you plied with tea.' And I felt weak with disloyalty. What I'd picked up, surely, from the air was the still-new physical excitement of their marriage! How bad to have forced my way into that, even in thought!

Olive kept me plied with tea, certainly. There was a looseness about that, as about everything she did. Her talk was poured out, too, teacups of talk with slopping saucers. The flat, her family, Hugh's family. And the Party. Hugh was important to it, she said—to the local branch. He sold more *Workers* than anyone. 'Everyone says what discipline he has.' She poured out that praise, and at once followed it with : 'I wish there were . . . I wish we had a little time to ourselves. It's sometimes . . .'

I wondered how Hugh could have wooed and wedded someone so, in every respect, gangling; so insecurely locked together, mind and body. Olive was a comrade, too; but how could she ever hold that stern doctrine inside her? In choosing her, part of Hugh must surely have elected for disorder, even derangement? Weren't there forces at work here not to be explained by his adamantly reasoned philosophy?

Oh God. What was this, now? So my sense of the unaccountability of persons was to prevent me from adopting a consistent view of the political world? I was to resist communism because communists were, on the edges of their lives —oh no, in the private centres of their lives—as mysterious and blind as anyone else? But Hugh held that everything could be explained by reference to doctrine. How follow a man who was unaware of the untidy and inconsistent essence of his existence?

When Hugh returned, we went to the local party headquarters. It was an evening of relaxation, Hugh said. A member, a professional tenor, sang . . . Schubert. He prefaced his recital with a reference to Schubert's position among the bourgeoisie, and to the role of *lieder* as beguilements provided for this class in nineteenth century Vienna. 'With their individualistic self-indulgences, their romantic extravagances of what they were pleased to call love, they rode on the backs of the toiling masses.' He spoke with a smile and concluded by saying that, all the same, these were songs of great loveliness; and one should be ready, especially on a Saturday evening, to take pleasure even when it sprang from the gifts of men who'd served the luxurious needs of a discredited class . . . But I sulked inside, as I listened.

The communist smile, I thought (and was not pleased by the thought), hardly covered all these . . . all these vital untidinesses . . .

It was 1939. 'Someone,' said Ned, 'has only got to say boo, and Europe will blow itself to pieces.'

Is it possible to write temperately about the run-up to the Second World War? It was curiously horrible—unlike anything that has happened since, however awful—because it seemed a matter of one's own world trying to legitimise, as neighbours, the inmates of a lunatic asylum. Well, no, not an asylum. The lunatics had taken over: obscenely sick, they had the keys, the run of the wards; all the doctors were dead or deposed. Methodically they were exterminating those who were incurably sane, making mad those who had a mere ordinary grasp of sanity. The world was fast becoming a dream inside the head of a psychopath.

Oddly, 1938 was worse than 1939. I suppose it may have been because the first taste of a supreme horror can be more frightful than any repetition. Or perhaps it was that in 1939, horror was eased by the sheer matter-of-factness of war actually being declared. The first was a nightmare one woke from—blearily, with deeply ashamed relief; on the second occasion one turned out to have been awake all the time. Something like that.

Over our time in the sixth form at school, the inevitability of war had hung. It may have been partly why I was such a wretched student. The path ahead was already erupting. Many of our discussions among ourselves made the rawest possible use of terms now almost bland with long employment. One of these was 'air raid.' Thinking back to what it meant to us in 1936, I see it as a term out of Grimms' fairy tales. Politics had become a matter of black forests, witches and wicked step-parents . . .

My grandmothers died within a few months of each other. The one in the mental hospital went first. By the coarsest of mistakes, when my mother called out, 'Granny's dead,' I thought she meant my other grandmother, and was unmoved. That little grey woman, my mother's mother, so long in the fading, had simply faded altogether. Herself a silence, she left a silence. Her parents (my mother said) after her marriage to my grandfather, no longer sat at their basement window, watching for her coming. They had been proud of her, a handsome girl, but then came the love child, the need to marry, the bad marriage. 'They would rather have followed her to her grave than seen her married to *him*. They never got over it. Never looked out of the window again.'

When the news came of my other grandmother's death, I did not at first believe it. She had made a profession of dying. There was a heartless story about Uncle Will, told in the family with the relief that heartlessness can offer. She'd summoned him on the grounds that her end was minutes away. 'Goodbye, Willie,' she'd whispered, affectingly. 'Well, goodbye then, Mum,' Uncle Will cried, with exhausted good-humour; gave his mother a hearty slap on the shoulder and left the room, whistling. But now she had really gone. 'It must have been,' I said, 'in her sleep; the only way she could have been taken.' I turned out to be right: she'd been found quite sleekly dead one morning. She had been the root of so much pain and enmity that I did not know how to be sorry. At the same time her going made me wonder deeply about her. We had settled for our story about the sort of human being she was. But where did it all begin? When she was a girl, what events

209

had determined that the worst and not the best of her should rule throughout her life? We knew only the woman, incorrigible; what about the child she'd been? And wasn't there, in her, some chemistry that had made quarrelsomeness and black egotistic humours, the family mark? It had joined, perhaps, with a peremptory sort of chemistry provided by my grandfather. All those men and women in the uncaptioned photo albums inherited from Aunt Ada: both sexes as tense as sword blades, leaning against tables, tight-lipped against backcloths; the legs of the men indeed like swords at rest, the breasts of the women fiercely contained! How explosive it had all been, that late Victorian and Edwardian world; such passion and temper packed tight in the sheaths and cartridge-cases of its clothing! Here it was, dying on the verge of Europe exploding, of huge historical tensions and national chemistries about to burn their world about them!

Grotesquely, the voice of what was happening seemed to be that of the Movietone News, at the pictures. The commentary, set at its usual pitch of comprehensive jocularity and lunatic elation—as if the voice of the news had been crossed with the voice of the cracker motto—spoke of floods, aerial flights, a Nazi rally. It struck me that Doomsday itself would have found Movietone News in its invariable mood of hollow jollity.

My father's *Daily Express* referred, with the most tender brutality, to 'our lasses', who should be conscripted as housewives 'as the frauleins are.' The Rev. Charles Blossom urged Herr Hitler to reflect on the virtue of patience. Let him think himself into that excellent cleric's own frame of mind. Then all the world would become Crawley Hill: irritable, a little, but mild, patient, nondescript . . .

But the world wasn't the Rev. Charles Blossom's to dispose of. Mild dullness wasn't its mark, at all.

'If', said my father, in one of those late-night monologues that aimed to make me declare myself, so that he could fly at me, 'if once you get it into your noddle that there's not much in this life worth living for, you won't worry.' Then he talked about war, as he had known it. It was, after all, for him only yesterday, a little more than twenty years earlier. 'You're all together, that's what you'll find, you've got guns and weapons, you don't see any danger. You're young. It's all a game. Rather exciting. Very nasty, but you're all together, you see.'

He was telling the story of his war for the hundredth time, to the same detail, as if he had never told it before. And my mother listened as if she had never heard it before, but restlessly ruffled the dress on her knee, longing for bed. 'I just do what I'm told,' he said. 'That's what I've learned about life. Do what you're told, and get your fun where you can.' When he tired at last, mother tapped me on the shoulder and, in one of her unsuccessful whispers, said: 'Talk! talk! talk!'

He went, then, to lock up for the night. There was a pattern to this . . . so familiar that one could easily fail to notice it. The front door opened; then the pause while he lay the night under examination. The clouds, the stars. All ticked off, as present. The street inspected for any nocturnal abnormality: a car outside a front gate ('Who the hell would visit the Wilsons?'), a couple in the shadows ('They could go elsewhere for that'). Then the milkbottles placed on the doorstep, ready for the morning. A sigh; the door closed and bolted.

In the core of the sky was the moon, and round it grey coils of cloud that spread through infinitely distant air in flat, motionless formations. In another dimension altogether, these nights, was the rapid searchlight, hurled by way of practice from horizon to horizon, obeying the orders of invisible soldiers. How to believe that, tomorrow or the day after, a fleet of planes, murderously intent, abnormal beyond my father's nightly managing, would inhabit what was now so lonely a heaven . . .?

9

How strange, adolescence and early youth! Here are all the elders, making their experienced use of a world well-known; and here among them are the young, treating the same geographical space as if it were new-found-land! Such collisions, between the sober grown-ups, and the younger people who might as well be dressed as conquistadors: roaring their rage as they encounter ancient inequity, crying out their amazement as, on their blank charts, they record long-established causes of human excitement. It was books and music, weather and London, girls and politics, that had me, as I walked about Crawley Hill in the late 1930s, writing notes on the backs of envelopes, confusingly in the pages of my reporter's notebooks —on the margins, when all else was used up, of bus tickets. Phrases for my diary; which agreed with every word I wrote. Such fulminations as to ways in which the world might (so very obviously) be bettered. Such assaults on sad seniors—Mr Trout, for example, whom my diary could not leave alone. Dammit, he was a secondhand Buddha, wasn't he, chubbily fixed behind his typewriter! Something editorial about a Buddha! Here were the suburbs, ugh, such dinginesses of brick, and above them, all round them, majestic arrangements of cloud, huge scribblings in the sky, every day different, every moment on the move!

More libraries! I had tickets galore to use in the Crawley Hill branch, as well as the one in West Green; these in addition to my Barton tickets. The amazing pleasure of reading something startling on the top of a bus! I was a top-of-the-bus man, in those days when buses had command of the roads; you were among the trees in summer, halfway to the clouds all the year round. From Barton to Crawley Hill was half an hour of the latest book from Jonathan Cape or Faber & Faber—whose colophons seemed, then, a guarantee of the literary fineness and urgency of anything they chose to publish. I was amazed by the different ways there were of writing about life. How find a voice of one's own among so many attractive kinds of voice?

God, yes, there I was on the top of the bus of life, it was a phrase I must offer to Mr Trout for his Jottings, awfully conscious of barely touching the ground at all. But what to do about the gulf between the great beauty and brilliance and mystery up there, and the mean banality of so much of everyday life? Didn't every piece of music you heard make a proposal to which our daily dispositions were no response at all?

I saw myself as an appalling prig—remembering what Williams had said about not regarding yourself as a superior person.

Into Williams himself I'd run, lately; he was, he said, in love. 'Are you having any, ah, experiences of the kind?' my old teacher asked, as if it were a matter of some book we might both have been reading. 'My dear chap,' he said, and gave his attention for a moment to the lighting of a cigarette. He'd always had a curiously intimate way with cigarettes : between his fingers they ceased to be commonplace tubes and became instead fluttering, dancing personalities—they seemed to *dance out*, as he spoke, his moods and meanings. I remembered, on the other hand, the severe stillness of his cigarette on occasions when he'd been displeased with me . . . 'My dear chap,' he said now, 'to get what you want in love you have to make sacrifices—small ones, big ones. You know, I'd do anything'— he laughed excitedly—'anything I had to do to smooth the way. You know, I'd write for *John Bull* if I had to!' His cigarette turned somersaults. 'It certainly is love that makes the world go round!'

I wrote to Ned about my dismal certainty that I was a prig. 'As to your high horse,' he wrote in reply, 'you don't have to get down from it : what you must do is help others up beside you.' I was confused by this new image : being on a high horse was somehow not as manageable an idea as being on top of a bus. But I felt uneasily comforted.

And really—I see now, trying to give an honest account of that distant self—really, it's never easy to grow up in a fashion not largely ludicrous; but it may be particularly difficult when the most important elders in your life surround you with rage for what you are. It was with the scholarship that it had begun to go wrong. My father had thought the scholarship would make me respectable, but in his terms it had actually made me profoundly unrespectable. It had made me, as he was always saying, someone who took life too seriously . . . Mother caught my eye one evening, in our crowded living room. What a recipe for domestic explosion it was, our having to spend so much of our time crammed together in that tiny room! Mother said: 'You're always thinking! I wish I could stop you thinking! I wish I could just do something that would stop it!' I had this hunted feeling of someone who was being constantly inspected for signs of being engaged in thought, being serious.

I could not see what they had against reading, and writing,

213

and thinking. And in any case, as I told my diary, it wasn't thinking, really. Years before there'd been a poem in the school magazine, the work of a real poet, no Wilson B. F. C. with his 'swart fingers' . . . and it included the line : 'Ink won't do your thinking for you.' Because I admired the poet, I believed this to be a pronouncement binding on us all. And since I knew I couldn't think simply by arranging ideas in sequence in my head (in my head was only this complex reflective tangle), I took it that I was simply incapable of thought. When I used ink, I certainly had a sensation as of ideas shaking themselves into order . . . but it must be an illusion. It took me many years to realise that with some of us, some focusing activity such as writing (it might be painting, I guess, or making music, or even talking) is required if something like thought is to occur.

But it wouldn't have done, in that touchy living room, to have told my poor mother, who had my happiness at heart, that the look on my face that worried her was no guarantee that I was thinking, at all . . .

Among mother's dangerous habits was that of finishing people's sentences for them. Sometimes it arose out of a kindly desire to save someone's breath. When it was my father who was speaking, it was often another sort of wish : to bring some long-winded and bossy pronouncement to an early end. So my father would hold forth about our prospects of survival should there be a war ('I'm not saying there will be one') accompanied by air raids ('I'm not saying there will be any'). 'Now, let's think for a moment about what your German bomber will have to face,' he'd say. 'First, how many German bombers are there? If you ask me, I'd say there are—'

'None at all,' mother would say crisply, and begin to rise from her chair.

'Oh, for God's sake! Where are you going? What do you mean, none at all? What are you talking about, woman? Why the devil don't you let a man finish what he's trying to say! No wonder you get the wrong end of the stick when you listen to—' Here, with rapid and practised scorn, my father listed a number of mother's favourite neighbours. It was his belief that they were a set of idle gossips ('Bloody women!') who filled each other with inaccurate news and bilious rumours, and that this effect was compounded in mother's case by her inattentiveness. 'Where the devil was I?'

Mother would say: 'I've got to go and boil a kettle.'

'Let the damned kettle wait a moment. Look here, there are probably only a quarter of the bombers they say they've got, they all tell lies about things like that—well, they come over, say a dozen, and what do they find they're up against? Well, our forces aren't going to be caught—'

'Redhanded,' mother would incorrigibly supply.

'*Redhanded?* My God! What do you mean, redhanded? They're not going to be caught *napping*, woman! Oh, for God's sake! What is the point of my trying to discuss anything?'

What he would sometimes discuss, to my mother's annoyance, was sex. It was often in relation to some aristocratic or even royal scandal. 'Well, he's always been much too interested in . . . what's below his navel.' 'Dick!' 'What's wrong with that? Haven't you got a navel?' My mother would be totally unwilling to entertain such an inquiry. 'He's coarse,' she'd explain to the surrounding air. 'He's always been interested in what's down there,' my father would insist. 'But so has she, I bet!' 'Dick! After all, she's—' 'I know very well who she is, my dear. They have the same arrangements as the rest of us, you know.' He was resolved, one knew, to reach his usual conclusion. 'Makes you wonder, though, why they make such a fuss. I mean, to have it—' ('Oh, Dick!')—'with Lord or Lady Muck, when it means trouble, when they could have it—' ('Oh, Dick!')—'with some little'—('Now, Dick, that's enough!')—'floozie who'd take her two-and-sixpence and make herself scarce. After all'—and my father would laugh loud and long—'they're all the same when the light's out.'

I would sit, thinking of Tess and shuddering with horror worse than my mother's.

. . . And yet it was Ned who had said: 'What is it but a small hole and a few inches of skin?'

I'd smiled: quite unready to express the actual feeling that flooded me as Ned spoke—one of shock and dissent. Surely anything whatever could be reduced to disgust by some such formulation! It occurred to me uneasily that what Ned had said was very close to my father's view of sex.

Not that I really knew anything about it. Even when Tess had said recently: 'Are you, sir, making the mistake of respecting my feelings? Are you being a perfect gentleman, do you think?', I had understood her only as one might understand a rarefied philosophical proposition. It had nothing to do with any actions upon which Tess and I might embark. Partly, I guess, this was poetic vagueness and loving patience; but partly it was because, for all my reading, I hadn't the faintest idea of the practicalities of making love. It was as remote as the idea, say, of flying an aeroplane, or playing the Emperor concerto in Queen's Hall. My sole experience of sex education, as it wasn't then called, was being taken aside by Williams, in his role as my housemaster. 'Ah,' he'd said, 'I have to give you senior fellows a talk about the facts of life . . . but only if you need it. You know everything, do you?'

'My goodness, yes,' I said. I'd just been reading the copy of Aldous Huxley's *Eyeless in Gaza* that he'd lent me—how could I confess that I knew nothing?

But Ned, I thought, was always likely to be more right, because so down-to-earth and undeceivable and intelligent, than I was myself. I was a romantic fool, I thought. I was a romantic fool and could never think in that way of the relations between man and woman. I should never be, like Ned, a courageous realist.

Though this did leave me convinced, I saw that my father was wrong, but Ned somehow right, for saying much the same thing . . .

'I don't believe,' said Tess, sadly, 'that you have any intentions at all. Not any practical ones, I mean.'

I proved her right by welcoming with a tender smile a statement that would have filled any reasonably alert lover with the most ominous gloom.

It was August 1939, and Tess went on holiday . . . 'With family,' she said, making a face. 'And family friends. Oh, my dear! It will be so stuffy! But sometimes one has to please them. Do you think? Perhaps you don't think one should?' I smiled in the manner of someone willing to turn this question over for weeks, if not years, before replying. We were occupying a favourite trysting-place: the Horse Guards Parade. We liked leaning against the plinths of soldierly statues; we liked kissing under those whiskered faces. Lord Wolseley we felt to be rather moved by our presence; we often imagined a secret smile under the marble moustache. This had been the scene of some of our earliest kissing : 'Pale beauty of proffered face,' my diary had noted; and then had mentioned all the clock faces that floated behind hers, and behind and above them, the ultimate in faces, that of the moon.

'You've really *got* to go?' and 'Oh !' she said. 'Oh !' Then : 'Are you going to say I can't?' A long pause : I was thinking that war might come before she was back . . . Then : 'It won't be long.'

She was not strictly accurate about that. The truth is that I never saw her again.

Crawley Hill Police Court : the morning of the first day of September, 1939. A succession of small cases : speeding, failure to pay rates, remarkable ignorance of the need to purchase a dog licence.

Suddenly Dingle of the *Monmouth Park Gazette* appeared and slid into his place at the end of the reporters' bench. He held an evening newspaper in his hand, and turned it so that all of us could see.

The headline, of the size that always made your heart jump, said : WARSAW BOMBED.

I saw that Hugh Cramm was smiling. He smiled as if the last line had dropped into place in a satirical poem.